THREE WAYS TO BE ALIEN

THE MENAHEM STERN JERUSALEM LECTURES

Sponsored by the Historical Society of Israel
and published for Brandeis University Press
by University Press of New England

For a complete list of books in this series,
please visit www.upne.com

Sanjay Subrahmanyam, *Three Ways to Be Alien: Travails and Encounters in the Early Modern World*

Jürgen Kocka, *Civil Society and Dictatorship in Modern German History*

Heinz Schilling, *Early Modern European Civilization and Its Political and Cultural Dynamism*

Brian Stock, *Ethics through Literature: Ascetic and Aesthetic Reading in Western Culture*

Fergus Millar, *The Roman Republic in Political Thought*

Peter Brown, *Poverty and Leadership in the Later Roman Empire*

Anthony D. Smith, *The Nation in History: Historiographical Debates about Ethnicity and Nationalism*

Carlo Ginzburg, *History Rhetoric, and Proof*

THREE WAYS TO BE ALIEN

TRAVAILS & ENCOUNTERS IN THE EARLY MODERN WORLD

Sanjay Subrahmanyam

THE MENAHEM STERN JERUSALEM LECTURES

Brandeis University Press

Historical Society of Israel

Brandeis University Press
WALTHAM, MASSACHUSETTS

Brandeis University Press /
Historical Society of Israel
An imprint of University Press of New England
www.upne.com

Manufactured in the United States of America
Designed and typeset in Arno Pro by Michelle Grald

University Press of New England is a member of the Green Press Initiative. The paper used in this book meets their minimum requirement for recycled paper.

Library of Congress Cataloging-in-Publication Data appear on the last printed page of this book.

5 4 3 2 1

For Ashok Yeshwant Kotwal

Contents

Illustrations

MAPS

FIGURES

Foreword : DAVID SHULMAN

There was a time, some five centuries ago, when restless Europeans headed east, as did many enterprising Iranians, and curious North Indians set out either for Central Asia or for the wild and barbarous lands of the Marathas, Tamils, and Telugus to the south. Most of them were men, though there were also some colorful, adventurous, polyglot women like Nicolò Manuzzi's English-Portuguese wife, Elisabetta Hardeli (or Elizabeth Hartley). The majority of the Europeans were driven — let's face it — by sheer greed, sometimes masked by an assumed missionary zeal or a taste for political intrigue. Some, however, were genuinely curious about the exotic cultures into which they had wandered, although even among this latter group there were figures like Manuzzi who, having miraculously survived some six decades in India, came to detest the place and its peoples. Homesickness, the intimate shadow of wanderlust, affected all of them to some degree and became a predictable topos in their records and letters. Pravara, the prototypical, middle-Indian hero of the sixteenth-century Telugu poet Peddana's novel *The Story of Man*, though consumed by a burning desire to see the remote places he has heard about, is unable to get through even a few hours in the Himalayas before desperately looking for a safe route home. For most adventurers of the sixteenth through nineteenth centuries, home was a place very far away.

Every one of these individuals carried with him or her a set of mental maps, usually fuzzy and unsystematic and full of gaps, often also dogmatic and condescending, about the outlandish cultural worlds to be encountered. In the works they have left us — travelogues, memoirs, endless letters, histories and pseudo-histories, rudimentary ethnologies, diaries — we find the not unreasonable presupposition that people back home are dying to hear the often self-aggrandizing account of the would-be hero's adventures and more than eager to learn about the peculiar ways of the distant East or North or South. In any case, the urge to report is a staple feature of this vast literature, in which a host of tricksters, charlatans, and operators try, usually unsuccessfully, to hide the true nature of their careers, and the borderline psychotics generally sound, well, insane.

One way to write the history of those centuries is to tell the story of those intersecting mental maps, which, naturally, tended to evolve along highly patterned lines and sequences. Such an integrated work would be one form of what Sanjay Subrahmanyam has aptly called "connected history" (he has published two remarkable collections of essays under this rubric). Connected history envisions a world so densely textured, so profoundly interlocking in causal processes, that even a slight shift at one point will produce change at many other points — a version of the so-called Butterfly Effect (if a butterfly flaps its wings in Beijing in the spring, by late summer hurricane patterns in the Atlantic will be affected). Over a thousand years ago, a school of Indian logicians, the Nyāya-Vaiśeṣika, discussed the notion of causal connectivity with a subtlety perhaps unparalleled in human civilization. They concluded that such consequential connections depend upon delicate, usually invisible, and always very partial contacts — mostly at isolated points — between complex entities whose internal composition is invariably altered by the contact; ultimately, such causal connections generate a second-order phenomenon, in the sense that a necessary meta-connectivity comes into being whenever something truly new emerges (they call this "connection born from connection," *samyogaja-samyoga*). Are modern historians capable of offering analyses of a rigor and imaginative density commensurate with such a description?

If they are, they would need to be someone like Sanjay Subrahmanyam, who has recapitulated in his own life most of the geographical trajectories I mentioned at the outset. Born into a family of Tamil Smarta Brahmins, the intellectual aristocracy of India, he grew up in Delhi and was trained, first in economics, then in economic history, in the remarkably effervescent environment of Delhi University in the early 1980s. He has lived and taught in Lisbon, Paris, Oxford, Los Angeles, and Jerusalem, to name but a few of the stations. He speaks flawlessly all the languages that were mother tongues to his sixteenth- and seventeenth-century adventurers (I once saw him learn excellent German in less than six weeks). His early work culminated in a historiographical masterpiece, *The Political Economy of Commerce: South India 1500–1650* (Cambridge University Press, 1990). In that book he focused on early modern southern India seen largely from the intermeshed perspectives of the foreign traders and companies — Portuguese, Dutch, Danish, French, and English — that established footholds along the coasts of the region. These perspectives have remained stable parts of his oeuvre, but quite rapidly, in his subsequent monographs, the center of attention shifted inland, away from the coasts. An astonishing wealth of source materials in Tamil, Marathi, Persian, Telugu, and other Indian languages came to enrich his narratives, now often more directly political and focused on states and state formation no less than on maverick entrepreneurs and "portfolio capitalists." Quixotic adventurers like Yacama Nayaka and Sultan Bulaqi march through Subrahmanyam's pages alongside the apparently endless series of homesick travelers I have already mentioned. Often we are allowed to watch these somewhat shadowy figures flit through sources in all the languages of their time, as if reflected from the surfaces of a vast chamber of mirrors, each mirror fashioned in its own, distinctive cultural matrix. Or, to switch the metaphor: the experience is something like watching a performance in the classical Kudiyattam tradition of Sanskrit drama from Kerala: what one sees, in great precision and slow detail, is the continuous, discordant mingling of incommensurate imaginations. This is the true, recurrent subject of Subrahmanyam's analysis and the real heart of his historical project. He reveals to us an often bizarre amalgam of diverse mental worlds that, in merging, mostly tend to the tragicomic, the ironic, and the doomed.

Some of his heroes and anti-heroes seem to elicit the author's empathy, as if the experience of sliding rapidly through radically distinct cultures, with its attendant incongruities and its occasional alarums and excursions, were very familiar to him. At other times, his tone is skeptical and — when it comes to impostors and con men like Manuzzi or cynical and predatory self-promoters like Anthony Sherley — even scornful. Occasionally, a poignant note creeps in, as when Subrahmanyam writes of "the subtle movement from a father of Turko-Persian cultural heritage" (the Micawber-like figure of Meale, hero of chapter 2 in this volume) to "a son [Yusuf Khan] who is far more Lusitanized but still 'of another law' — that is to say, still a Muslim." And, rather like Conan Doyle's famous teasing references, in the Sherlock Holmes stories, to cases that for one reason or another went unrecorded — like that of Mr. James Phillimore, "who, stepping back into his own house to get his umbrella, was never more seen in this world" — Subrahmanyam's pages are filled with brief, tantalizing references to such redoubtable characters as "the Venetian merchant Andrea Morosini, resident in Aleppo, [who] was a major source of rumors" or Giovanni Tommaso Pagliarini, "a knight of the Order of St. Lazarus who had been the cupbearer of the Papal nuncio at Prague," at one point a secretary of Sherley's. One would like to know more about such people, and I am certain Subrahmanyam would indeed be able to fill in the picture with still more juicy details. My only complaint, intimated above, has to do with the inevitable dearth of compelling female characters to set beside the lurid rogues and bewildered innocents who fill the pages of this book.

Two of Subrahmanyam's characteristic methodological devices deserve explicit formulation, though they are not, of course, uniquely his. First, he has happily reversed, or perhaps shattered, the Eurocentric lens that still focuses so much of modern world history. He is writing a history of human civilization, and we can be sure that it will be a history with a great many focal points and shifting perspectives, and that it will not particularly privilege the role of Europe or succumb to the still amazingly resilient, implicit teleology of so much Western historiography. His Iranian and Sumatran entrepreneurs, loquacious Mughal wanderers, and Central Asian millenarian rebels will easily stand their ground beside their Dutch, Iberian, and Venetian (or for that matter, Chinese) counterparts. Second, there is much to be said for foregrounding expressive figures from the intercultural margins, which often provide the historical narrative with a clarity and drama not so readily available in the political or socioeconomic centers of power. In general, it seems, it is the periphery that is the site of lasting cultural innovation. Indeed, Subrahmanyam loves the multi-lingual, usually agitated peripheries and the human anomalies who inhabit them; he naturally gravitates to these interstitial eccentrics, as Jonathan Spence has done in his classic studies of early modern China and Japan. The margins, in short, tend to be at once emblematic and entertaining — no small virtue. In Subrahmanyam's hands, history does not provide moral object lessons, but it definitely has the capacity to fascinate and amuse.

Subrahmanyam is a master of wide-ranging collaborative projects, as a look at the notes to this volume will immediately disclose. He has worked closely with the great historian of Mughal India, Muzaffar Alam, with Velcheru Narayana Rao, and with many others, including myself. I don't think I can fully convey the somewhat dizzying effect of writing a book or an essay together with him. One has to be prepared for a continuous flow of witticisms and occasional prickly comments in half a dozen languages; and there is the secondary (or perhaps it is a primary) benefit of consistently excellent Indian cuisine. One thing, in any case, I can say with confidence, after long experience. Subrahmanyam has the historian's instinct for a mode of understanding, or of visionary reconstruction, that Johan Huizinga correctly characterized as transcendent. This mode requires several active metaphysical assumptions.

For example, unlike me, Subrahmanyam still truly believes in the reality of time.

On that same note, let me add that Sanjay Subrahmanyam delivered the Menachem Stern lectures in Jerusalem in early January 2007, to a large, typically heterogeneous and multi-lingual Israeli audience very familiar with the shadowy domains of marginality and all the drama, sorrow, and effervescence that naturally belong there.

Preface

This is actually an uncomplicated book, which (alas) as usual took far too long to complete. Visits to Jerusalem have been a regular feature of my life since the mid-1990s, owing largely to my long friendship and ongoing collaboration with Velcheru Narayana Rao and David Shulman. Cooking sambar with David and Eileen in their "Kattappomman" residence, and improvising music with Tari, Misha, and Edani — these have been recurrent themes of my visits there, interspersed with some academic and other activities of course. We all recall too the effects of the fumes of red chilies on Narayana Rao's hapless onetime neighbors in French Hill. The visit in early 2007 that was occasioned by the lectures that are at the heart of this book was no exception to our rule, though I did get the opportunity in addition to stay at the splendid Mishkenot Sha'ananim, and visit the old city or Bait al-Muqaddas as often as I wanted to wander its streets, besides going to the opera in Tel Aviv, and taking in many other sights and curious experiences linked to *Ta'ayush*. I was also almost arrested for jaywalking on King George Street, which I am told is a fairly typical Jerusalem tourist experience (though David and I have also tried this out in Philadelphia, near Thirtieth Street). On this occasion I was equally fortunate to receive the very generous hospitality of various persons: Gadi Algazi, who accompanied me on a splendid day-long visit to the Sea of Galilee or Buhairat Tabariyyah; Ornit Shani, specialist of Gujarat's unhappy politics, who eased the not-negligible pains of departure; Fredrik Galtung, who taught me much more about Palestine than I ever dared to ask; Michael Heyd, whose invitation lay at the heart of this visit, and whose hospitality was ever present; Yosef Kaplan, who was ever charm and intelligence combined; Yohanan Friedmann, an enigmatic and legendary character for me, and who lived up to everything I had heard about him; Miriam Eliav-Feldon, an old friend and ever-delightful host; Benjamin Arbel, whom I was honored to meet for the first time and learn a great deal from very rapidly; and many, many others, to say nothing of the familiar pilgrimage to meet Shmuel Eisenstadt in the Jerusalem version of Tiananmen Square. These were among the busiest two weeks of my recent life.

It was a privilege for me to deliver the Menahem Stern Jerusalem Lectures in January 2007, in memory of a great and prolific historian of the antique world who had been tragically killed there over seventeen years earlier. It was an honor but also frankly a cause for trepidation. For no historian — and certainly none of my generation — can probably feel confident of holding his or her own in a line of past speakers that included such figures as Carlo Ginzburg and Peter Brown (and half a score of others). Further, I am no specialist of the world of classical Western antiquity; but then this was surely known to those who invited me to Jerusalem. Rather my work usually revolves around India, not as a closed civilization but as an open door, a revolving door even one might say, or a *carrefour* to use the felicitous term of my late colleague at the EHESS in Paris, Denys Lombard. Perhaps my hosts here were inspired then by the phrase *Hitbollelutu-temiyah* (Acculturation and Assimilation) which appears as the title of a work that Menahem Stern edited together with Yosef Kaplan, and which appeared in 1989. For although the general title I had given to these three lectures (and, with a minor modification of an article, to the book that derives from them) was "Three Ways to Be an Alien," they were certainly concerned with processes of acculturation and assimilation, as well as their limits, and the historical reasons for these limits; and in more general terms, I should underline that my own work as a whole as well as in these lectures speaks to issues of mutual perceptions across cultures in a way that was probably rather familiar to the historian to whose memory they are dedicated.

In the final analysis, my immodest impression is that the lectures went off quite enjoyably, and the audience was kind and even rather generous to me. The discussions were long and engaging, especially after the second lecture. The questions were at times searching and always thoughtful, which has not necessarily been my experience in North America. The separate session with the graduate students was one that I found rather stimulating. Throughout, the efficiency of the staff of the Israel Historical Society was remarkable, and Maayan Avineri-Rebhun was a model of organizational rigor and grace before, during, and after.

The title of the lectures, as Michael Heyd was quick to spot, derives from the first and best-known book (dated 1946) of the Hungarian writer and humorist George Mikes (1912–87), who on occasion did write serious work on the Hungarian secret police and other subjects. (Mikes also once wrote: "It was a shame and bad taste to be an alien, and it is no use pretending otherwise. There is no way out of it.") It follows a sort of case method, and focuses on a few individuals in the sixteenth, seventeenth, and eighteenth centuries who found themselves in awkward situations of intercultural communication, the "travails" of the subtitle. It seemed an appropriate subject for the place where the lectures were delivered, a fact that was clearly not lost on the audience (as Richie Cohen dryly pointed out in discussion that followed the last lecture). I should stress the appropriateness of the subject too for a resident of Los Angeles. Since I have come to live in that city in 2004, a constant question to me by friends living elsewhere and visitors to LA has been of whether I feel somehow "alienated" there. My response, which no doubt informs this book, is that whatever alienation I feel has less to do with the place than the people; to my mind, social relations must always lie at the core of the answer to such a question.

The individual chapters that make up this book have had varying gestations. The work on Miyan 'Ali bin Yusuf 'Adil Khan of Bijapur, which occupies the second chapter, goes back to various stints I had in the Torre do Tombo in Portugal in the late 1990s, when I was laboriously mining the *Corpo Cronológico* collection *maço* by *maço* rather than calling for individual documents using their often unreliable summaries. José Alberto Tavim and Jorge Flores helped me obtain reproductions of a few documents later, and Jorge has been a ready interlocutor as these texts were written. The collaboration with my old friend Maria Augusta Lima Cruz on editing and annotating the *Década Quarta* of Diogo do Couto also helped me clarify many thoughts. The third chapter on Anthony Sherley stems from conversations with Décio Guzmán and Serge Gruzinski on the subject of the past of "connected histories," and a very rough first version was presented at Gruzinski's seminar at the EHESS; later, and more polished, versions were also presented at various occasions at UCLA, at the Australian National University, and at the ECMSAS in Manchester. (A second section of that lecture, on François le Gouz de la Boullaye, has not been included here and will be developed on a separate occasion.) It also reflects, in an ironic way, on my own family and its ongoing engagement with realpolitik. As I was completing the book, I was fortunate enough to find a new edition of Sherley's *Peso político* as well as of another minor text by him, but these did not alter my conclusions significantly. The fourth chapter, on Nicolò Manuzzi, is again based on a rather old project of mine, which I initially presented at the Wissenschaftskolleg zu Berlin in 2001. It has undergone much modification since then. My greatest debt here is to Piero Falchetta of the Biblioteca Nazionale Marciana in Venice, who was very helpful to me when I used that collection in the summer of 2006. Ebba Koch was most encouraging with regard to this project, as was Velcheru Narayana Rao when he heard the first version of the chapter a decade ago in Berlin. Audiences at Duke University, the University of Delhi, the Scuola Normale Superiore (Pisa), and Cornell University also made useful comments on draft versions of this chapter.

I owe much to several other people in putting this book together, many more than the size of the book possibly warrants. Muzaffar Alam has always been there when I needed him. Carlo Ginzburg was there too as a sort of formidable taskmaster who did not even know that he played that role. To him and Luisa Ciammitti, I owe many thanks in relation to my visits to Venice, Pisa, Siena, and more. Caroline Ford graciously accompanied the work and tolerated its author's eccentricities, which were surely not a few. Fernando Rodriguez Mediano helped me with a crucial text at the closing stages of the book.

While writing this book, I have naturally puzzled as usual over the real nature of the audience for which it might be intended. My intention here remains to go beyond a simple academic readership, and that — if no one else — at least nonacademic members of my own family might read it. But it is also owes much to my many friends who have taught me that it was necessary to reach beyond the usual frontiers of which academic convention makes us prisoners. They include Ken McPherson, an old friend of twenty-five years standing from Australia, who sadly passed away as this book was nearing completion. Ken encouraged me enormously when I was but a young scholar in the mid-1980s. I think too of the late Jean Aubin, whose shadow falls across these pages, as it surely does over all those who write these kinds of histories.

The book is dedicated to a friend who is an omnivorous intellectual, but not really a historian; and who welcomed me to Vancouver at a time some years ago when I too was a sort of alien. He shares a bit of his name and some qualities with Arun Kolatkar's Yeshwant Rao.

THREE WAYS TO BE ALIEN

1 Introduction

THREE (AND MORE) WAYS TO BE ALIEN

Why cross the boundary
when there is no village?
It's like living without a name,
like words without love.

— Tallapaka Annamacharya (fl. 1424–1503)[1]

CROSSING BOUNDARIES

"From the day that I returned to this country, I have had neither pleasure nor rest with the Christians and even less with the Moors [Muslims]. The Moors say I am a Christian, and the Christians say I am a Moor, and so I hang in balance without knowing what I should do with myself, save what God [*Deus*] wills, and Allah will save whoever has a good comportment. . . . Today, the knife cuts me to the bone, for when I go out into the streets, people call me a traitor, clearly and openly, and there could be no greater ill."[2] These words were apparently written in Portuguese (albeit in *aljamiado,* or Arabic script) by a fairly obscure Berber notable and "adventurer" in the vicinity of the port of Safi in the Dukkala region of Morocco, Sidi Yahya-u-Ta'fuft or Bentafufa (as the Portuguese liked to term him).[3] They may be found in a letter he sent to a Portuguese friend called Dom Nuno, but also in another version to the king of Portugal, Dom Manuel, sometime in late June or early July 1517, about seven months before the writer was perhaps predictably assassinated—literally stabbed in the back—in the course of a mission on behalf of his Portuguese allies by his Berber compatriots. They point to a situation where Yahya had fallen deeply and irrevocably between two (or more) stools, a process that had begun in 1506 as the Portuguese gradually moved to capture Safi and to fortify themselves there. The political and social context was undoubtedly a complex one, where different groups and interests pulled violently in varying directions. There were, to begin with, the Muslim residents of the city of Safi itself, with their own internecine quarrels. In the countryside around were both Arab and Berber clans and groups, in attitudes of lesser or greater hostility with regard to those in the town. Then we find a number of significant Jewish merchants, often refugees from Spain and Portugal, with whom Yahya was periodically accused by his rivals of being in league. At some distance, but with a lively interest in matters in Safi, were the Hintata *amīrs* at Marrakesh with whom Yahya was charged with carrying on a treacherous and secret correspondence where he allegedly pleaded that he was a "Moor and more than a Moor." And finally, in Safi itself and in Portugal were the servants of the Portuguese king with whom Yahya was ostensibly allied, but who accused him periodically of all manner of ills, from exceeding his competence as a mere official and *alcaide* (or *al-qa'id*), to taking bribes, to making claims that he himself was no less than the "King of the Moors [*rei dos mouros*]."

What does the historian of the early modern world make of such a figure as Yahya-u-Ta'fuft? How typical or unusual are he and his situation, and why should this matter to us? What are the larger processes that define the historical matrix within which the trajectory of such an individual can or should be read, and how meaningful is it to insist constantly on the importance of such broad processes? Should the individual and his fate be read as a mere refraction of the times, or can we tease out more from the "case study" even by the process of accumulation?[4] There are no easy answers to any of the above questions, as historians working both within the domain of microhistory proper and from its fringes will gladly concede. The individual with his forensic characteristics is at one level the obvious and irreducible minimal unit for the historian of society (or what the economists might call the "primitive" for purposes of analysis); but at another level, historians in the past century have been both attracted to and repelled by the individual for methodological reasons. For those who wish to conjugate the practice of history with insights from individual psychology (and beyond that, from psychoanalysis), the central place that must be given to the individual is very nearly self-evident. Humanist traditions in history writing also remain attached to the individual figure as a peg upon which to hang much that would be difficult to set out cogently otherwise. There is also the powerful hold that biography has on the popular imagination in the past two centuries, as one can see by inspecting the shelves of the rare bookstores that can still be found today in large North American cities. Clearly readers both on university campuses and in airports would prefer a biography of President John F. Kennedy to a social history of the United States in the 1960s, or an account of the love affair (real or embroidered) of Prime Minister Jawaharlal Nehru and Edwina Mountbatten to a historical account of the political dimensions of the language problem in India in the first decade after independence.

There are many from within the social sciences who have railed against this tendency, from a variety of standpoints. A long Marxist tradition of historiography asserted its opposition to the promiscuous mixing of biography and history, disdaining the former as a mere reassertion of the prejudices of writers in a somewhat heroic vein such as Thomas Carlyle.[5] The thrust here was to argue that what biography fostered was a quite mistaken, and decidedly romantic, notion of historical agency, which was vested in key individuals. Late in the twentieth century, a celebrated sociologist in the Marxist tradition continued to inveigh against "the biographical illusion."[6] But historians constantly found ingenious ways around these objections, even when writing the biographies of those classic subjects, kings and emperors. Among these one can count a great medievalist's quite recent account of the French king Saint Louis (Louis IX, 1214–70), which disarms its potential critics with the question: "Did Saint Louis [really] exist? [*Saint Louis a-t-il existé?*]."[7] However, a set of objections were also raised from a quite different viewpoint, namely that of the early post-structuralists, with their claims in the 1960s regarding the illusive nature of the idea of authorship and their radical demotion of notions of "intention" with regard to the production of texts. If extended ever-so-slightly, the dissolution of the author of a text could soon be transformed into the dissolution of the author of any act; the weight might then naturally shift to the infinite ways of reading or perceiving an act, which also rendered more or less irrelevant considerations regarding the intentions of its alleged author. The tension between structure and agency was thus radicalized, if anything, in this process. In such a context, the resort to biography could then be posed as a way of reasserting the centrality of historical agency.

But the question then arose: whose biography? A median solution may have suggested itself to social historians licking their wounds after the multipronged assault outlined above. To be sure, one could "sociologize" one's history, resorting to descriptive statistics if not actual cliometrics, and thus make the individual and the problem of his or her historical agency disappear for a time while redefining the nature of historical inquiry as focusing on the collective or group. Or again, one could accept one of the central premises of the post-structuralist challenge and agree that history and literature were essentially not distinct; as Roland Barthes would have it, that history writing did not "really differ, in some specific trait, in some indubitably distinct feature, from imaginary narration, as we find it in the epic, the novel, and the drama."[8] What remained then would be to produce a narratological analysis of historical practice and turn the mirror on historiography itself in a sort of infinite regression. But if this did not appeal, a third solution did exist: namely to seek out the "unknown" individual, the person *lambda* as the French would have it, as a resolution to the structure-agency tension. Here then was a way of meeting two significant objections at the same time. First, at least on the face of it, the heroic-romantic temptation was seemingly avoided or at least postponed until the moment when the "heroism of the ordinary" as a construct might itself be called into question.[9] Second, the individual in question could be made to face both ways, toward structural questions and away from them. Agency could be restored through an evocation of uncertainty, of hesitation, of the forked paths where choices needed to be made by individuals. Further, even if it contradicted the idea of the "modal biography," the justification of the well-known microhistorian Edoardo Grendi could also be deployed in the opposite direction, by situating the individual within the category of the "exceptional normal [*l'eccezionale normale*]," in other words in a language that evoked the statistical distribution but also mildly subverted it.[10]

The debate was rendered even more complex by the interventions of scholars of literature, many associated with the movement known from the 1980s as "New Historicism." It is to one of these, Stephen Greenblatt, that we owe the celebrated phrase "Renaissance self-fashioning," which has very nearly been elevated to the level of a slogan in some circles. It would seem that the reference here is, in the first instance, to the far earlier claims of Jacob Burckhardt with regard to the emergence of a new sense of the individual in the context of the Renaissance, associated in turn with texts that are explicitly concerned with issues of self-presentation such as Benvenuto Cellini's diary. Of the sixteenth-century artist and *bon viveur* Cellini, Burckhardt wrote in a passage that is justly celebrated: "He is a man who can do all and dares do all, and who carries his measure in himself. Whether we like him or not, he lives, such as he was, as a significant type of modern spirit."[11] One is propelled here by a sense of a powerful will, a strong sense of individuality and a freedom from the ascriptive requirements that might have mattered in an earlier, say "medieval," social structure. Such an individual is thus able to preserve himself (or herself) in both an active and a passive-defensive mode; the latter creates the requisite freedom from ascriptive structures that might be seen as the sine qua non of the modern self, while the former is a more creative aspect, of the man "who carries his measure in himself."[12]

However, a second look at notions of "self-fashioning" current in the 1980s quickly reveals how great a distance has in fact been traversed from Burckhardt. If daring and frankness may be said to characterize the Renaissance individual in the received formulation of the nineteenth-century historian, the individual engaged in "self-fashioning" seems anything but liberated from constraints. Rather, what we have is deviousness, a somewhat twisted defensive posture, a constant and nervous resort to masks of one and the other kind, as if living were an endless costume ball from which one might be summarily expelled by surly footmen. For Greenblatt, then, "in the sixteenth century there appears to be an increased self-consciousness about the fashioning of human identity as a manipulable, artful process," a process in short that is bound up with theatrical modes of role-playing. There is more of this, for we learn too that self-fashioning "always involves some experience of threat, some effacement or undermining, some loss of self."[13] We thus come to be located, in many ways, at the very antipodes of Burckhardt's conception of the unfettered agent "who can do all, and dares do all."

What has transpired in the interim to transform Burckhardt's individual who dares to paint himself in the boldest colors into Greenblatt's feral survivors, scrabbling somewhat desperately in Renaissance society for the wherewithal to survive? The simple answer may be the intervening shadow of the Foucauldian moment. For the "self-fashioning" individual of Tudor England liberates himself from nothing; he is only passed on from one ascribed form of subservience to another, "from the Church to the Book to the absolutist state," or from the stirrings of rebellion to an eventual acceptance of nothing more than "subversive submission." There is a basic historical and contextual contrast that underlies this however. Clearly the Italy of fragmented states in the sixteenth century was anything but an all-powerful absolutist monarchy. Whoever individuals such as Cellini had to answer to, it was not to the likes of Queen Elizabeth or, a half century later, Cromwell. A large weight is thus placed on transformations in the nature of the sixteenth-century state as a regulatory and disciplining institution in order to explain the particular forms that "self-fashioning" took under the Tudors. Little wonder then that we have the following lapidary phrase from the pen of Greenblatt: "we may say that self-fashioning occurs at the point of encounter between an authority and an alien."[14]

Where does such a discussion leave us with respect to an understanding of the figure with whom we began: Sidi Yahya-u-Ta'fuft of Safi? The historiography already offers us a variety of solutions. A leading scholar of sixteenth-century Morocco sums up the matter thus from the relatively dispassionate perspective of political economy.

> [I]n the first decades of the 16th century, Portuguese administrators relied heavily on the services of allied tribal leaders to exploit inland areas economically dependent on the ports of Safi and Azemmour. Occasionally, they went so far as to appoint a local ruler by royal decree when it suited them. The most notorious example of such a ruler was Yahya-u-Taʿfuft (d. 1518), a Berber adventurer from the village of Sarnu near Safi who was brought to power by a Portuguese-engineered coup that ousted the previously dominant Banu Farhum family. As *qa'id* of the city and its rural periphery, Yahya-u-Taʿfuft was paid a yearly salary of 300 *mithqāls* (about 30 ounces) of gold plus one-fifth of the booty taken in raids conducted against tribes considered to be hostile to Portugal. In addition, he could count on approximately 10,000 *mithqāls* in bribes or "donations" from merchants and other individuals seeking his aid or protection.[15]

The same historian then goes on to detail the various abusive practices of Yahya and his like: first, their use of a "band of mercenaries" who collected taxes from village and tribal lands and punished pastoralists through "brutal and destructive raids," thus using their alliance "with the Portuguese to amass large fortunes"; second, the fact that Yahya directly trivialized the "form and content of Islamic law in the region," by arrogating to himself "the authority to promulgate a personal *qānūn,* or extra-Islamic body of regulations, that took precedence over all other forms of legality"; and finally, his collaboration with the "legendary captain Ataide of Safi" in order to organize raids as far as Marrakesh, where "Yahya-u-Taʿfuft's men insolently banged their spears on the locked gates of the half-deserted city that had once been the capital of the mighty Almohad empire." Yahya is thus clearly seen to be an accomplice, if not more, in "the short-sighted and rapacious policies of both the Portuguese crown and the captains who served in the region [which] significantly contributed to the ruin of Portugal's African commercial empire by destroying the stability of the local Moroccan socioeconomic structures upon which the supply of goods guaranteeing its African trade network depended."

This macroscopic vision gives us limited insights into what might have been the lived world of such a man, let alone what might have prompted him to write lines such as those with which this introduction commenced. This Yahya might have had problems with local Muslims, but surely he should have been well treated by the Portuguese, for whom he was apparently an agent, a *comprador* of sorts. A rather different reading from that presented above is available to us in a more recent study, focusing on the question of "honor" in general, and the rivalry between Yahya and the Portuguese captain of Safi,

Nuno Fernandes de Ataíde, more particularly.[16] We are reminded that in spite of the fact that he spent two long sojourns in Portugal (from 1507 to 1511, and again from 1514 to 1516), and that he appears to have gained direct access to the king, Dom Manuel, Yahya never succeeded in penetrating the world of the *fronteiros*, the Portuguese settled in Safi itself. Whether on account of their visceral dislike for Moors of all stripes, or because of competition within the field of honor, it is argued that they continued to exclude him, plot against him, write letters of complaint about him, and—eventually—may even have had an indirect hand behind his assassination. This is a decidedly more sympathetic portrait then, when compared with the one presented above: here the Berber notable is a victim of local Portuguese machinations, whom even the protection and approbation of the king cannot eventually rescue. Yahya's "self-fashioning" is decidedly in a characteristically defensive mode, however little it may have had to do with the Renaissance as such. However, the sources of his defensiveness, and of his wearing of a series of masks, seem to stem not so much from his encounter with a centralizing or absolutist monarchic state but from his difficulties with a coherent social group. Thus, writes Matthew Racine, "as a member of the local elite (*a'yān*), Yahya felt that he had the status necessary to be treated as a member of the Portuguese noble elite, not to mention the confirmation of that feeling that he had received on numerous occasions from the Portuguese monarch himself. However, the *fronteiros* were an honor group to which Yahya could never gain complete admission. Because he was a Muslim, he was not trusted to be honorable or loyal despite proofs to the contrary, and despite nearly unwavering royal support."[17]

At the heart of the matter was, of course, the fact that Yahya remained a Muslim, a "Moor." The fear manifestly remained in the minds of some—though not all—Portuguese that their initiatives and plans in the region around Safi would be subverted were they to fall, proverbially, into "the gross clasps of a lascivious Moor." However, the matter is even more complex than the foregrounding of issues of "honor" might suggest. Portuguese overseas settlements and colonies in the sixteenth century, including those in North Africa, were usually riven by a tension between those with strong ties to the metropolis and those who were more locally rooted (such as the *fronteiros*). Nuno Fernandes de Ataíde does not seem to have had such a degree of local insertion, to the extent that he himself admitted that he needed Yahya as a "go-between [*terceiro*] between myself and the Moors."[18] In this, he was quite different from one of the Portuguese with whom Yahya had particularly close relations, namely a certain Dom Rodrigo de Noronha, whose nickname of *o aravia* ("the Arabic-speaker") tells its own tale.[19] Further complicating the matter is the existence of a number of Muslims converted to Christianity, whose "true" identity at times lies concealed behind the bland front of a Portuguese name. One of these was Ataíde's notional second in command, a certain Lopo Barriga, who held the post of *adail* (for the Arabic *al-dalīl*) and knew the terrain well enough to be charged with the organization of the regular raids into the territories of hostile Muslims (*mouros de guerra*, as distinct from the *mouros de pazes*). A number of converts also held the post of *almocadém* (from the Arabic *al-muqaddam*), and were in charge of surveying and defining the routes to be followed during the raids (or *cavalgadas*).

Manifestly, Yahya did not choose to become a Christian, although the option was open to him. Had he done so, he might have received the habit of the military Order of Christ from the Portuguese monarch, as did a certain Pero de Meneses, a converted Muslim who served as *almocadém* of Arzila. Other converts and apostates from Islam such as a certain António Coutinho were sufficiently well inserted into Portuguese high society to eat regularly at the table of high noblemen such as the Count of Redondo, side by side with the other Portuguese *fidalgos*.[20] Again, this was not the route that Sidi Yahya chose to trace. We are thus left with the complex characterization of his posture and strategy that comes to us from the pen of the late Jean Aubin, who studied the materials relating to his career most closely.

> Sidi Yahya U Ta'fuft, whether from 1511 to 1514, or from 1516 to 1518, did not behave as a puppet [*fantoche*] auxiliary. A Moorish ally, he remained true to his faith and maintained his liberty of action, and was accepted as such by the patrons he had at the Manueline court. He was careful to protect his fellow-Muslims from the abuses of Portuguese legislation. He demanded that none of the *mouros de pazes* be enslaved, or be sold by a Christian, nor that one Moor be sold by another, and that no Moor who had come to trade at Safi could be seized. Dom Nuno Mascarenhas was obliged to have orders from the King [of Portugal] read out in the *souks* which had been inspired by the lobbying of Sidi Yahya. At the same time, he obtained an indefinite delay in the payment by the Moors of the ecclesiastical tithe that the Bishop of Safi had imposed on them as residents of his diocese.[21]

Aubin is thus inclined to see Sidi Yahya as "controversial and enigmatic," but attributes this to the complex nature of his political vision. In 1506–7, he was "one of those Berber chiefs who were inclined towards a fruitful Luso-Moroccan *entente*, and at the same time opposed to the extraterritoriality of the Portuguese factories, and *a fortiori,* to the presence of garrisons." Though deeply disappointed by his treatment by the Portuguese, he twice rejected (in 1514 and in 1517) the overtures of the Wattasid rulers of Fez to join their camp. At this later date, it is still highly probable, in Aubin's view, that Yahya was attempting to maintain a tributary relationship to the Portuguese for the *mouros de pazes* without allowing the direct conquest of the region.[22]

But how much honor (*honra*) could a Moor have after all? Othello and Iago were not the only ones to ponder this question.[23] Portuguese views of Yahya constantly return to this issue, posing Islam and honor as antithetical in many crucial respects. It was one thing for the Muslim residents of Safi to write to Dom Manuel in 1509 that they "had not found anyone better, more loyal, more sincere, and more lacking in any vice, than the Shaikh Yahya ben Ta'fuft." But from the point of view of Ataíde, even any signs of good organization he showed were sinister: "to carry out these affairs in such an orderly way does not come from a Moor, but I suspect it originates with the Jews, his friends, who are duping this treasury." Given Yahya's well-known dealings with the Jewish merchant Yitzhak ben Zamerro, the finger could quite easily be pointed in the direction of a Muslim-Jewish conspiracy against the Christians. Ironically, among those who held to this thesis was Rabbi Abraham Rute of Safi, an unflinching enemy of the Ben Zamerros, and trenchant critic of Yahya.[24] But many modern historians have held to the view that a common language of honor in fact bound together Christian and Muslim in the North African context. Thus, writes one author: "It is clear that Yahya believed honor was affirmed by victory and conquest performed in the name of the king and with the blessing of God. Like the Portuguese, Yahya believed that the performance of martial deeds and their acknowledgement by the monarch was central to honor." At the same time, it is noted that "if the Portuguese accepted Yahya into their honor group, thereby admitting his parity with them, some aspect of their claim to superiority (religious or otherwise) over Muslims would be compromised."[25] Here lay the rub. It is unclear how easily and consistently the shared vocabulary of honor could trump that of religious difference. A Portuguese governor in India put the matter effectively when he wrote the following words to the queen in 1567: "I did not come to this land [India] for any other reason nor for any other end than to serve the King with much love and truth, and this I am trying and will try to do so long as I have this post and my life lasts; for I understand that in this way I give satisfaction to God and to my honor [*satisfaço nisto a Deos e a minha homrra*], which are the things which every honorable man is most obliged to take into account."[26] Not for no reason then did Sidi Yahya bring both Deus and Allah into the same phrase when expressing his discontentment in the letter we cited at the outset. But in reality — despite the many ambiguities he leaves us with, the source of the divergent interpretations discussed above — here at least, there were no doubts about which of the two he preferred.

TRICK OR TREAT?

This is because he did not make another, further choice: he did not opt for dissimulation in matters of faith. Many others in the Mediterranean world of the sixteenth century did so under a variety of circumstances. Spanish or Portuguese soldiers who were captured in North Africa would routinely convert to Islam, and if they made their way back at a subsequent date to their homeland, would then claim that they had been obliged to do so — while remaining truly Christian in their hearts.[27] Communities of renegades flourished in the Ottoman domains, and some again made two or even three moves across the religious divide, asserting each time that their ostensible adherence to the other faith was mere dissimulation. In Algiers, it was estimated that in the 1630s there were as many as eight thousand renegades, who — however useful they were to the political powers of the time — were also regarded with much suspicion and disdain.[28] Much — perhaps too much — has also been made of a single responsum (*fatwā*) given by Abu'l 'Abbas Ahmad al-Maghrawi al-Wahrani, a juriconsult in the city of Oran to the Muslims of Andalusia in 1504, stating that in view of their pressing needs, they could in fact conceal their true religion and agree to practices imposed on them by Christians (including the worship of Jesus and the Virgin, drinking wine, and eating pork).[29] Certainly the text seems to have been copied and even translated by the *moriscos* in sixteenth-century Spain; but scholars have sometimes tended to downplay the fact that this *fatwā* was meant explicitly to oppose another, far more stringent, opinion given by a prestigious *muftī*, Ahmad bin Yahya al-Wansharisi, who proposed that all Muslims leave the domains of the Catholic monarchs immediately.[30] In reality a larger body of opinions on the question exists even within the Iberian sphere, some of it sympathetic to the idea of Muslims continuing to live for pragmatic reasons in lands ruler over by the infidels (*kuffār*).[31] Further, other *muftīs* in prestigious centers such as Cairo also issued interesting rulings in this regard which — albeit at a greater distance from Europe — are not devoid of significance.[32]

Dissimulation was of course a well-known practice among crypto-

Jews or *conversos,* and had a variety of other proponents in sixteenth- and seventeenth-century Europe, as well as among Shi'is in the Islamic world.[33] But it was a practice born of coercion rather than choice, the resort of persons faced with intolerant state or quasi-state institutions such as the Inquisition. Besides Muslims and Jews, they also came in the sixteenth century to include Protestants under pressure who continued to claim Catholic identities, often identified under the broad head of "Nicodemites."[34] In these instances too, we return to Greenblatt's conception of a "point of encounter between an authority and an alien." However, it has become increasingly commonplace for historians to find a different sort of dissimulating figure in situations of encounter in the early modern world: the trickster. This is not dissimulation in extremis; rather it is *homo ludens* at his finest, dissimulation by choice or out of playfulness. The vision is one of protean actors who change their form and appearance, speak in this tongue or that, and quite cheerfully contemplate existence through the prism of trickery: in short a particular species of "larrikin" if one were to evoke contemporary Australian usage.[35]

The initial purpose of such a conception (harking back no doubt to both Ulysses and Aeneas, and their use of trickery and deception) may have been to find some relief in the unremittingly oppressive and tragic narratives that most early modern encounters seem to carry with them. To make la Malinche, who accompanied Hernán Cortés to Mexico-Tenochtitlán and later bore him a son, a playful figure may stretch the documentary evidence, but it can perhaps help lighten the preoccupation with the devastation wrought by guns, germs, and steel. The path in this direction had already been traced some two decades ago by James Clifford in evoking the figure of Squanto or Tisquantum, a Native American of the Patuxet tribe. Clifford wrote of the delicious irony of his being one of the first natives to encounter the Pilgrims in early seventeenth-century America as follows: "But have not travelers always encountered worldly 'natives'? Strange anticipation: the English Pilgrims arrive at Plymouth Rock in The New World only to find Squanto, a Patuxet, just back from Europe."[36] The implication of course was that Squanto, a worldly-wise trickster figure, then led the Pilgrims a merry dance in their dealings with the Wampanoag leader Massasoit or Ousamequin, despite the fact that he was trusted by neither party.[37] But Squanto's history prior to 1621 and his meeting with the Pilgrims is (to the extent we know it) often less than playful or trick laden; it includes being kidnapped by a certain Captain Thomas Hunt in 1615, a sojourn of some years in England (where he managed to learn some English), and an eventual return to America in 1619, where he lived for only another three years before dying of smallpox. As a commentator on Clifford's short passage has remarked of his vision, it is "generous, but a bit too breezy, inasmuch as it makes it seem as though Squanto had just decided to take off and see a bit of the Old World rather than having been carried forcibly to England; that he had just had time to unpack before hurrying down to the shore to complicate the Pilgrims' vision of the New World."[38]

Historians should be warned perhaps that the depths of the matter where early modern tricksters are concerned have already been plumbed by writers of fiction. Some fifty years ago, the novelist John Barth explored the issue in his massive and brilliant comic novel *The Sot-Weed Factor* (1960), concerned with life in colonial Maryland in the late seventeenth century. Moreover, Barth was no ordinary novelist but an aficionado of both American colonial history and the picaresque novel, from Cervantes and Alain-René Lesage, author of *Gil Blas,* to Tobias Smollett and Laurence Sterne. His massive novel ostensibly concerned a certain Ebenezer Cooke, a poet and incompetent traveler, with a marked resemblance to Candide; Cooke is also the author in the novel of a violently satirical poem titled "The Sot-Weed Factor" that denounces life on and around the tobacco plantations of the American East Coast. Barth in fact plays throughout with the reality of a poem and author who really exist in the historical record, save that he constantly transforms them to his own ends.[39] For in the novel, Cooke is balanced against the central character, a protean trickster figure by the name of Henry Burlingame III. Here the novelist, by the deft use of parodic exaggeration, shows us how the "trickster" is in fact precisely a trope of the fevered early modern imagination, as reflected in the picaresque novel itself. No one is ever who or what he or she seems to be, and Burlingame repeatedly warns Cooke of this through the use of bogus (largely sexual) proverbs such as "There are more ways to the woods than one." The positivist historian is put on his guard as well: what if a missing fragment (such as one that Barth concretely imagines) were indeed to turn up of the journal of the celebrated Captain John Smith from the early seventeenth century?

But the central issue in the work remains the unstable nature of identity, between Proteus and the Heraclitus of "everything flows and nothing stands still." In the course of the novel, Burlingame thus transforms himself periodically into most of the major characters, including figures who are in radical opposition to one another. He is at some point Lord Baltimore, but also appears as other figures such as John Coode, Nicholas Lowe, Timothy Mitchell, and Peter Sayer. Eventually, matters are resolved to some extent—

if that is even possible — by the revelation that Burlingame, who is presented as a foundling, is in fact of Native American descent, an odd version of the *coureurs des bois*.[40] But the personage himself is quite reconciled to his lack of a proper "identity" as others might wish it. "There is a freedom there that's both a blessing and a curse, for't means both liberty and lawlessness. 'Tis more than just political and religious liberty — they come and go from one year to the next. 'Tis philosophic liberty I speak of, that comes from want of history. It throws one on his own resources, that freedom — makes every man an orphan like myself and can as well demoralize as elevate."[41] The novel ends, as it were, with the dissolution of Burlingame as a figure; but Cooke — the Candide who is tied to his Cunégonde, or Joan Toast — remains to face the banal and brutal realities of the real colonial world. The fantasy of the trickster is excellent as long as it lasts, a great diversion to be sure, but we are left to wonder in how many senses it does come "from want of history."

For despite the many, and quite well-known, instances of imposture that characterize intercultural dealings in the early modern world, it is easy to exaggerate the protean character of identity.[42] It was distinctly easier to impersonate someone in particular than assume, in the face of a discerning audience, a series of cultural attributes one did not in fact possess. This may be why it is necessary to take with a large grain of salt the constant claims by Christian travelers that they were able to impersonate Muslims well enough to travel  with them in groups, or even to enter the holy cities of Mecca and Medina. To be sure, the absence of a series of as yet undreamt-of forensic measures, from photography to the fingerprint, limited the technologies of identity verification available to the early modern state — even the ambitious absolutist one. Still, it is remarkable how those who attempted to pretend to be something (as opposed to merely someone) they were not were regularly unmasked. An example is provided to us by the Orthodox Russian merchant from Tver, Afanasii Nikitin, who by a series of accidents and errors found himself in the Bahmani Sultanate in west-central India in the late 1460s and early 1470s.[43] Nikitin decided as a measure of precaution to claim to be a Muslim merchant by the name Khwaja Yusuf Khorasani, and there was also a practical side to the claim given that Muslim traders were often taxed at a lower rate than their Hindu (or rare Christian) counterparts. He was no doubt counting on the fact that his fair complexion and looks would help him pass as a distant (*āfāqī*) Muslim, when faced with local converts and Hindus. It is clear however that he was exposed soon enough, and that the local governor in the town of Junnar, a certain Asad Khan, found out about his true identity and upbraided him for his pretence. Later, he even came to be taunted by Muslims in the Deccan for being neither a Muslim nor even a good Christian. To carry off this change in identity could not have been easy. Did Nikitin know how to perform Muslim prayers, or even recite a few Qur'anic verses? Was his Persian, such as it was, not marked by traces of an exotic accent? Such traces may not have revealed him to some Hindu interlocutors, but the elite of the Bahmani Sultanate was composed in good measure of Iranian and Turkoman migrants who could have soon pierced the veil. The facility of imposture would thus have depended on a number of factors: first, how exotic the identity one assumed was (Khorasani was here just not exotic enough); second, the degree of ethnographic information that one's interlocutors possessed. Indeed, even a personal imposture — as opposed to a cultural one — was not always easy; when a man presented himself to the Portuguese authorities in western India in the early 1630s claiming to be the lost Mughal prince Sultan Bulaqi, they simply sent a Jesuit to meet him who had known the real Bulaqi in the Mughal court. The imposture was revealed in a matter of moments.

THE ETHNOGRAPHIC FIX

It has sometimes been claimed that the early modern period sees the birth of ethnography, and even of anthropology.[44] There is an evident paradox here deriving from the tension between the claims linking modernity and individualism on the one hand, and the essentially collective character of the ethnographic enterprise on the other. But seen very broadly — and shorn of specific scientific claims — ethnography, of course, may be as old as writing, as old as the stereotypical representation of groups based on some empirical foundation. It makes use of a series of other genres such as cartography, travel texts, gazetteers, and administrative manuals, but also of visual representations such as the notion of a "typical couple" belonging to this or that group, or of scenes allegedly characteristic of the lifestyle of a particular group. A classic example of a writer with ethnographic claims from before our period is Giraldus Cambrensis or Gerald of Wales (1146–1223), whose works also clearly served a function in relation to projects for the conquest and subjugation of Ireland, among other places.[45] To the extent that ethnography was linked to travel on the one hand, and to the identification and management of difference in an imperial context on the other, it had nothing particularly Western or European about it in reality, as a perusal of literature from the Arabic-speaking world and from China confirms;[46] there does remain some question however on the distance to be traversed between loose ethnographic practice and a more rigorous comparative ethnology with claims to some form of completeness.

Ethnography, depending on the institutional context of its practice, can in turn lead to processes of ethnogenesis, a form of collective "self-fashioning" if one will. The object, rather than merely being reported on, proves to be malleable, redefining itself through a familiar application of the larger "observer effect." The claim has been made with regard to phenomena such as "caste" in colonial India (from the late nineteenth century onward), where it is a well-known proposition by now that colonial ethnography when linked to the census and its administration led to important changes in caste composition and ranking, and also exacerbated caste rivalries and hardened previously fluid boundaries.[47] In order for this to be the case, it is important that the state machinery possess both disciplining and persuasive powers, but at the same time that these should not be total or all-encompassing, allowing some margin for maneuver on the part of social groups. More generally, the relationship between the ethnographic object and the observer has frequently been captured in recent times through such formulae as the "invention of tradition," where one sees the shadow of the figure of the "trickster"—albeit a sort of collective trickster.[48]

The underlying purpose of such exercises is to de-naturalize what has often been portrayed as "primordial identity" or given ethnicity, based on kinship, language, descent, or even the opposition between, say, priestly and warring roles in a society. Effectively, politics and political negotiation come to impregnate all forms of group identity formation here, and politics in turn is principally seen as located in the links that tie the state and state power to society at large. In other words, by a curious and unintended effect, the central actor in such historical analyses is always the state, and no group or individual is seen as even possessing the possibility of an existence or identity outside the sphere of interaction with state power. This argument, for the primacy of a particular form of the political—like the work on "Renaissance self-fashioning" discussed earlier in this introduction—again bears the traces of a particular reading of the work of Foucault. It may be interesting to attempt to see how well it works in relation to a rather different conceptual scheme, that of the ethnically constituted trading group sometimes referred to as the "diaspora."

Although long used from its Greek origins, *diaspora*—"a scattering or sowing of seeds"—was deployed as an analytical concept only from the early

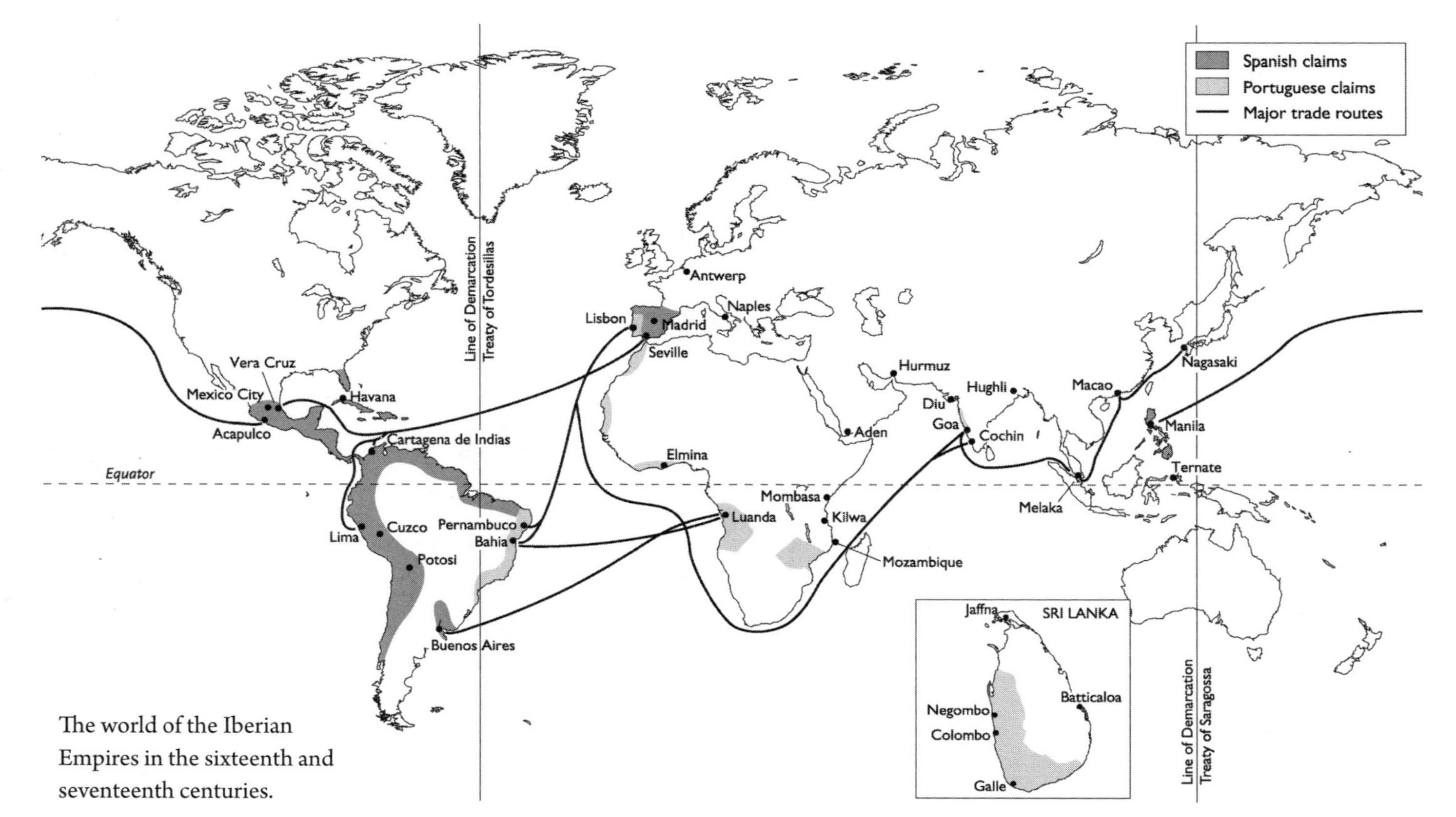

The world of the Iberian Empires in the sixteenth and seventeenth centuries.

1970s forward by Abner Cohen with regard to the Hausa in western Nigeria, and then popularized in the next decade by Philip Curtin in a wide-ranging and transhistorical study of merchant networks the world over.[49] Now in common use, it tends to have two quite distinct meanings: a medieval and early modern one, and a nineteenth- and twentieth-century variant. In the latter temporal context, it is assumed that one is dealing for the most part with a world of constituted nation-states, which then allows us to speak of the citizens (or former citizens) of a state as being in diaspora when they emigrate. These could be laborers as much as merchants, and both temporary and longer-term migrants. In the medieval and early modern situation, however, the focus has very largely been on merchants and entrepreneurs. Among these, some groups have a particularly favored empirical place: Jews, Greeks, Chinese from Guangdong and Fujian, and in recent times Armenians.[50] It is to the last instance that we may turn below to illustrate the complex negotiations of selfhood and alienation in a collective and early modern context.

While texts in Armenian speak of an engagement with the trade of the Indian Ocean in medieval times (in relation to trading ports in Sumatra, for example), it is in the sixteenth century that we find a particularly significant number of entrepreneurs who are clearly denominated as "Armenian"—in the Ottoman Empire, Iran, Mughal India, and beyond.[51] By the seventeenth century, a veritable stereotypical representation exists of "the Armenian." This image includes remarks on their religion (and proximity to Monophysite Christianity), on their dress—which also finds visual representation in woodcuts attached to travel-accounts like that of Nicolas de Nicolay (1517–83)—but also regarding their comportment at large.[52] Such remarks could be quite hostile, even when they came from other Christians. Here, for example, is the French East India Company merchant Georges Roques in the late seventeenth century.

> Let us now pass on to deal with the trade of the Armenians, where one shall see no less cunning, but rather if you wish even more chicanery than with the Indians. . . . This nation is even more cunning than the Indian *sarrāfs* [bankers] because the latter are simply concerned with what brings them money. The former, more enterprising, engage in everything that comes before them, and know everything about the price of goods, be they from Europe, from Asia, or from other parts, because they have correspondents everywhere who inform them of the true value in each place. Thus, they cannot be misled in their purchases. As they are great misers and work incredibly towards saving, and never over-price

> goods, they contribute to it through their low living expenses, to which they are naturally accustomed on account of their very low origins.[53]

This is a deeply uncomplimentary portrait, composed of the most abject stereotypes: cunning, chicanery, miserliness, low origins, and miserable lifestyle. The end point is to suggest however that all these unworthy aspects finally do lead to an enviable result, namely that of making the Armenians formidable competitors. But the other side of the coin concerns what manner of collaborators or partners they might make. Here, the French view tended to vary considerably depending on the proximate circumstances. By the time Roques wrote, these circumstances were none too good. This is the reason for his round condemnation, all the more remarkable in view of the fact that his text was not intended for publication but rather for circulation within the limited circle of the French Company. Here then is how his description continues.

> There are an infinite number of these merchants in the kingdom of the Moghol, Bengal, Pegu, Siam etc, and a great quantity in Surat, which has led us to know them profoundly. They are descended from the caste that the great Chaabas [Shah 'Abbas] king of Persia, brought from Armenia in order to have them live in his kingdom; and he gave them a suburb close to his capital which is called Julfa, in order for them to settle and live there using the largesse of that great prince and the gardens that they still cultivate. They benefited to such an extent from the neglect that Persians demonstrated in regard to the worth of trade that, in the end, they have brought everything into their hands and have created five or six very powerful households [*très puissantes maisons*] through which everything passes on account of the work of their servants who are dispersed through the whole world.

Here Roques passes rather coyly over the very violent process of expropriation and displacement through which the Safavid ruler Shah 'Abbas (r. 1587–1629) in fact brought the Armenians to settle in New Julfa, a suburb of Isfahan.[54] His principal purpose in the description is to argue, after all, for seeing the Armenians not as victims but as predators; for the real victims in his vision are the French, who have been duped by a certain number of individual Armenians whom he has in mind. Roques has a number of ironic remarks to make about their social comportment as well. "Though Christian, like other agents they take up with women in every place that they trade in order to have one at home. They intrigue in the affairs of governors to have their money better placed, and by this means manage to obtain their protection so that if their master seeks them out, or if he sends out a notice to retrieve his goods, he cannot obtain justice." The French Company agent brings out the curious mixture of behavior that characterizes the Armenians in his view. "In dealing with foreign nations, they are as refined as crude peasants, [but] they have become subtle and cunning in trade so that it is difficult to contract with them without being duped. Even if you are in agreement regarding all the articles on the basis of a paper signed by both parties, you cannot assure yourself of the execution of your contract. They are like those who play at billiards who, by a little trick [*par une bricole*], manage to get the ball to their goal and always have some proposition that they have not explained and which they have in mind, and which they will use when they want to break off or when they find a better option elsewhere."

Behind these propositions of a rather general nature, Roques in fact had some rather particular dealings in mind. He refers to these briefly, while noting that on "fifty occasions, to my knowledge, they have proposed rather important dealings which would be good for them and for the Company." However, he claims that the great difficulty lies in the incoherent fashion in which their trade is organized; each principal in New Julfa has several agents, who act in order to attract as much capital as they can to begin with. Once established in a distant spot however, they proceed to cheat their master as well as all others with whom they are engaged. Ostensibly based on kinship, trust, and servitude, the whole Armenian network in Roques's highly cynical view is based on the desire to collude in order to destroy the trade of other nations ("*ils s'ameuteront comme des chiens courant pour faire échouer les autres marchands*") through unfair competition.

Curiously, however, what lay behind this series of generalizations and claims of a broadly ethnographic or pseudoethnographic nature was a set of extremely specific operations. In 1664, the French minister Jean-Baptiste Colbert had supported the creation of a new French East India Company, or *Compagnie des Indes,* to rival those of the English and Dutch.[55] The problems that were faced were however numerous. Though the French (and especially merchants from Normandy) had indeed had periodic dealings with India since the sixteenth century, and individual merchants and entrepreneurs had also traded there overland in the seventeenth century, the degree of accumulated commercial knowledge was somewhat limited. Colbert's initial tendency was hence to draw heavily on the knowledge and experience of François Caron, a French Huguenot and former Dutch East India Company official with first-hand dealings in Taiwan and Japan. Since Caron did not have a great deal of knowledge with respect to the western Indian Ocean — whether the Persian Gulf or India — it was thought sound to find a counterpart who did. Colbert chose an Armenian Catholic by the name Martiros Marcara Avanchinz, who had arrived in distressed circumstances in Paris and claimed to belong to "one of the most considerable and comfortable of the houses, that Shah Abbas called the Great, transferred to Hispahan from Armenia Major."[56] The Armenian had considerable experience in the jewel trade, had spent time in Rome, Naples, and Venice as well as Livorno, and also claimed to know India well, having several brothers who were based there.

Marcara eventually accompanied Caron to India and was named director of all the factories to be set up in India and Persia, but their relations turned sour very quickly. In the welter of accusations and counteraccusations that were later exchanged, it is unclear what precisely transpired. Tensions seem to have been high already initially while at Surat, and Caron clearly wished constantly to assert his hierarchical superiority over his Armenian colleague. In a dispute over indigo purchases, he had Marcara shipped off a first time in chains to Madagascar, where he was absolved of all charges and returned to India. But difficulties continued, not merely between Marcara and Caron but also between the Armenian and various French employees of the Company. In 1669, the French thought to open a factory in the prosperous port of Masulipatnam on the east coast of India, and Marcara was dispatched to negotiate a royal order (or *farmān*) for this from the Qutb Shahi Sultan at Hyderabad. He seems to have managed the task very ably, thanks to his dealings with a certain Aqa Nazr Beg (or "Anazarbec"), a high-placed Armenian convert to Islam at the court, and to the fact that he had direct access to the Sultan's nephew. But the multilingual Marcara, who was able to deliver courtly discourses and write letters in Persian, obviously aroused the worst suspicions of his French colleagues, this in spite of the fact that he was able to extract a most favorable *farmān* in early December 1669. Shortly after this success, instead of being rewarded for it, he was summarily and rather brutally arrested on the orders of Caron and sent back to France, where he arrived after an extended and painful journey via Brazil in 1675. The Armenian now took legal recourse and sued the Company, and the trial dragged on for several years. In the end, Marcara won his case after strenuous efforts, with a royal verdict pronounced in his favor in 1685; but he could not obtain financial satisfaction even as late as 1688. However, the real damage had already been done to the French commercial reputation in both Iran and India. French relations with Armenian merchants remained bitter for long afterward, and it is an echo of this sourness that we find in Roques.

Can we discern what the underlying causes were for this peculiar falling-out? We may of course turn to the nature of some of the personalities involved, notably the authoritarian Caron. However, the key to the matter seems to lie in the stereotypical view that most European employees of the French Company had of the Armenian as early as 1667. Somewhat at a loss in India, their only recourse would otherwise have been to use Portuguese speakers as go-betweens, which was the eventual solution they adopted after 1690. Marcara, on the other hand, frequented the extended Armenian network, and also had extended access to Iranians, such as Yar Beg, the governor of Masulipatnam, and other highly placed members of the Qutb Shahi court. This may have been an asset but it was also a major liability, since it made him eminently opaque in the eyes of men such as Caron. The latter, we should remind ourselves, prided himself on his ethnographic skill and had authored and published a work on the "mighty kingdom of Japan [*machtigh koninghrijck van Iappan*]" based on his extended stay there.[57] It seems however that he found Marcara as an Armenian to be impenetrable, and this was a view that was carried over into later writers such as François Martin, the founder of French trading fortunes in India. Martin was to claim in his memoirs that the French had no way of knowing who Marcara really was: "He passed himself off as a gentleman from an illustrious family in Armenia," he wrote, but added that it was easy enough to claim this "since the Armenians are capable of everything."[58] He also cast doubt on the sincerity of Marcara's conversion to Catholicism, and noted that he had diverted most of the Company's purchases and sales to the hands of other Armenian intermediaries. The close-knit nature of the Armenian network, and the internal bonds of trust and reputation that held it together — which have usually been posed as one of the main assets the community possessed in trade — were in this instance the source of the problem.[59] Marcara to the French was thus not an individual but a chameleon, a trickster from a community of tricksters, than whom (to quote Martin once more) "there are no bigger cheats and double-dealers." Ethnography here aided the creation and reinforcement of negative stereotypes, leaving the individual little margin for maneuver.

In the Age of Discoveries therefore, there were indeed more ways to the woods than one, but there were also several that led nowhere. Accustomed as we are to celebrating the cosmopolitan, and the person who crosses cultural boundaries with a certain facility, we should not assume that such persons were always valued in past societies. The Spanish historian García-Arenal reminds us of how in the early modern Mediterranean even the renegades were constantly under pressure to fix themselves and their identities. "There was still a social distrust that kept these renegades at a distance. The renegade or *'ulj* was, even in terms of his name, both a witness to a crossing-over and to its limits. In the Maghreb, the renegades came to constitute a 'caste' with an important political and military role. On the other hand, they were situated in a restrained space, a political and social space which was specific to them, closed off above all in relation to the rest of Muslim society and which was defined in terms of either clientship or family relationships with their master or the sovereign."[60]

A great wanderer of the late fifteenth and early sixteenth centuries, the Mughal prince (and later emperor) Zahir-ud-Din Muhammad Babur begins his memoirs as follows: "In the month of Ramadan in the year 899 [June 1494], in the province of Fergana, in my twelfth year I became king."[61] Babur wanted his readers to understand that he knew very well who he was. He was destined to end his years over thirty years later in the Indo-Gangetic plain, in a climate he disliked, but his origins—both geographical and in terms of lineage—were eminently clear to him. He was a descendant of the great conqueror Timur, and the son of 'Umar Shaikh Mirza, whose death in an accident opens the memoirs of Babur. For all that his memoir is a deftly constructed personal document, it depends crucially time and again on the support provided by larger received structures: place, lineage, and religion. This was not the experience of the bulk of those whom we have looked at briefly in the above pages, nor will it be the experience of those who appear in the pages that follow. The reader will judge where the norm lies, and where the exception. My own sense for now is that the fate of which Yahya-u-Ta'fuft complained was perhaps not so unique after all.

2: A Muslim Prince in Counter-Reformation Goa

The Jew said to him [the captain of Surat] . . . that he should hand the fortress over to the Portuguese and that they would make him captain of Goa and would marry him to the daughter of Meale. He replied that that was all very well so far as life in this world went, but what would he do in the next?

— Fernão de Álvares, SJ, at Daman (1561)[1]

THE MAKING OF PORTUGUESE GOA

Goa, the city and the territory around it, is a place that somehow tends to attract and accumulate clichés, and this was already the case in the sixteenth century. *Goa Dourada*, "Golden Goa," was the phrase that was deployed by many contemporary travelers as well as later historians to evoke a place that, on account of its dense landscape of churches, was also glibly termed "the Rome of the East." A verdant location at the place where two rivers — the Mandovi and the Zuari — entered the Arabian Sea, it was seen as an ideal situation for a port that would direct commercial maritime traffic to the advantage of the power that held it, even though it was not situated at one of those dramatic "choke-points" that made for the prosperity of Aden and Hormuz to the west, or Melaka farther east. Goa in 1510, when it was conquered, then lost, then rapidly conquered once again by the Portuguese under their ferocious governor, Afonso de Albuquerque (admiringly nicknamed "the Terrible" in sixteenth-century texts), competed with a series of other ports, Honawar and Bhatkal farther south along the coast of Karnataka, as well as Dabhol and Chaul farther north. On the other hand, Mumbai (known to the Portuguese as "Bombaím") was still an ill-defined set of islands, creeks, and inlets, and could hardly be seen as the ideal location for the center of an extended enterprise such as the Portuguese *Estado da Índia* (or "State of the Indies") was turning out to be.

The heart of the territory of Goa was an island some 166 square kilometers in extent known as Tiswadi (or "Tissuari" to the Portuguese, from *tīs vādī*, or "thirty settlements"), where the sixteenth-century city denominated Goa was located. If one included the adjoining islands of Chodan ("Chorão" to the Portuguese) and Divar, as well as some other smaller ones, the area was collectively designated as *Ilhas*. In the years from 1510 to 1530, the status of Goa in the overall scheme of the *Estado* was still somewhat uncertain. Melaka on the Malay Peninsula, the focal point of important trading routes to the Spice Islands of Southeast Asia as well as across the Bay of Bengal, was also seen as a center of prestige and a lucrative spot to preside over as captain. For sentimental and strategic reasons, many also preferred Kochi (or Cochin) in the further southwestern part of the Malabar coast, the port where the Portuguese had taken refuge in 1500 after being forced out of the great commercial entrepôt of Kozhikode (or Calicut) when they had attempted clumsily to impose themselves by force. Kochi by the 1520s was more than a simple place for many Portuguese in Asia; it was instead the symbol of a certain vision of things, an implicit blueprint for an *Estado da Índia* where the Portuguese Crown would wear its power lightly, and leave most significant initiatives to freebooters, corsairs, and aristocratic entrepreneurs. But the years immediately following the death of Viceroy Vasco da Gama (who breathed his last in Kochi on Christmas Eve 1524 only a few months after arriving there) did not prove kind to the protagonists of the primacy of Kochi. Rather, the regime of the powerful, enigmatic, and long-serving governor Nuno da Cunha (1529–38), who had been nominated by the court of Dom João III to settle affairs in Asia after a deeply turbulent period of internecine quarrels among highly placed *fidalgos* and their clients, asserted the primacy of royal power, and also considerably consolidated the Portuguese presence along the west coast of India. The new Portuguese territories were mostly located in the so-called "Northern Province" (*Província do Norte*), and were acquired at the expense of the sultanate of Gujarat, formerly a powerful and expansive state in coastal northwestern India. Gujarat in the early 1500s was perhaps the most powerful of the northern Indian states, seemingly poised to expand far inland into both central India and the heartland of the Indo-Gangetic plain. Instead, in the course of the early 1530s, it collapsed dramatically when faced with the challenge of the rising Mughal dynasty, which had irrupted into northern India in the mid-1520s. The ambitious and charismatic sultan Bahadur of Gujarat (r. 1526–37) was thus obliged not merely to curtail his expansionary ambitions but to cede territories to the Portuguese, who pressed on his maritime flank even as he turned to face the Mughal threat. These included coastal lands to the southern fringes of his sultanate (in the area of Mumbai), as well as the port of Diu, strategically located to control trade with the western Indian Ocean.

In this new set of circumstances, Goa emerged as the logical center of the *Estado da Índia,* a position it effectively held from the early 1530s. Contemporaries began to use terms like *chave* (key) or *cabeça* (head) as metaphors to speak of Goa. A characteristic evocation appears in an anonymous text from the early 1580s, describing the Portuguese Indies to the Habsburg ruler Philip II, who had recently assumed control of the Crown of Portugal.

> The city of Goa, head and principal seat [*cabeça e assento principal*] of the State that the Crown of Portugal possesses in the parts of the Orient, is situated in an island of the same name, along the northern bank of a river called Pangim, two leagues to the interior from its mouth. This island shares borders with the lands of the *Hidalcão,* a very powerful king who is the lord of the greater part of the Kingdom of the *Daquem* [Deccan]. The separation from the mainland [*terra firme*] is effected by a very narrow divide that comes from two rivers which descend from a mountain range (which they call the *Gáte*), and which enter into the sea here creating two most excellent and large harbors, capable of receiving many ships, lying north and south respectively.[2]

We shall return presently to this *Hidalcão,* who in fact plays a rather major role in the pages that follow. The text then goes on to note that there were a number of passes that connected Goa to the interior, and that four of these were heavily fortified; all of them were nevertheless defended by garrisons, and all equally possessed customs-houses (*alfândegas*) which regulated trade from the island into the mainland.

Astonishing though it may appear, we have very few detailed maps of the city of Goa in the sixteenth century. One of the best representations comes to us from the 1590s, accompanying the travel account of the Dutch traveler and spy Jan Huyghen van Linschoten, whose *Itinerario* contains a candid (if colored) account of Portuguese strengths and weaknesses in Asia; it should ideally be read together with Manuel Godinho de Erédia's slightly later map from about 1620.[3] Linschoten's depiction (like that of Erédia) has the south at the top of the map and the westerly sea to the right, and we can effectively follow the Mandovi River eastward from its mouth, where we at once encounter the monastery of the Magi (*Reis Magos*) often used by entering and departing governors and viceroys as a staging post in relation to Goa proper. Sailing upriver beyond Panaji (or Pangim), we pass a set of islands to our left of which the most important are Chodan and Divar mentioned above. Facing Divar on the right are first the assorted docks (*a ribeira grande* for oceangoing ships, the *cais de Santa Catarina* and the *ribeira das galés* for the construction and repair of galleys). Eventually we come to a small inlet leading into the customshouse (*alfândega*), which is a part of a complex including the great bazaar and fish market, the weighing station (*peso*), and a *bangasal* (from the Malay *bangsal*, a shed or storehouse for foodstuffs), which Linschoten oddly describes in his gloss on the map as "the place where one sells firewood [*de plaets daer men't barnhout vercoopt*]." Running east to west from the weighing house and parallel to the river are first the prison (*tronco*), then the viceroy's (or governor's) residence, and eventually the royal hospital and the mint. The central axis of the town is however the great north-south commercial street termed the Rua Direita, a busy market with shops and public auctions (*leilões*) of both goods and slaves. If one were to take this up from the river, one would soon come to a square on the right denominated the *Terreiro do Sabaio* ("Sabaio's Square," on which more below), around which we would find loosely agglomerated the archbishop's palace, the seat of the Municipal Council, the See Cathedral, and the Holy Office of the Inquisition, the last of which was located within a building still denominated the Casas do Sabaio in the seventeenth century. This appears in some sense to represent a first core of public buildings defining a center to the town, a poor relative of the Zócalo in Mexico City. Still pursuing our southward path along the Rua Direita, we would come quickly to the Holy House of Mercy (Santa Casa de Misercórdia), as well as the abattoir and the old pillory, which seem to be at the secondary heart of the town as it is depicted by Linschoten. At the southern end of the urban space along this axis, one eventually would find the church of Our Lady of Light and the gallows.

Despite the fact that Velha Goa today is no more than a set of vestiges, with no apparently discernible urban structure, enough remains of the buildings shown in Linschoten's map for us to be able to orient ourselves using him (and then Erédia) as a guide.[4] These surviving buildings include the See Cathedral and the Chapel of St. Catherine, though the visitor is somewhat disoriented today by the dominant presence of slightly later buildings that Linschoten does not depict such as the convent of St. Cajetan and the Basilica of Bom Jesus — begun in 1594 and completed in the early seventeenth century — where the remains of St. Francis Xavier are preserved, but still a minor presence in Linschoten's map. The Viceroy's Arch, where ceremonial entries were made from the river — for example by the viceroy Dom João de Castro in the 1540s — corresponds to the passage into the Rua Direita from the riverbank, but was again completed slightly after Linschoten's time.[5] Also absent from his depiction in the very same vicinity (though farther east from the arch, and close to St. Cajetan's) is the stripped-down portal denoted as a vestige from the palace of the *Hidalcão*. Devoid of any inscriptions in Persian or Arabic, it is still clearly Indo-Persian in style, and an enigmatic reminder of the fact that this "very powerful king who is the lord of the greater part of the Kingdom of the *Daquem*" (to use the words of Philip II's anonymous informant from the 1580s) was once lord of Goa too.

By Linschoten's time, despite his own rather confused claims, few Muslims remained in Goa beyond the resident ambassadors of neighboring Muslim sovereigns and their retinues. In contrast, in 1510, when the Portuguese conquered the town, they had found considerable numbers of both local and migrant Muslims there, aristocrats and prebend holders of the grants known as *iqta'*, petty warriors, traders, and artisans.[6] A number of them were immediately put to the sword in late 1510 at the moment of conquest, and their widows taken into the households of the Portuguese conquerors, who were notoriously short of female companions from Iberia. Between 1510 and 1540, a certain laxity with regard to religious difference seems to have characterized Goa, and it is probable that no one looked too closely into the religious beliefs or practices of these women. A somewhat similar policy was followed in Portugal itself after the forced conversion of Jews and Muslims in 1497, when a moratorium of a generation's duration was declared with regard to enforcing religious practices closely.

But by 1540, matters were beginning to change in Goa, with respect not only to Muslims but also Hindus. In that year, a quite systematic campaign of destruction was carried out with respect to several hundred Hindu temples in Tiswadi, as well as in the islands of Divar and Chodan. Pressures mounted for Hindus to convert as quickly as possible to Christianity, and these pressures would have grown stronger with the arrival in 1542 of the first Jesuits in Goa. The Jesuits chose to locate their principal church — that of St. Paul — somewhat to the southeast in the town, though not quite as far out as the lagoon or the church of St. Lazarus. A rough road led south from their church to the Passo de Santiago, from where one looked across to the mainland. If one wished to return north to the real centers of power on the riverbank, one took the Rua de São Paulo and eventually the Rua do Açougue (or Slaughterhouse Street), which led to the *Misercórdia* and the old pillory, before turning onto the Rua Direita. Still, from this ex-centric location, seemingly far more modest than even that of the Franciscans — who as earlier arrivals occupied a prime spot right by the See Cathedral — they exercised a considerable influence over the cultural politics of the town, eventually providing the whole of the *Estado da Índia* with a patron saint in the form of that rather severe and dyspeptic Navarrene Francis Xavier (1506–52), who had himself spent appreciable amounts of time cooling his heels and grumbling in Goa.[7]

A MUSLIM FLY IN THE OINTMENT

By the 1560s, the religious "cleansing" of Goa proposed by the protagonists of the Counter-Reformation and other obdurate Catholics was well under way. In about 1600, a quite reliable estimate would place the town's population at about 75,000 of which some 55,000 were notionally Christians (including 1,500 Portuguese), and the remaining 20,000 Hindus.[8] What then can one say about the former Muslim population? Here, for example, is the account of the Venetian *bailo* Daniele Barbarigo, reporting to the Senate of the Serenissima in 1564 after his return from Constantinople, with a panoramic view of Indian Ocean trade. "Besides there is the city of Goa, which is an island, and in the city the river enters via two mouths, and parts the land, and makes an island of it; and the whole island of Goa is 16 miles long and as wide again. It is a most lovely city, which is the seat of the viceroy who governs all of India on account of the King of Portugal. And in this island, there is not even a single Moor of the Mahomedan sect [*non vi sta pur un moro della setta maomettana*], but only Christians and Gentiles."[9] One can discern a scarcely concealed envy in the tone of Barbarigo, who obviously had spent long months gazing out from his residence in Pera (today's Beyoğlu) across the Golden Horn at the domes of the Topkapı Saray and the silhouette of the Hagia Sophia, to say nothing of the other mosques with which the great architect Mimar Sinan was beginning to decorate the skyline of Constantinople.[10] But he was not quite right. For there were still Muslims in Goa in the 1560s, of which at least one conspicuous example could be found in the records of the times.[11]

In a letter composed in Goa on 30 November 1557 to his colleagues in the Company of Jesus at Coimbra, the celebrated Jesuit Luís Fróis wrote the following: "In this city was converted a Mooress of great quality, a daughter of the Moor Meale, to whom the kingdom of Balagate rightfully belongs. And since there are many particular and notable things to recount in the matter of her conversion which you will greatly rejoice to hear, I will write of it in another letter with the aid of Our Lord."[12] This might appear to be a rather mysterious and enigmatic reference on the face of it. Who could this "Meale" be? Why did the "kingdom of Balagate" belong to him? And finally why was there a Muslim woman of "great quality" resident in Goa with her family in the late 1550s, when Barbarigo believed in 1564 that there was not a single Muslim left living there who was worth mentioning?

Happily for us, the Jesuit Fróis did indeed keep his promise to his colleagues, and a bare two weeks later wrote another far more detailed letter regarding *l'affaire* Meale, with his addressee on this occasion being the Jesuit Francisco Rodrigues in Portugal. He began the letter with a rather rapid explanation of the identity of the person whom he saw as the principal protagonist in the matter. It runs as follows: "Meale, as you would have already learnt there from persons who have returned from here, is a Moor who is already of a certain age [*já de boa idade*], prudent and experienced and, in the opinion of the Moors, a great follower of Muhammad and well-versed in their scriptures and Qur'an [*muito versado nos moçafos e alcorão*]."[13] Fróis then continues by affirming that "it is to him, it is said, that by rights the kingdom of the *Idalcão*, which is very large, in fact belongs," and goes on to mention without a great deal of detail that there has been an attempt in the past "to put him in charge of his kingdom." He then adds the following rather elaborate explanation: "Through his legitimate wife, this Meale has two sons and a daughter, who said that her father wished to marry her with the oldest son of the *Izamaluco*, heir to that kingdom, or with the son of the king of *Bisnagá* which is one of the richest and most opulent kingdoms in these parts of India. His residence is here on this street, close to São Paulo; and as it is the custom among the Moors, especially here in these lands, to keep their women and daughters confined in the highest degree, it appears that this daughter found it a relief and recreation in her very narrow confinement to keep her ears open to the doctrine that the boys here sang in the street, both when they came to learn in the college, which is every day, and when they came and went from the schools."

In other words, we have a Muslim prince from the family of the aforesaid *Hidalcão* or *Idalcão*, former lord and master of Goa, with a residence still in the very heart of the city of Goa in the Rua da Carreira dos Cavalos, very close to where the Society of Jesus had its own principal residence. The suggestion is that this prince was busy negotiating the marriage of his daughter and that the candidates were, on the one hand, Murtaza, the son and eventual successor of Husain Nizam Shah (r. 1554–65) of Ahmadnagar (the *Izamaluco* or Nizam-ul-mulk of the letter), or—rather more improbably—a prince from the nearby Hindu kingdom of Vijayanagara (*Bisnagá*). The letter of Fróis now continues: "To this was added the fact that next door to them there lived a most noble and virtuous woman, who was the wife of Diogo Pereira, whom I already mentioned in another letter, both of whom are solely friends of the Company, and who greatly frequent our confessions and communions, and from whom the College receives much charity. It seems that they [Pereira's wife and Meale's daughter] talked through the windows concealing it from the father and mother. Maria Toscana, wife of Diogo Pereira, was so zealous for the good of her soul and persuaded her with such vehemence to become Christian, that when this had gone on for an entire year, she [the girl] began to give some positive signs of this."

Now, the diligent historian of Portuguese Asia in the sixteenth century should be familiar with the Pereira-Toscana couple mentioned above. The Diogo Pereira of the 1550s should not be confused with his homonym Diogo Pereira "the Malabar" (to cite his odd nickname), a rather important character with regard to the Portuguese presence in Kochi in the first half of the sixteenth century. Our Diogo Pereira is quite different, the son of a certain Tristão Pereira and an unnamed Indian woman, and known in the Portuguese chronicles of the epoch as the envoy sent in the 1550s to the court of the Gujarat Sultans, but also quite centrally implicated in the negotiations surrounding the foundation of the City of the Name of God in Macau at the very end of the 1550s.[14] A close friend and ally of the Jesuits (and a personal friend of Francis Xavier himself), as Fróis mentions in his letter cited above, he was equally known for his close dealings with the governor of the *Estado da Índia,* Francisco Barreto. Here then is the larger political context for the conversion of the daughter of Meale. If we continue to follow the narrative logic of Fróis's letter, little by little the daughter found "in her soul such a new desire and ardor to convert that it was a truly strange thing, but the thing that most affected her was seeing that she had no one with whom she could communicate, and that if her father found out that she wanted to become Christian, she would not escape death." It turned out however that the girl's life was not quite as "confined" (*emcerrada*) as Fróis's letter would initially have us believe. Quite on the contrary, it seems that she understood Portuguese and that she was frequently visited by Maria Toscana, who was a "great friend" of hers, and on one occasion had even spent the night in the house of her Portuguese neighbor while Diogo Pereira was away in China on one of his commercial trips.[15] Meale was clearly not keeping as strict a watch on "his women" as he might. However, despite this porosity, it was quite another matter to introduce a Catholic priest secretly into Meale's household for the purposes of conversion, and even more difficult to carry the girl off to church to baptize her in secret. The sole solution was to evoke temporal power, and ask for the direct intervention of the governor. Not for nothing was Goa a Catholic territory at the high tide of the Counter-Reformation after all.

The conspiracy, for it was no less, was eventually mounted in the following fashion. Diogo Pereira, through the mediation of the rector of the Jesuit College of St. Paul, Father Francisco Rodrigues, managed to speak directly to the governor Francisco Barreto, and "as a sign of how much [the girl] wanted to become Christian" showed him a jewel belonging to Meale's daughter, with the statement from her that "her father . . . was a native king [*rey natural*] even if he had been deprived of his kingdom, and . . . that all her relatives and descendants partook of royal blood, but that His Lordship should be the protector of her temporal life, in the face of the so-great perils that confronted her." The governor, if we are to believe the characteristically smooth Jesuit narrative, was greatly impressed by this declaration, and all the more so by a gift that Diogo Pereira offered him of "one of her [the girl's] diamonds set in a ring." This was a moment of great emotion: the governor "could not hold back his tears, raising his hands to heaven and giving thanks to God that during his government he could see the conversion to Christianity of the most noble woman since the time that this land had been conquered by the Portuguese." It was decided to swing into action on 10 August, "the day of the glorious St. Laurence."

We may still follow the prolix letter of Luís Fróis. On that day, he writes, "the governor decided he would go to hear Mass and the sermon in this College [of St. Paul] and that on the way, before he reached the church, he would take her away from her father's house." The girl had already been warned of the affair and was waiting inside the house with bated breath when Francisco Barreto came to the door of Meale's house accompanied by "many noble *fidalgos*," as well as by "two or three of the married and most prominent women of the city in their palanquins," among whom one could count Maria Toscana, the gray eminence of the entire operation. The narrative continues: "And Meale when he saw the Governor dismount at his door, and especially on a holy day on his way to church, he was greatly perplexed by the novelty of the affair, and not understanding why he came, sallied out to receive him down below at the door. And the Governor told him the reason why he came to speak to him, and how his daughter wanted to become Christian. Meale, who was most heavyhearted and also doubted that such could be the case, responded that he did not believe that his daughter wanted to become Christian. Then the Governor asked him if he recognized the ring that he carried, and on recognizing it he began to concede that it might be so."

During this whole conversation, the Portuguese women led by Maria Toscana had mounted their own guerrilla campaign. This is what Fróis's letter leads us to believe at least.

> While they were still exchanging these words, the women went up to fetch the girl who was upstairs, and she was so ready to go that she met them halfway down the steps, and at once clutched on to Maria Toscana. But since it seemed to the women that while the Governor was negotiating they should wait upstairs, they climbed back up with her. The girl's mother, when she saw the Portuguese women in her house, began to be nervous and have doubts about what was in store; she seized the girl and sat her down next to her, drawing her head to her bosom for greater security. At that moment, when they were all seated, it seems that one of the Moors overheard what the Governor was discussing below with Meale. He rushed up the stairs and in their language told them how the girl wanted to turn Christian and that all those people had come to take her away on that account.

We pass now to the most dramatic moment in the whole narrative, when the text of Fróis's letter seems drawn to a near-allegorical representation of the process, almost worthy of a painting in oils.

> Upstairs, both the girl's mother and the other female relatives who were there in the house rose up, as did all the other women servants, with great outcries and shouts, and pulling harshly on her, all the Mooresses tried to throw her down a trapdoor [*por huma porta d'alçapão abaixo*]. The Portuguese women grabbed hold of the girl from the other side, so that the struggle assumed such proportions that all their hair came undone, though — as I have said — these women who went there were among the most noble and dignified of this city, and would normally have taken it as an insult if the Mooresses had dirtied their velvet dresses with their hands, let alone treating their persons in such a rude fashion. The girl, agitated on account of all these dealings, and even more so wounded by the painful and dolorous words of her mother and female relatives, well my dearest friends, you can see in what state of anguish she would have found herself. Still, her determination was such that with her eyes closed, she would not let go of Maria Toscana and the other Portuguese women, and seeing that one of the Mooresses had seized the throat of one of these women with her hands, she reproached her so bitterly that, taken aback, she ceased to attack her.

The delight of the Jesuit author at this sixteenth-century equivalent of female mud wrestling can hardly be concealed by his dignified prose. The episode wound then to its conclusion. The governor himself, "hearing from down below the roars and outcries that were going on," rushed up the stairs; the Muslim ladies of the household ceased their resistance, and the girl was carried away rapidly by the Portuguese in the palanquin of the governor, which was already at the door of the house. She was taken first to the house of Diogo Pereira and Maria Toscana, where she was provided with a change of clothes; instead of being "wrapped up in some cloths as was their custom," she now emerged with "a rich dress in the Portuguese style" to respond to the questions of the governor and the chief magistrate (*ouvidor-geral*). Five days later, on 15 August, she was baptized in the Jesuit church and received the name of Dona Maria de Além-Mar (or "Lady Mary from Overseas"). On that occasion, she received from the hands of the governor himself "a grant in the name of the King" of one thousand *pardaus* a year in rents; and according to the Jesuit chronicler Sebastião Gonçalves, some years later "married Jorge Toscano, brother of Maria Toscana, who later was captain of Cananor [Kannur in Kerala], and was a lady of great Christianity and honor until she died in childbirth."[16]

As for Meale and his wife, this was for them a moment of great disgust and humiliation. The Jesuit letters assure us that the mother "shaved her head as a sign of her sadness, and with the vehemence of her sentiments fell ill and was very unwell." However, a few days after the daughter's baptism, they seem to have become resigned to their fate; if we follow Fróis's letter, "some days later, it seems that the father and mother wanted very much to see the girl; the Governor took her there in person with Maria Toscana, and in the evening went back to fetch her to his own house." The Portuguese thus kept the girl; the Moor had to be content with his sighs. And, in order to lend his account that little human touch, the Jesuit author adds the following anecdote. "When she was carried off from her father's house, one of her little eunuch boys [*hum eunucozinho seu*] ran after her, very lively and smart, clutching on to the clothes of the Governor, and swearing by the cross that he wanted to become Christian too. And he climbed into the carriage with his mistress, and when he had become Christian she ordered that he be placed in this College in order to learn the doctrine, where he is nowadays."

MORE ABOUT MEALE

It is scarcely a secret that the Iberian presence in both Asia and America in the sixteenth century provides evidence of various cases of "native" princes who entered the political sphere of magnetism of the colonizing power, serving eventually as agents, informants, hostages, and even at times quislings and guinea pigs.[17] There thus existed from early on a process of negotiation between the two (or at times three, or even four) sides in the affair, in a spectrum of possibilities that at first sight might seem rather limited, but which in reality did leave a certain amount of margin for maneuver.[18] This is a situation that can be looked into with respect to a certain number of specific cases, of individuals who crossed political and cultural frontiers with a certain facility, despite the fact that they were at the same time subject to constant suspicion.

In this chapter, my own purpose is to study over a period of roughly three decades (between 1540 and 1570) the career of one of the principal protagonists of the episode in late 1557 discussed above, the aforementioned Meale or Mealecão. He is a character whose name must be familiar enough to the readers of the principal chronicles of sixteenth-century Portuguese Asia, and notably the works by Gaspar Correia and Diogo do Couto.[19] That said, a great deal of confusion surrounded the personage, leading a historian of western India as late as 1983 to devote a short essay to attempting to sort out who he really was.[20] To be sure, he was a prince from the ʿAdil Shahi royal house of Bijapur, as we see from the claim that it was to him "that by rights the kingdom of the *Idalcão*, which is very large, in fact belongs." But which prince, and descended from whom? Even the contemporary chroniclers cannot agree on this and attribute locations for him in the ʿAdil Shahi genealogy that are highly dubious.[21] Now our knowledge of fifteenth-century Goan history is undoubtedly fragile. It seems the territory was controlled by the Vijayanagara Empire till about 1472, when it fell into the hands of the Bahmani sultan Muhammad Shah III. From the 1490s, as the sultanate began to fragment, the region came under the control of a certain Yusuf ʿAdil Khan Sawaʾi, of Turkoman extraction from the Iranian town of Sawah (or Saveh, northwest of Qom), briefly mentioned by Marco Polo, and dominated in the fourteenth and fifteenth centuries by Sunni Muslims of the Shafiʿi school. It is the term "Sawaʾi" that is at the origin of the Portuguese term *Sabaio*, which is in turn at the root of such expressions as the *Terreiro do Sabaio* or the *Casas do Sabaio*.[22] Yusuf seems to have arrived in India in the 1480s as part of a group of slaves or servants in the entourage of a rich horse trader. We have an interesting account of his origins from the pen of the chronicler Dom Fernando de Castro at the close of the sixteenth century.

> According to the general opinion of those who know the origins of the fortune of this *Sabaio*, they say that he was a native of Persia, born in the city of Sabá. When he was a young boy, he was given as a servant [*criado*] to a great merchant, and he was so good at carrying out his trade, and he served his master with such fidelity and love that he received great concessions from him and came to accumulate a great capital from him. So it happened that he was sent to India with a consignment of horses, in which affair he managed to multiply the value of the goods that he carried from his master by four times more than he had hoped. The merchant on seeing such a great multiplication as well as the fidelity he possessed, sent him off once again with a cargo of fifty horses, but before he reached India, two-thirds of them died on account of the poor voyage, and the others that remained to him he sold for 6,000 *pardaus*. And seeing the great extent of the loss and fearing that he would not be well received by his master, either because he did not dare to return to his land with such a loss, or because Fortune called on him for better things, he decided to remain in the kingdom of the Deccan with the money he had made from the horses, and went off to live in the city where the king resided.[23]

This version corresponds quite closely to that put out in a certain number of Persian chronicles as well (and notably the *Tazkirat al-Mulūk* de Rafi'-ud-Din Shirazi, which identified Yusuf as the son of one Sultan Mahmud Beg of Sawah), and is far more plausible than the alternative version (by the great chronicler Firishta) that casts him as the long-lost son of none other than the Ottoman sultan Murad II (d. 1451).[24] At any rate, we are aware that he had risen to prominence in the Bahmani Sultanate by the late 1480s, and held the title there of 'Adil Khan. When the sultanate began to totter after the death of its great *wazīr* Mahmud Gawan Gilani, Yusuf 'Adil Khan was one of those who managed to profit from the situation, together with Burhan Nizam-ul-mulk and Quli Qutb-ul-mulk. He thus hived off the southwestern section of the Sultanate, including the territory of Goa, and installed himself in what had hitherto been the provincial town of Bijapur. It was under his control that the Portuguese found Goa in 1510, and on his death in October of that year, he was succeeded by his son Isma'il, who seems to have continued the humbler title of 'Adil Khan rather than assuming the more elevated title taken later of 'Adil Shah ("Just King"), from which by a process of metatheses we get the term *Idalxá* in Portuguese.[25] Isma'il 'Adil Khan, who lost control definitively of Goa in November 1510 to the Portuguese, remained on very poor terms with them through his reign, until his eventual death in 1534. It was only from the time of his successor that the title 'Adil Shah was eventually adopted in Bijapur, probably after the last of the older line of Bahmani sultans, Kalimullah Shah, was formally dethroned in the 1530s.[26]

The succession stakes were now open. Court politics in the early Bijapur Sultanate seem to have still functioned within the template provided by the Bahmanis: the main line of tension separated a Twelver Shi'i group (comprising Persian and Turkoman migrants in large numbers) closely oriented toward the Safavids, the dynasty that had recently come to power in Iran, and a group of native-born Muslims who saw the others as "foreigners" (*āfāqīs*), and preferred the ecumenical Sunni-inflected Islam that had taken root in the region under the influence of charismatic figures such as the Chishti Sufi Sayyid Muhammad al-Husaini, known as *Gesudarāz*—"He of the Long Tresses." As the century wore on, other groups would emerge into prominence in the Bijapur court, notably Maratha Brahmins and East African (or Habashi) migrants. But in the 1530s, their role was minor. Isma'il 'Adil Khan seems for his part to have had a noted preference for the Iranians, and had aligned himself closely with first his homonym Shah Isma'il Safawi (d. 1524), and then with the latter's son Shah Tahmasp (r. 1524–76). Bijapur's principal port, Dabhol, kept alive a vital link with the Persian Gulf, which brought not only horses and war materials but Iranian migrants eager to try their luck in the Deccan.

These Iranians seem, rightly, to have been nervous of Isma'il's son Ibrahim. An experiment was thus tried with the other son, Mallu Khan (whom historians have sometimes confused with our "Mealecão"), but this proved to be of short duration. Soon after, he was deposed and Ibrahim did succeed. It soon became clear however that he had a strong penchant for Sunnism, visible in the changed form of prayers in Bijapur's mosques. Opposition to his rule began to crystallize around a great Iranian noble of Turkoman ethnicity, Yusuf Lari, holder of the important title of Asad Khan, whose power base was in the town of Belgaum (not far into the interior from Goa). Asad Khan decided not to reach forward into the younger generation of Ibrahim 'Adil Shah's competitor siblings, but instead to a prestigious figure of the past. The man he chose as an alternative to Ibrahim was thus the younger son of the founder of the dynasty, Yusuf 'Adil Khan. This was a certain 'Ali (known in a familiar fashion as Miyan 'Ali, with *Mīyān* being an affectionate title used even today in India), at that time resident with his wife and sons in the court of Sultan Mahmud Shah of Gujarat, where he enjoyed a prebendal income. How had 'Ali wound up in Gujarat? We can by no means be entirely certain. The version given us by the Portuguese chronicler Diogo do Couto is, as is usual with this prolix writer, quite elaborate. He reports how Asad Khan, described by him as "governor of all the Deccan," had "at the death of *Malucão*, the son of *Ismael Idallcão*, decided to raise up as king Mealecão, son of *Sufo Idallcão* who had been master of Goa." However, he did not succeed and instead Ibrahim was placed on the throne. Couto is unique among Portuguese sources in treating the new sultan as "a very good man and of good character [*muito bom homem e de boa natureza*]," and states that it was on this account that he initially decided to free Meale, who was languishing in prison. The chronicler equally reports that he arranged Meale's marriage at this time with "a princess who had been brought up in the house of the queen [of Bijapur] . . . belonging to the caste of the ancient kings of *Xarbedar* [the Bahmani sultans of Bidar]." However, the sultan's ears were soon poisoned by jealous courtiers, and he grew suspicious of his uncle, the more so since it was known that he was closely tied to Asad Khan. Fearing death or imprisonment, Meale eventually chose the course of prudence, and hence asked for (and received) permission to perform the *hajj* pilgrimage to Mecca and Medina. Turned back by bad weather, and robbed at Zeila in East Africa, while on a ship that had set out from Dabhol in April 1541, he had then made his way to Surat, from where the Gujarat sultan Mahmud had received him well at his court in Ahmadabad, "giving him a household in conformity with his quality and a town by the name *Nagara* and its villages, which yielded ten or twelve thousand *pardaos* for the expenses of his household."[27] Such courtesies were commonplace in the Indo-Muslim sultanates, and each of them normally hosted a set of exiled princes from their neighboring dynasties. This was a matter of a shared political culture, but also seen as sound from the viewpoint of realpolitik. The Gujarat sultans thus also hosted 'Alam Khan Lodi, the brother of Sultan Sikandar Lodi of Delhi (d. 1526), for long years, much to the irritation of the early Mughals.

Asad Khan Lari's plan in the 1540s centered on the project of persuading 'Ali to return to Bijapur from Gujarat. To implement this, he seems to have decided to use the Portuguese as go-betweens, and the time seemed singularly propitious. The impulsive and rather eccentric Estêvão da Gama—who had led an expedition as far as Suez—was about to be succeeded as governor by Martim Afonso de Sousa, well known for his interest in and sympathy for intrigues in the sultanates of the area. Sousa had been a rather close companion for a time of Sultan Bahadur of Gujarat, who had rather mysteriously drowned (or been killed) while meeting the governor Nuno da Cunha off Diu in February 1537. It was to this new Portuguese regime that Asad Khan turned to implement his vision. The Goa administration accepted to play its part, and a group of Portuguese headed by a certain Sebastião Lopes Lobato was dispatched to this end to fetch 'Ali bin Yusuf 'Adil Khan from Gujarat. We do not know what exactly Lobato dangled in front of the Muslim prince's eyes by way of bait; he certainly promised him Portuguese support in a project to become sultan, and he must equally have told him he would be treated well and with dignity while in Goa. Here then is how "Mealecão," the Portuguese version of Miyan 'Ali bin Yusuf's name, eventually found himself in the capital of the *Estado da Índia.*

But even the best-laid plans of Iranian grandees need their share of luck to be carried through. Instead, shortly after the arrival of 'Ali and his family in Goa, disastrous news arrived from Belgaum: Asad Khan Lari had suddenly sickened and died, leaving a good part of his accumulated fortune in the hands of a great Iranian merchant, a certain Khwaja Shams-ud-Din Gilani.[28] This is how we find the context for the incidents of this period set out for us in a contemporary letter written by one Manuel Godinho, a burgher resident (*casado e morador*) at Goa in these years, and directed to the king of Portugal, Dom João III. "The old 'Adil Khan [*Ydalcão o velho*], the father of the one who reigns now, purchased a slave of the Turkish nation and made him a great lord, and he was captain of a city called Bilgão; and at the time that I came to India, he was [still] called Sufolarym [Yusuf Lari] and they say that at that time he had revenues of 500,000 *pardaos*. And thereafter the old *Ydalcão* died and this other one who is his son [Ibrahim] gave him the title of *Açadacan* which is like *Dom* among them, and they say that he would have had revenues of 800,000 *pardaos* and the treasure [*tisouro*] he possessed was very great."[29]

Our analysis of what happened thereafter is helped by two letters written from Goa by the captain of that city, Dom Garcia de Castro, in December 1543, a year into the government of Martim Afonso de Sousa. In his first letter, dated 3 December, Dom Garcia reports to the king Dom João III concerning the activities of the governor in order to confront the perceived menace of the Ottomans (*Rumes*), on the one hand, and also recounts in a rather discreet manner the strange (and abortive) project of Martim Afonso to sack the great Hindu temple of Tirupati on the other (the so-called "viagem do Pagode"). He then touches on the presence of Meale in Goa and its significance.[30]

After the governor left here [for Tirupati], a few days later some great revolts began among these lords of the Deccan against the *Ydalcam* with a view to deposing him, for he was a tyrant and man of dissolute life [*omem de mao viver*], and in his place and state to put in one of his uncles, a brother of his father, who is called *Myalyquão*, a man who has great credit among them and is considered to be virtuous, and it has been a long time that they have wished to make him their master. He was in Cambaia [Cambay, i.e., Gujarat] having run away from the *Ydallcão* who wished to kill him. The person who persuaded him most and worked hardest to put this affair into effect was our neighbor *Acedecão*, who brought in the *Yzamaluco* [Nizam-ul-mulk] and the *Verido* [Barid Shah] against the *Ydallcão*, and they invaded his land and took almost all of it, and he was in a state of utter defeat; and he being in such a state, with everyone's consent and the participation of the great part of the captains of the *Ydalcão*, it was decided to send for *Mialycão* in Cambay to make him master of the state of the *Ydalcão*. And for this they had no other option than to ask for my help since the governor was not present, in particular *Acedecão* who was the principal agent, and the most implicated in the affair, since he was openly declared to be in rebellion against the Ydalcão, and so he sent a message asking me for a small vessel [*fusta*], armed and prepared to bring this man whom they wanted as their lord [*senhor*].

The suggestion here is that Asad Khan Lari was able to create an alliance with the Ahmadnagar sultan Burhan Nizam Shah (r. 1508–53), whose interest in Bijapur was also linked to the fact that he was Isma'il 'Adil Shah's brother-in-law, as well as with 'Ali Barid Shah (r. 1542–79), ruler of the relatively minor central Indian sultanate of Bidar. The negotiations with Goa would have taken place sometime in the months of September and October 1543, given that Martim Afonso left the city on 2 September, immediately at the end of the monsoon season. Thus, despite the governor's absence, as well as that of a number of other key actors who accompanied him on his raid, Dom Garcia appears to have been confident enough of the tone of the administration to act decisively. "I discussed what should be done on this matter with Dyogo da Silveira and other appropriate men who were here, and I found that there were some opinions against what I wanted to do, which was to send for him [Meale] and work to bring him here, since some good service to Your Highness was bound to follow from this; and I commended myself to God, and sent for him, because when things are done with a good intention and without ulterior motives or malice, God favors and helps them as we presently came to feel. So I sent Bastião Lopez Lobato for him, who acted in this matter exactly as I ordered, which he followed." The career of this Sebastião Lopes Lobato is known to us through a large set of documents from the period, and we know that a few years later, in 1547, he would rise to high office as *ouvidor-geral* of the *Estado da Índia.*[31] Lobato left Goa for Gujarat then in his vessel, and once there managed via the help of some Muslim intermediaries to enter into contact with Meale, who "although in Cambay, had lands, and revenues and a great house." The initial idea, once Meale had been persuaded to leave behind this rather comfortable lifestyle for the risky venture that was proposed, was to take him to the port of Banda (near Vengurla), "which is a port belonging to *Acedecão* ten leagues from here [Goa]." It is reported that Meale himself was rather enthusiastic at this point: "he dropped everything as soon as he saw the message and got into the vessel [*fusta*] one night with just his wife and sons and came along." But by the time the ship arrived in Banda, matters had changed. To return to the account of Dom Garcia de Castro:

> Since the Moors are rather inconstant in all matters, they became slack with the *Ydalcão* since they believed he was defeated, and he regrouped with the substantial help that he had from the *Madremaluquo* ['Ala-ud-Din 'Imad Shah of Berar] and came back against *Acedecão* in order to destroy him. And when things were in this state, Mialy arrived in Banda, and found that it had already been taken by the *Ydallcão* and was forced by him to come and place himself in this city [Goa], which was considered to be very bad by the old hands in this land among whom one can count Pero de Faria, and even if it seemed so to them, I for myself thought that God must have arranged matters in this way for the greater service of Your Highness, and I had him disembark and welcomed him very warmly.

In his second letter, dated 29 December, Dom Garcia returns with further details to the same subject, and also recounts the posterior evolution of the political situation. This is a rather astonishing transformation in many ways.

> After I wrote to Your Highness, other things transpired concerning the arrival of this Moor [Meale] in this city, which it became necessary to write about, and I give many thanks to Our Lord that things are going from good to better. When it was known for certain in the *Balagate* that this man whom I had sent for had come and was in this city, the *Ydalcão* as a man who was deeply implicated in this, sent his ambassadors here to the governor, and promised him a great sum of money if this man was not allowed in any way to enter the *Balagate. Acedecam* also sent a certain number of his captains with many men to Ponda, which is the spot closest to this island, and also sent his ambassadors equally promising a

great deal of money if this man was handed over to him so that he could be made *Ydalcão,* since the *Yzamaluquo* and the other lords of the *Balagate* were a part of this alliance. Things being in this situation, the affair was forced to the point that the governor was obliged to go to his council, and then to the city and its people [*povo*], and it was decided rather to accept the offer of the *Ydalcão;* and Your Highness ought not to assume that this matter was quite so light or so easy to decide, and both sides had so many justifications that it had been a long time since one had seen a matter that was so difficult to decide, and thanks to Our Lord to whom I always commended myself in this affair, the governor chose the best option, and accepted the offer of the *Ydalcão* and sent for his ambassadors, and told them that bearing in mind the old friendships that the Portuguese had with their lord, the *Idalcão,* which Your Highness had with special orders ordered him [the governor] to maintain and keep, and that he in the name of Your Highness had declared himself for the *Idalcão,* and had decided to keep the peace with him forever, and that he accepted from him the lands of Sallsete and Bardes which the *Ydalcam* gave him by way of friendship and of his own free and good will, of which they made solemn acts with all the good declarations that Your Highness will see over there. I refer to these for they have been carried out by the governor Martim Afonso de Sousa who, besides the fact that his intentions are entirely addressed to the good of the service of Your Highness and the profit of your treasury, has many other qualities by way of knowledge and decision, and Your Highness should be sure that he will in his time perform his entire service with every perfection.[32]

From the obsequious tone and contents of the letters of Dom Garcia, we can rapidly comprehend that we are dealing with a partisan of the same political conceptions that drove Martim Afonso de Sousa; for him, the up-and-down dealings regarding Meale were pretty much part of the normal functioning of the *Estado da Índia.* There was clearly a problem to be resolved here, and this concerned the "penumbra" of Portuguese Goa. To be sure, the island of Tiswadi itself as well as the adjacent small islands had been acquired by the bold acts of conquest of 1510. But to the immediate north lay Bardes or *Bārā desh* (the twelve territories), a space somewhat larger than what the Portuguese already held in 1540, extending as far north as the 'Adil Shahi fort of Shahpura (Chapora) and its river. South of the Zuari River was the even larger territory of Salcete (from *Sasasta* or sixty-six settlements), a space that went as far south as the lands controlled by Vijayanagara and its vassals. These territories had the potential to provide a small but significant agrarian hinterland for Tiswadi of a sort that the Portuguese had dreamed of from the 1520s. The presence of Meale in Goa provided Martim Afonso and his entourage a brilliant solution to this problem. By threatening Ibrahim 'Adil Shah with the imminent return of his uncle, a solution could be found that was exactly equivalent to the concessions that Nuno da Cunha had extracted from the sultans of Gujarat less than a decade earlier in regard to the *Província do Norte*.[33]

But there were further complications to the matter, as seen from the second letter of Dom Garcia de Castro. He writes:

> Since the arrival of this man [Meale] in this land was generally profitable, both in terms that has happened so far and from whatever else can be hoped for in the future, since the *Ydalcão* is a youth, and a man of dissolute habits and bad customs, and is surrounded by men like himself, as a result he can never be at peace either with his own people or with his neighbors, on account of which we have a great threat [*sobroso*] to him in the form of this man [Meale], since everyone wants him for their overlord; and thus, when the *Ydallcão* dies, it is this man by whom the kingdom will be inherited. Thus, in every way, the coming of this man to this land was a great service for God and Your Highness, and it shows clearly that this work was performed by His Hands, because my knowledge and efforts would not have sufficed for me to take such a heavy task upon myself, as it was to send for this man against the advice of all the experienced men in this land; and when I decided on this affair, I commended myself to Our Lord, and He gave him to me and I accepted him [Meale], and whatever happens to him, we should be thankful to Him [God]. And since I am too small to be able to give thanks [to God] for so great a deed, Your Highness — whom all of this concerns — would do me a very great honor if you were to thank Him on your behalf and that of everyone.

The arrival of the prince from Bijapur in Goa is thus posed as nothing less than providential, a matter in which the hand of God can be discerned. The plan that is being proposed is the following: the governor Martim Afonso and his henchman Dom Garcia awaited either the death of Sultan Ibrahim from his "dissolute habits" or further rebellions against him. At this point, the time would come to bring Meale out once again from cold storage and deploy him as a potential successor. The immediate complication was however the disappearance of a crucial ally within the Bijapur polity itself. Dom Garcia's letter thus continues:

> After accepting the terms of the *Idalcão*, once all the articles had been signed, the death of *Acedecão* took place, and thereby the *Ydalcão* seized hold of his lands and fortresses. And the principal ambassador whom *Acedecam* maintained here [in Goa] in regard to all these matters was a very honored Moor by name *Coge Sameçadym* [Khwaja Shams-ud-Din], a great intimate of his, with whom the governor had particular dealings so that he should give him [Martim Afonso] a great sum and quantity of money that *Acedecão* had placed in Cananor in some residences that this Moor had constructed there, and this for certain, and the Governor hopes for sure to send the good news to Your Highness by these ships; and for these reasons and for many others, it can be said that Our Lord brought this man [Meale] to this city, and thus I hope that his arrival will be for the good and expansion of Your Royal State, and also I hope with the greatest confidence that Your Highness will not deny me the honors and benefices that I merit on this account; and I believe for certain that the governor Martim Afonso will write to Your Highness that it was my care and industry that brought this man to this city.

This is a brief reference here to an important affair of the 1540s, that of the so-called "treasure" of Asad Khan, which the Iranian merchant Khwaja Shams-ud-Din Gilani had in his safekeeping in his residence in the northern Kerala port of Cannanore (or Kannur). This money was eventually largely swallowed up, or so it would seem, by Martim Afonso himself.[34] Dom Garcia, having ensured that his own diligence has not passed unnoticed by the court in Lisbon, now continues by reflecting on the situation with respect to the newly acquired lands in Bardes and Salcete.

> The lands of Salscete and Bardes are pacified, and the *Ydalcão* has given his royal orders [*seus farmõis reais*] and letters that are attested and sworn on his scriptures [*nos seus moçafos*] to the effect that he grants these lands to Your Highness, and to all your successors in the kingdom of Portugal, which comprise the *tenadarias* of Salsete and Bardes of which I already went and took possession, and I placed them peacefully under Your Highness with the local people [*a gente da terra*] being most content and satisfied about this, and they give revenues of 45,000 *pardaos* which is a great help to sustain this land. Everything else that concerns this affair Your Highness will learn from what the Governor writes.

The finances of Goa, always in a precarious state, are thus posed in the letter as having attained a considerably greater stability as a consequence of this masterstroke. But the situation was, in reality, even more complex. For the person of Meale, or 'Ali bin Yusuf 'Adil Khan, was of far more complex utility in the conceptions of Martim Afonso de Sousa and his circle. This is revealed to us by other correspondents of the Portuguese king who also resided at this time in the capital of the *Estado da Índia*. One of these was precisely one of those "old India hands" disparaged by Dom Garcia de Castro in his letters, namely the former captain of the fortress of Melaka, Pêro de Faria. In a letter written nearly two years later, on 11 November 1545, he reports to the king on a series of matters before entering into the affair of Asad Khan, here posed by him in far larger geopolitical terms involving the threat presented by the Ottomans in the western Indian Ocean.

> Dom Grasya [de Castro] when he was captain of Goa sent to Cambay for Myale, and on his account the said Miale in person is in this city of Goa. *Açadaquão* sent Coje Samasadim since he had great trust in him; indeed, he trusted him with so much money so that he could bring Myale. And if I speak of Dom Grasya, I am also obliged to speak to Your Highness of myself for if Your Highness has some-one who carries out his service in this matter, it is I who have done so. I shall not speak of Martym Afomço, for it is enough that he is governor; I will only speak of Dom Grasya, since he sent for Myale in Cambay for him to come to this city, and I contradicted him before everyone in the council, and said that it was not correct nor in Your Service to break the peace with the *Idalquão* simply in order to favor one of his slaves, which is to say *Asadaquão*, against his own king and master, even though *Asadaquão* might order 90,000 *pardaos* to be handed over, for since God would see that we were not being true, He would turn against us. And since *Hasadaquão* was old and a foreigner, he was a rotten cable on which to attach the [ship of] service of Your Highness, and that we would then have great wars and the *Idalquão* would nurse a great hatred against the Portuguese and that he would install the Turks in his ports and fleet, for he had many and very well-supplied ports and the fleet of the Grand Turk needed wood, linen, iron, many food-supplies, and besides this also good ports, and that this would create the possibility — were he to make war on Your Highness — for the Grand Turk to find ports and protection for his fleet and people, and that they would take advantage of this far quicker than had been considered. And [I gave] many other reasons all founded in the service of Your Highness, and three of us held to my opinion and I will count myself first as a villain since I was the first to state this opinion, and only then the Vicar-General and Luys Falquão, when we were twenty and odd in the council and all the others were of the opinion that Myale should be sent to *Asadaquão* and all the more so since *Asadaquão* was giving

> us 90,000 *pardaos*. Still, what I said appeared sound to Martym Afonso your governor, because I said that since he would be creating travails for the residents of [Goa] by way of famine and war he should advise them of what had been said in the council, and he called in the Municipal Chamber, and everyone then agreed that they should not break with the *Idalquão*, and everyone agreed now with my opinion. Then, with the arrival of Myale, a mere five or six days later *Asadaquão* died, so that once Myale stayed Coje Samaçadim stayed on too, so that Your Highness became heir to a million in gold [*dum comto douro*] besides the mainland [*terras firmes*] which now belongs to Your Highness, and with the money that the *Idalquão* gave besides acquired the lands, as well as [the money of] *Asadaquão*.[35]

In this self-serving letter then, all the good that came out of the negotiations can entirely be attributed to the sagacity and vision of Pêro de Faria. Neither the governor nor the captain of Goa can be seen to have had any good sense at all. But Faria does not tell us of how far the machinations had gone either; for this, we need to refer to another letter written from Goa, this one of 23 December 1545, by António Cardoso, secretary of the *Estado da Índia* at the time, and equally addressed to the king Dom João III. This letter lays bare an even more peculiar transaction that was being contemplated at the time involving Meale. It appears that Sultan Ibrahim, becoming restive with the presence of his uncle at Goa for over two years, had begun to treat with Martim Afonso concerning the possibility of purchasing the prince and his family for a suitable sum of money. The governor and his entourage were quite content to mull over this possibility, and had even come close to agreeing on a price; the only problem was that at this point the new governor, Dom João de Castro, arrived in Goa. Thus, we have the letter of António Cardoso:

> My Lord. After the last letters had been sent to Your Highness, the *Ydalcão* sent three of his captains back here with the ambassadors whom Martym Afonso de Sousa had sent him regarding the affair of Mealle Quão which has already been written about to Your Highness, and they come with many men on foot and horseback, and are six leagues distant from this island of Goa hovering between peace and war, requesting the Governor that he hands over Mealle and his wife and sons and that they will give 50,000 *pardaos* to the ambassadors which was the price that they agreed upon even after the Governor Dom Johão de Crastro had arrived in this land, without having his agreement nor a word from him agreeing to do so aside from the council that the Governor held on this subject

> with all the *fidalgos* in India; and the whole populace has asked him that such an agreement should not be confirmed nor carried out, and that they would prefer to have war all their lives with the *Idalcão* if he wants to make it for this reason. The Governor has responded to them giving his reasons for not being able to hand over this Moor to them unless he has orders from Your Highness to do so, as I believe can be seen there from the letters that on this matter have been written from one side to the other. It is fifteen days since they have been exchanging these messages, and the Governor has held himself up as best as he could and now we simply await a response from the *Ydalcão,* and may it please God that it might be reasonable so that we can remain on good terms and in friendship, but they are ready for all sorts of ill and subject to various twists and turns, but they are more fearful of us than we are of what they are doing, since the Governor has ordered some roadworks to be constructed on the mainland with tumult and the setting off of munitions.[36]

The same situation of heightened tensions and preparations for war is mentioned in another letter of the same time, this one written by a certain Pêro Fernandes. This letter, written from Goa on 20 December 1545, openly mentions "the great peril in which Martim Afonso de Sousa has left this land because he contracted with the *Idallcão* to hand over Meale to him for 50,000 *pardaos,* a contract that could not be implemented as it would be against any kind of justice and equity and the service of Your Highness, and against every divine and natural law, which forbid one to sell for money someone who of his own free will placed himself in our hands, trusting in our good faith and truth, without sinning against us, or against our king and law."[37] The letter then continues with a particularly bitter attack against the former governor and his manner of proceeding.

> And even so the Governor has on two occasions asked for the opinions of the *fidalgos* and the principal persons in this land regarding this matter, and all of them with one voice, with no variation, decided that Meale should not be handed over on any account. And it is feared that now the *Idallquão* would want to insist on the contract that was made with him, and on this account block the passage of supplies from the mainland and place this island in the travails of war, which travails were caused by the greed for 50,000 *pardaos,* besides the many other [problems] with which Martim Afonso leaves India, and it lacks a proper armada and these ships and foists that remain here are all rotted and worm-eaten, and an infinity of money will be needed to repair them.

We also have a letter from Ibrahim 'Adil Shah to the governor Dom João de Castro, in which he complains (at least implicitly) of the behavior of Martim Afonso in this matter. But we are equally aware that notwithstanding this complaint, the new governor closed the door to these negotiations.[38] Here is how he himself presents matters in his own letters to the king in Portugal. In a letter from Goa written on 2 September 1545, he declares:

> In the castle of this city I found as prisoner a Moor, Mealecão by name, to whom the kingdom of the Deccan belongs. The summary of what happened with him is as follows: this Moor fled from the Deccan fearing that the Hidalcão would kill him, and took shelter in Cambay, where he received favors and honors from the king of Cambay. Thereafter, there were differences between the Hidalcão, and Acedacão, and Inisamaluco, and the group opposed to the Hidalcão decided to ally with Dom Garcia de Castro, who was at the time captain of this city, so that he should send for Mealecão to make him king, since all the populace wanted this, and because it came to him by right, and on account of the ill deeds, tyrannies and cruelties of this Hidalcão.[39]

Castro then proceeds to recount the familiar story of how Sebastião Lopes Lobato was sent to Gujarat by Dom Garcia, carrying letters from Asad Khan, and of how Meale was brought back to Goa. Then Martim Afonso de Sousa, who had been absent on his foolhardy raids, returned to Goa and began to negotiate with the Bijapur sultan "so that he would give him the *terras firmes*, which is Bardes and Salcete, and 80,000 *pardaus* in cash if he did not hand Mealecão over to *Acedecão* and the captains of the Deccan kingdom, and that he would instead send him to Malaca." Castro proceeds to note how in 1545 the governor proposed to Sultan Ibrahim that he would sell Meale to him for 50,000 gold *pardaos*, and how he negotiated this through Krishna, the *tanadar-mór* of Goa, and a certain Galvão Viegas. However, just when the negotiations had reached a ripe point, Castro himself arrived and intervened. The proximate cause for his intervention was a petition that he had received from Meale himself, insisting on "how discredited the name of His Highness would be in these parts if they sold him to the *Hidalcão*, after having been called on by us to be king, and his having placed himself in our hands, believing in the assurances that had been given him in the name of His Highness."

Castro professes to have found this moral argument regarding "great dishonor and little credit" a convincing one, to which was added the fact that if Meale were indeed handed over, he would at once be killed, whereas while in Goa he still represented a useful threat or "pawn" (*penhor*). His view was unanimously confirmed by a council that he summoned soon after, whose signed opinions he gather to send back to Portugal. But Castro even seems to have found Meale a sympathetic figure overall. He writes:

> This Meale ate at his own expense, and no one gave him anything from the treasury of Your Highness, which seemed very bad to everyone, and he complained to me about it. So that I, on seeing that it was on his account that we received so many thousand *pardaus* in revenue from the mainland, and that he had come to the city of Goa having faith in us, and that he had lost the revenue and grants that he had from the king of Cambay, and that he also was and is in a condition where he could become king of the Deccan, it seemed to me only just, and worthy of the virtue of Your Highness that he should be maintained at the cost of your treasury. And on discussing this with the Financial Intendant and the other officials, I ordered that he be given 1,500 *pardaus* each year to help him maintain himself; which was seen as very good by everyone, principally by the free Moors who are our neighbors.

Castro also grew greatly annoyed with the ambassadors who had been sent to Bijapur by Martim Afonso, since they refused to obey his orders and cease the negotiations. Thus, on 15 October, he passed an order to the effect that Galvão Viegas should be beheaded in the public square at Goa for his attempt "to sell Mealecam for money," alleging besides that he had received a bribe from the sultan for this. Fortunately for Viegas, the sentence was commuted at the request of the Goa Municipal Chamber. In letters exchanged with Ibrahim 'Adil Shah in the same month, Castro also firmly rejected the proposition that he should hand Meale over, stating that "instead he would keep him in his liberty with much honor."[40] The situation turned very tense, with an 'Adil Shahi blockade of Goa, and a counterthreat by Dom João de Castro that he would "take Bilguião [Belgaum] and there raise Miale up as king." Eventually, with Ibrahim under increasing fiscal and financial pressure — with "all the Deccanis openly starting to murmur against the Idalcão and demanding that Miale be made their overlord" — a treaty was signed between the two in February 1546 in which a compromise was struck. Castro agreed to the following: "that concerning the affairs of Miale, that I would be obliged to keep him and his sons prisoners, and in such confinement that no person on behalf of the lords of the Deccan, nor of the *Niza Maluquo*, nor the king of *Biznaguaa*, nor from the lands of Malavar, nor from the kingdom of Cambay will speak with him."[41] This situation was to be maintained until an 'Adil Shahi embassy had been sent to Portugal to negotiate the situation directly with Dom João III. In effect, therefore, Meale once again came more or less to be deprived of his freedom. To be sure, we know that he did make one visit to Kannur (or Cannanore in Kerala) at this time with Khwaja Shams-ud-Din, but as late as February 1547, it was noted that the arrival of a letter for Meale from Dom João de Castro at Diu set off rumors in Goa that "Your Lordship had written to him of his great friendship, and ordered him to be freed [*o mãodaves soltar*]."[42] We shall return below to the restrictions placed on him.

The wanderings and tribulations of the Portuguese ambassador to Bijapur, Galvão Viegas (who also incidentally held the post of *alcaide-mór* of Goa), were also not quite over. Less well known perhaps is the role played by the celebrated Goan Brahmin Krishna, *tanadar-mór* of the island of Goa, who had also earlier been sent by Martim Afonso de Sousa to the court of Ibrahim 'Adil Shah to prosecute a series of negotiations. When one reads a letter written from the court at Bijapur by the said Krishna on 6 December 1546, a great deal of light is shed on a certain perception of the legacy of Martim Afonso.[43] In this letter, written to the king of Portugal, the *tanadar-mór* mentions an earlier letter (unfortunately lost to us), which he had sent to Portugal through a certain Micer Bernaldo Nasi (almost certainly a Sephardic Jewish trader), describing "the affairs of the *Idallcão* and of *Açadecão* and Myalle to which Your Highness did not respond." The letter then continues:

> And though I have written to Your Highness as I have said, still I am thinking of writing about some things that are happening at present, and [how] I perish in this *Ballagate*. Your Highness will be aware that when *Açadequão* rebelled against his lord the *Idallcão*, I worked in such a way that there were two lands by name Salesete and Bardes belonging to the *Idallcão* that passed to Your Highness, which were rented out for 48,000 *pardaos em tangas* every year, besides the 42,000 gold *pardaos* in cash, and I worked it in such a way that the *Idallcão* granted all the money of *Açadecão* that was in Cananor to Your Highness, and the grant that the *Idallcão* made of this money was done in a letter to me that he wrote, which Martim Afonso de Sousa asked me for and then took away with him.

Writing then from the area known as the *Bālāghāt*, the area above the Western Ghats, Krishna thus returns here to familiar themes: the famed "treasure" of Asad Khan Lari, but also the initial grant of Bardes and Salcete made by the same Asad Khan to the Portuguese in the 1530s, prior to the whole affair involving Meale. He too, like every other letter writer we have looked at, boastfully places himself at the very center of the action, and makes himself out to be the key intermediary in dealings between the *Estado da Índia* and the sultanate of Bijapur. But more than any other writer, he presents the arrival on the scene of the new governor as posing grievous problems. For it would appear that in the course of 1546, Ibrahim 'Adil Shah had once more seized a good part of Bardes and Salcete.

> And in the meantime, the said governor Martim Afonso and the *Idallcão* contracted that in exchange for the said two territories that the *Idallcão* had given Your Highness, that the said governor would send Mialle and his sons to Mallaqua; and since the said governor did not comply with the said contract, and since the *Idallcão* was very close to breaking the peace, Martim Afonso sent me with an embassy to the *Idallcão*, and had me ask him how much he would give if he handed over Mialle to him. And the *Idallcão* responded to me that this was no friendship he had with the king of Portugal if it came down to handing over Mialle, his own uncle, for money, and that he should be handed over without it; but that he would give 50,000 gold *pardaos* for a jewel that should be given to the Queen, our mistress. And the said Martim Afonso though it well to hand over Mialle and his sons to him in exchange for the 50,000 gold *pardaos*, and with this message he sent Gallvão Vyeguas so that the *Idallcão* might swear before me and Gallvão Vyeguas according to his faith that he would not harm, nor blind, nor kill the said Mialle or his sons, and only confine them in a fortress, and the *Idallcão* swore to it in the abovementioned manner.

So, if Krishna may be believed, there was an effective accord between the governor and the sultan that went beyond the mere exile of Meale and his family to Melaka; but there were also some assurances given — for what they were worth — that neither he nor his family would be harmed. This was where the arrival of Dom João de Castro came in.

> And at this point, there arrived the governor Dom Joam de Castro, and as soon as the *Idallcão* learnt of his arrival, he sent him a letter saying that he should abide by the contract that the past governors had agreed to with him, and at the same time I and Gallvão Vyeguas wrote another letter to the Governor giving him a detailed account of everything from the beginning to the end as he was your governor, and he replied to us that he was very glad to learn of our embassy and that if we had not been relieved it was because the *Idallcão* was occupied in his wars, and that as soon as he was free he would relieve us, and that he would make us grants in the name of Your Highness. And after this the *Idallcão* sent

> over the 50,000 gold *pardaos* and his captains for Mialle, and the said Governor did not wish to comply with the contract of Martim Afonso, on account of which the *Idallcão* was greatly disgusted and displeased, saying that he was astonished at the governors of Your Highness, who came every three years, and one made an accord in the name of Your Highness and the other undid it and poorly abided by it, and he did not understand whom he could trust for in spite of their always being sent by Your Highness, they were not alike.

These critical remarks, astonishingly accurate and perspicacious regarding Portuguese elite factionalism in many respects, were particularly apposite in regard to the difficult transition between Martim Afonso de Sousa and Dom João de Castro. Krishna's letter then concludes by describing the bitter consequences of such changes and instabilities in Portuguese policy.

> And for this reason it has now been over two years that we have been kept in this *Ballagate*, and since the Governor Dom João de Castro did not honor the contract of the Governor Martim Afonso, he made a fresh contract with the *Idallcão* to the effect that he would hold Mialle prisoner in this [*sic*] fortress of Goa, and the said two territories that had thus been given over would remain with Your Highness forever, without saying anything more or less about us either at the time of the negotiations or afterward, though we came here in an embassy on the orders of your Governor. And now that the Governor left for Diu, the *Idallcão* has once more seized hold of the two territories, saying that he had only given them on the condition that they would keep Mialle prisoner in Mallaqua and that since the Governor had not abided by what the governor Martim Afonso had done, he would take away the said lands. So that Gallvão Vyeguas and I having come here on the orders of your Governor for affairs of your service are perishing in this *Ballaguate*. We ask Your Highness that since we are your servants, and since I am such an old and ancient vassal and servant, that Your Highness should write a letter in a most firm way to the *Idallcão*, and make efforts to free us from this captivity, and that you should not abandon us among the Moors for we pertain to Your Highness. And Your Highness may well believe that it appears to be an unjust thing among kings and lords that we, despite pertaining to Your Highness, are left helpless in this *Ballaguate*. For the rest, Your Highness may do whatever he thinks is most in his service and I shall say no more.[44]

This letter, with its pathetic tone and its bitter critique of Dom João de Castro, was written at the end of 1546, before the campaign that the governor and his son Dom Álvaro de Castro mounted in 1547 to recover the lands of

Salcete from Bijapur. We are aware that in this latter year, there were a series of encounters and battles, not only in Ponda and Salcete, but also in the 'Adil Shahi port of Dabhol much farther to the north, which was attacked by the Portuguese. Dom João de Castro, after his victory at Diu against the forces of the Gujarat Sultanate, also attempted to profit from the new conjuncture and the freshly won prestige that he possessed: according to the contemporary chronicler Leonardo Nunes, on account of his "most mortal hatred of the Moors, principally the *Idalcam*, on account of the issues he had with him," the governor now even "came to conceive in his spirit of working to deprive him of his kingdom in order to hand it over to Mealle, or give it over to his neighbors."[45] He thus sent out two fresh embassies, one of a certain Duarte Barbudo to Burhan Nizam Shah of Ahmadnagar, and the second of Tristão de Paiva to the ruler of Vijayanagara. A letter from Paiva, written in the city of Vijayanagara on 16 February 1548, deals with his relations with Aravidu Rama Raya, the great warlord and éminence grise of the kingdom at the time. In a discussion with Rama Raya, his brother Venkatadri, and a certain Dilawar Khan (a Muslim general in Vijayanagara service), the Portuguese ambassador spoke first of the great victory of Dom João de Castro against Bijapur, "in the battle he had at Çalcete with the captains of the *Ydalquão* and through the great destruction he had visited on the coast." But the focal point of the discussion, if Paiva may be believed, was this issue: "what approach should be taken to make Meale into the *Ydalquão*."[46] Perhaps as a result of this cunning political pressure from a potential alliance against him, Ibrahim 'Adil Shah had to desist from his project to recover Bardes and Salcete in 1548, and instead signed a fresh treaty of peace with the *Estado da Índia*. In December that year, a few months after the death of Dom João de Castro, the sultan even sent a letter to Dom João III in Portugal.

> This love and friendship I declare to the [lord] most resplendent like the sun — may his star and fortune be most high! — the lion of the sea and the land, the King Dom Joam, the king of Portugal, may God extend the days of his life and of his reign and royal state until the day of judgment. I could find no better time than now to give you an account of what I have in my intentions. Your Highness would be aware of how when the *Rumes* [Ottomans] came, I went to the aid of your people on account of the love I have for your service as I believe Your Highness would already have come to know, and from that time on you were pleased to maintain a friendship with me and give permission to the Viceroy to make [peace] with me, and he wrote to me about this at great length and

> with many offers on account of which a great friendship was established between us which will last forever on both sides, with truth, until the very end, day by day, and it will keep on growing with the help of God.[47]

The letter then continues in the same exalted tone, typical of the Persian diplomatic correspondence of the period, but the significant fact is to discern the underlying shift in terms of political and diplomatic relations. To be sure, whether he was speaking of 1538 or 1546, we can be certain that Ibrahim 'Adil Shah was stretching matters somewhat when he claimed that "when the *Rumes* [Ottomans] came, I went to the aid of your people."[48] But what is significant is that the letter does not contain a single reference to Meale. No longer was he an imminent threat, obsessively referred to as he had been in every contract and negotiation between Ibrahim and the Portuguese governors since 1543. No longer a "prince in the deep freeze," was he then no more than a curiosity by 1548, a museum piece like so many other native American, African, and Asian princes in the Iberian world?

THE VOICE OF MEALE

We have so far managed to avoid engaging with the voice of Meale himself. What might he himself have thought of all these ups and downs? We are aware that the prince — like other members of his family — knew Persian and Turkish; by the late 1550s, he had also acquired a modicum of Portuguese. The few letters we have from him are written not in Persian but in Portuguese, and bear the unmistakable marks of having been composed by a professional scribe. They do however carry a valuable mark, a Persian seal that identifies the letter writer as *'Alī bin Yūsuf 'Ādil Khān*; had any one of a number of historians in the twentieth century thought to decipher this seal, they might have saved themselves endless speculation on whether Meale was in fact his nephew Mallu Khan or even the latter's brother 'Abdullah. The first of his own letters that survives, written to the king Dom João III in December 1548, presents us with a rapid view of events that is rather different from all those cited above.

> Your Highness will be aware of how I was brought to this city on the orders of Martym Afonso de Sousa your governor who was here, at the time that he resided in India, at which time the captain [of Goa] was Dom Garcia de Crasto, who on the advice of *Acedequão* had me brought to this city of yours of Goa,

> where I was held prisoner in the fortress for four years and deprived of my liberty. I had been in Cambay, where I formerly was, most peacefully and greatly favored by the king of Cambay — I and my wife and sons — and he had given me 10,000 *cruzados* a year for my expenses, and he gave me permission to come and go wherever I pleased. And from that state, I was brought and kept in this fortress of the city of Goa at great expense to myself. And later, when the Governor Dom Joham de Crasto arrived, and came to gather information of my imprisonment, he wrote to Your Highness of how I was a prisoner in this city and had me freed from prison and gave me my liberty outside the fortress, and Your Highness ordered that I should be given 2,000 *pardaos* for my expenses which was given to me by the Governor Dom Joham until the time that he died, and he honored me greatly — all at the orders of Your Highness.[49]

This is a clear enough plot sequence. To begin with we have Meale in a state of bucolic and luxurious living in Gujarat; then the voyage under false pretences to Goa followed by a bitter imprisonment; then, eventually the liberation by Dom João de Castro. A series of phrases now follows applauding the fine character and noble conduct of that late governor. Meale now returns to what led him to leave Gujarat in the first place.

> I cannot neglect to mention the great abuses that were done to me here by Dom Garcia, who sent for me in the name of Your Highness through Bastiam Llopez Lobato, with other Portuguese men in his company, when I was in Cambay; and this was because I knew that Your Highness was a great king and lord, and that in your kingdom matters are dealt with honestly and in a similar way among the Portuguese [in general] because they bear the name of Your Highness, for it is known everywhere that in the whole world there is no king who is more true. On which account, on hearing the great name of Your Highness, I came here with my wife and sons, where I find myself very poor and consumed, selling off the jewels of my wife and children and everything else I had at home to sustain myself, and many of the servants in my house left me on seeing my great poverty, and one of my sons left me without ever coming back. On account of which I ask Your Highness for permission to be able to come and go wherever I please, and even that I might go back to my lands, and that no Governor who is appointed to India, nor any other person should have power over me or my affairs, and that I can also leave with my wife and children.

The whole matter is thus posed in terms of a very courtly discourse, referring to the justice and truth of the Portuguese king, in marked contrast to the flagrant injustice practiced by his subordinates in India. Of particular significance is the insistence on the liberty of movement, and the right to return "to my lands." These were rights that Meale would continue to claim until the end of his life, without ever gaining entire satisfaction in the matter. Since it is likely that at this point Meale's grasp of Portuguese was not quite good enough, it is probable that he used a series of intermediaries to draft the letter. The letter is also written in a good and clear professional scribal hand, the same that has written "Meale/can" on the two sides of the Persian seal. It would seem very likely that Meale disposed of the skills of someone such as the well-known interpreter António Fernandes, whom the Jesuit historian Georg Schurhammer has identified as a "converted Moor" and a relative of Meale's close associate Khwaja Shams-ud-Din Gilani.

We can thus identify with some likelihood, if not entire certainty, the social network that 'Ali bin Yusuf 'Adil Khan made use of in the first decade or so of his stay in Goa. This was a network of social and commercial relations that he had in part inherited from Asad Khan Lari, who — as we well know — had maintained particularly close dealings with Khwaja Shams-ud-Din on the one hand, and with one of the richest Portuguese settlers (*casados*) of Goa on the other, Rui Gonçalves de Caminha. So influential was Caminha, and so indispensable his support for the finances of the *Estado*, that he even came to be named *vedor da fazenda* (or intendant of finances) during the government of Dom João de Castro.[50] The dealings of Meale with the Iranian merchant and his Portuguese associate appear clearly in a series of documents from the period.[51] The interest that the prince from Bijapur had in developing his own trade seems to have been linked with these networks; we may thus note that in his letter to the Portuguese king of 1548, he asked for "permission to be able to send one ship [*huma nao*] wherever I please, and that in no place where you have a fortress or city should they ask me for [customs] duties." The next year, he asked the king for permission to go to Portugal, no doubt in order to present his case in person at the court there. On this occasion, he wrote to Dom João III: "I ask Your Highness to send me an order [*huma provisão*] so that along with my wife and children I can go to the lands of Your Highness and come back to this city, and that you order the Governors of India and the captains of the fortresses that they let me go and come back by sea."[52] The permission does not seem to have been granted. In any event, these were relatively calm years in Meale's life. He did gain a series of grants from the

Portuguese court, albeit not everything that he asked for. A letter by him to Dom João III from the end of 1551 gives us a sense of his situation some eight years after his arrival in Goa from Gujarat.

> My Lord: I, Mialycão, make it known to Your Highness how this year I received a letter from you with a benefice of 2,000 *cruzados* in revenues each year for my sustenance, on account of which I rejoiced greatly, and I kiss the royal hands of Your Highness for the said benefice that was granted to me. Since the fame of Your Highness is so great that it runs through this world, I would consider it a great favor if you were to be pleased to order that I be given license to leave this city with my wives and children and all my household wherever I should wish to go, and that my departure should not be forbidden by any person, which I would consider a great favor. Let me also say that I rejoiced greatly with the arrival of Dom António de Noronha as Viceroy of India, as he is an able person for this [post] without any greed at all, who serves Your Highness well and with great honesty, and I have spoken many times with him and I always found that he responded well, and he did me great honor and was welcoming, and he has a very good reputation here. This year my mother died, on account of which I was greatly bereaved [*fiquey muito nojado*] and if Your Highness were to give me permission to depart, it would be a great favor and I would be satisfied. May the Lord God always keep watch over Your Highness, and extend your life and state by many long days. I say it thus so that it may come true. I kiss the royal hands of Your Highness. From Goa, today, the last day of November in the year 1551.[53]

The scribe in this letter has a poorer turn of phrase, and also commits errors of grammar, but the central thrust is clear enough. Meale clearly continued to receive news from Bijapur, in relation to his extended family. It is unclear who his mother was: Was she the legendary Punji Khatun (referred to by Couto as "Babúgi Fatima"), who allegedly intervened in the succession struggles of both 1510 and the mid-1530s?[54] We are even uncertain as to Meale's real age, though he was clearly born some time before 1510.

Ironically, the desire expressed in his letters — to be able to return to the interior — was eventually sublimated, but in circumstances quite different from those that Meale might have had in mind. This had once more to do with the evolution of political circumstances in the Deccan in the mid-1550s. The Portuguese viceroy at Goa by now was no longer Dom António de Noronha but Dom Pedro Mascarenhas, a veteran diplomat and soldier, and he came to know in 1554 of a series of negotiations that were under way between two relatively new and energetic rulers in the area, Husain Nizam Shah (who had just acceded to the throne at Ahmadnagar), and Ibrahim Qutb Shah of Golkonda.[55] Initially in alliance with Aravidu Rama Raya at Vijayanagara, they seem to have thought once more to put pressure on Bijapur, taking advantage of the discontent there of a number of principal figures, especially a certain Iranian notable titled 'Ain-ul-mulk Gilani, described by the chronicler Diogo do Couto as the "governor of the whole Concan [Konkan], and in terms of his power and authority, another *Acedecan*."[56] 'Ain-ul-mulk, who had formerly held the title of Saif Khan, had for a time been in Ahmadnagar service before being tempted over to Bijapur with grants of land and the promise of power. Since the early 1550s, however, his relations with Ibrahim 'Adil Shah had steadily deteriorated, leading to a number of armed conflicts with the sultan from his base in the town of Satara, to the northwest of Bijapur. Mascarenhas seems to have taken counsel from the principal *fidalgos* of the time, and they agreed on this occasion to launch into what was after all a rather risky venture, counting on the aid of 'Ain-ul-mulk Gilani and a certain Salabat Khan to raise Meale to the throne. Mascarenhas however insisted on leaving Vijayanagara out of the equation for fear that Aravidu Rama Raya might wish to profit from his success and "be seized by the greed to once more become master of the island of Goa." It is in this larger context, a coherent narrative of which is provided to us by the chronicle of Couto (on which more below), that the archives yield up a significant document, in the form of a contract signed on 30 April 1555, by which the *Estado da Índia* proposed to take Meale to the fortress of Ponda "on this side of the *Gate*," where he was to declare himself sultan of Bijapur before entering his erstwhile lands with the aid of a Portuguese force. What follows below is the first part of the text of the "contract" between the viceroy and the man who is here newly termed "Meale Ydalcão."

> In the name of God amen. May those who see this contract be certain that in the year of the birth of our Lord Jesus Christ of 1555, on the 24th day of the month of April in this city of Goa in the residences of the fortresses thereof where there now resides the Most Illustrious Lord Dom Pero Mazcarenhas of the Council of the King, our master, and his Viceroy in these parts of India, in the presence of his lordship and also of Meallecam, true successor to the state of the *Ydalcam*, it was declared by the latter that the said state belonged to him as the legitimate son of *Yçufo Ydalcam* [Yusuf 'Adil Khan], as his grandson *Mallucam*, son of *Ysmael* who had succeeded to the said state on the death of his said father and older brother to him Meallecam had died without a legitimate heir, and his [Mallu's]

eyes had been put out by *Ybraemo* [Ibrahim] who now possesses the said state unjustly, as he is a bastard son of his said brother [Isma'il] born through a concubine of his [*huma sua manceba*], who — being a tyrant — exiled him Mealle, and took away all his revenues out of fear that the grandees and notables of the state would accept him as king and overlord. And that from his exile, he had been called by some of them so that they could hand over his state to him; and that on coming to this city, on account of the death of Acedacam, a principal actor in this affair and in the kingdom, this could not take place and ever since then he had remained in this city even though in the meanwhile, past Governors had greatly desired to bring this case to a conclusion and had attempted many times to effect this without being able to do so. And that now Our Lord, as a just judge showing the way for him to receive his due, had permitted that the said *Ybraemo* should be detested by the grandees of the kingdom, who have differences and wars with him, and hence offer to give him, Meallecam, possession of the said state. And since they cannot accomplish this without the help and favor of His Lordship who represents the person and state of the said Lord [Dom João III] whose Viceroy he was, and from whom he Mealle had received shelter and many honors and grants, and sustenance for his person and household for all the time that he had resided in this city, which is to say more or less thirteen years, and so he requested on his part that he should see fit to order him taken to Pomdaa, which is one of the fortresses of the said state [Bijapur] which is on this side of the *Gate*, and give him the permission for this, and the favor and help that His Lordship might consider necessary for him to be restored to his due. And that in recognition of this considerable benefit and grant that he hoped would be done for him, by way of taking him to the said Pomda, and also on account of the many other benefits that he had already received, he promised from now onward to the King of Portugal, our master, that he would be true to him and would follow and effect all his orders entirely so far as matters concerning the jurisdiction over the lands that were offered to him; and that he would be a friend of the state of His Highness, and of all those who were friends of the Portuguese, and opposed to their enemies to whom he would not in any way give any help or favor, but would instead persecute them to the extent that his forces permitted, and that he would in person attend to this if it were necessary.

And that he gave to the said Lord [Dom João III] from today onward, forever, for him and his successors in the kingdoms of Portugal, all the rights that he had and could have in any manner that might be, over the cities, towns and places, rivers and seaports, that had pertained to the lordship [*senhorio*] of this city of Goa in the time of the Moors and the Gentiles, which lands of Goa commence

> from the river of Setamcora in the *tenadarya* of Samvisar which are the limits of the lands of the Canaras of Garçopa and which end at the river of Tanbono in the *tenadarya* of Salsy which is called Achera; and from the pouring waters of the *Gate* to the sea, with all of the Comcam [Konkan] from Parboly, with Dabul and its territories also entering and remaining within this demarcation.[57]

This was in effect an enormous concession, involving much of the maritime front of the Bijapur Sultanate, from Gersoppa in the south to Dabhol and beyond in the north, and effectively including all the lands west of the Ghats. Still, before giving all this away, it was necessary first to control it. We may follow the progress of Meale using the chronicle of Couto, but also the contemporary letters of a certain Rodrigo Anes Lucas, secretary of the *Estado da Índia*. From the latter more than the former, it is clear that a key personage in this affair was still the indefatigable Khwaja Shams-ud-Din Gilani; the third member of their old alliance, Rui Gonçalves de Caminha, had already died in around 1550. In this expedition, Meale (now termed more respectfully as "Aly Idalcam" by the Portuguese) was accompanied by two of his sons, Muhammad Khan ("Mamedecam"), and Miyan 'Abdul Qadir ("Miabedulcadir"), both of whom also signed the contract with the *Estado*. A clause stipulated that "he, the said Meallecam, was pleased that, for greater security with respect to what was promised in the contract, he would leave his wives in this city of Goa, and also his daughters and one of his sons, all of whom would not leave this city until the King, our master, was in possession of all the lands contained and declared in the said contract." On 2 May, the secretary Lucas found himself in "the fortress of Pomda" with various other Portuguese *fidalgos* who had been sent out by the viceroy. From this point on, Meale was addressed as "Your Highness" by the Portuguese, at least for a certain time. Contemporary documents show that Meale was now usually accompanied by Diyanat Khan, who held Ponda on behalf of Bijapur, by a certain Khwaja Pir Quli ("Coje Percolim"), known as a translator and intermediary in various Portuguese chronicles, and by his two sons; on the Portuguese side, those present among the notables included the captain of Goa, Gaspar de Melo de Sampaio, a certain Martim Afonso de Miranda, as well as Dom Francisco Mascarenhas, Gonçalo Correa, Francisco de Melo, and António Ferrão.

Couto's chronicle adds details to this account, and even if we need not always trust his version, we should refer to it at least briefly. Though these events happened before his time in India, he claims to have been well informed of all the details, and even names one of informants, a certain Dom Fernando de Monroy. We are thus given a lavish account of the preparations in Goa before the expedition set out, including an elaborate ceremony at the *terreiro do paço* involving "a lovely platform with a full awning over the top [*hum formoso cadafalso, toldado todo por sima*]," decorated with rich carpets and precious cloths, where Meale was taken in procession from his house by the viceroy on horseback, accompanied by his sons. It was here, according to Couto, that the contract was in fact signed. The next day, the viceroy and Meale, accompanied by some three thousand soldiers in five companies, departed for the *Passo de Santiago* to prepare the eventual passage to Ponda. The chronicler makes it plain from the start, however, that the expedition was somehow jinxed. Already, when an advance party of Portuguese reached Ponda, a violent quarrel broke out between Martim Afonso de Miranda and Francisco Barreto (the latter described cuttingly by Couto as "naturally arrogant, a friend of his own honor and of the need to command"), and the viceroy himself had to intervene. A second ceremony followed at Benasterim, where many salvos of artillery were fired, and it was only then that Meale was sent on his way to Ponda.[58]

Four months later, little concrete progress had been made on the military front, in part perhaps on account of the intervening rainy season. Meanwhile, the viceroy Mascarenhas had sickened and died shortly after his return from Ponda at the age of seventy, claiming that the exertions of the journey, and the need to placate quarrelsome *fidalgos*, had hastened his end. Ironically, his successor was just one of those contentious men, Francisco Barreto. So it was that on 31 August, Lucas, the secretary of the *Estado*, found himself "in the village [*sic*] of Bilgam [Belgaum], limit of the territories of Pomdaa in the tent of Senhor Francisco Barreto, captain-general and governor of these parts of India." Also present in the tent were Salabat Khan, a certain Asad Khan (not to be confused, of course, with the other who had died in 1543), and "Cotatacam" (perhaps Khairat Khan), all of whom had been sent there by 'Ain-ul-mulk Gilani, besides Diyanat Khan, Meale, and his sons. Lucas describes the scene: "It was said by His Lordship [Barreto] to the said captains that since they had come to serve the *Ydalcam Aly*, as was declared in the letters of accreditation that had been sent to him by *Aynel Maluco*, that he was content to hand over the person of the said Ydalcam to them, and he had liberated him several days before at Pomdaa." Clearly then, Meale had been considered as a prisoner, or a captive, or in some unfree mode, until that point. The Bijapur representatives then made various oaths on the Qur'an (*no mossafo*), professing loyalty to Meale as well as their willingness to implement the contract signed by him.

However, another letter from the same Rodrigo Anes Lucas, this one written from Goa on 22 December 1555, shows us a totally transformed situation. The secretary wrote to Dom João III now in the following somber tones.

> My Lord. In this Konkan expedition [*nesta empresa do Comquão*], the viceroy Dom Pedro entered while calculating the losses and the profits that this *Estado* might have, asking for many opinions from the captains and *fidalgos* on whom Your Highness most depends here for your service. And so, since it appeared to them that the time was opportune, since the old Idalcam was besieged, with his own people and captains against him, and since Mealle and *Coje Cemaçadim* were interested in organizing his departure, arguing for the great profits that would result in the future for the King our master, as well as the fact that the neighboring kings of the *Estado* were each of them in difficulty with their own revolts so that no alliance between them could be formed with rapidity; and since everyone present understood that the needs of this land were such that whoever governed it could not allow it simply to be consumed, but needed to propose new remedies and cures, they advised him, and he [the Viceroy] with their support decided, taking into account these and many other things, that he should permit Meale to go ahead, and with some help. And those who were most positive about this were Dom Antão de Noronha, Dom Diogou d'Almeyda [and] Vasco da Cunha. Francisco Barreto, Dioguo Alvez Telez [and] Dom Joam Lobo also agreed to it, though they put forward some of their doubts and these may be found in the particular opinions [*pareceres particulares*] as the general ones were joint."[59]

So, whatever the doubts, it seems that the viceroy Mascarenhas could count on a sort of broad consensus among the *fidalgos* and men of experience; at any rate, the individual opinions have not been found so far in the archives. However, the secretary then goes on to describe, perhaps with a certain cynicism, how matters moved forward from there.

> Once the task had begun, as the particulars began to emerge more clearly, each one began to truck and trade with the words that he had said, and on hearing some news of difficulties, returned to the doubts and fears which they had pointed to, and if the news was good they would concede [the project], expecting that it would succeed; and so matters have gone until today, the 22nd

December, when they have ordered the withdrawal of the garrisons that were in Curale, Bamda and Pomda, and this because word has arrived that *Aynel Maluquo*, and Mealle and all of his party have been defeated by the old Ydalcam with the help of the king of Bisnaga, who in exchange for 300,000 *pardaos* that were given to him, came to his aid and lifted the siege. And that *Aynel*, Mealle and the Coje [Shams-ud-Din] were in the power of the *Inyzamaluquo* [Nizam-ul-mulk] in whose direction they had withdrawn. With this outcome to what had been begun, each one who has put his signature and opinion to this [project] will work here and make efforts over there [in Portugal] to redeem himself, admitting to some blame if he feels he bears any; and it must all be at the cost of the honor and intention of the Viceroy who is with God, for he entered into this in cold blood, and having sketched it out first with all those whom he should have consulted, weighing everything for and against, all the good and bad aspects of the enterprise, and the unlikelihood of there being a shipwreck; and having found that the service of his Highness would be put to little prejudice, and finding it a good expedient toward a good deal of profit, put it up and offered it to God to this end."

The chronicler Couto, in his usual fashion, has a far more elaborate narrative, full of all sorts of intrigues and counterintrigues. In his account, Meale was first taken from Ponda to Belgaum, and from there to Hukeri ("Cheri"), where he was met by 'Ain-ul-mulk and various others. Meanwhile, Ibrahim 'Adil Shah had been fully informed of the scheme that was being hatched, as well as the fact that the Portuguese viceroy had decided in his wisdom to exclude Vijayanagara from the alliance. He thus sent messengers on the one hand to Aravidu Rama Raya asking for help, and on the other hand offered a huge sum of money to 'Ain-ul-mulk if he would only hand over Meale to him. The latter, in Couto's account, was sorely tempted indeed, and only desisted eventually because he was shamed by Salabat Khan into not doing so. However, a Vijayanagara army under Aravidu Venkatadri (brother of Rama Raya) was dispatched northward to help Bijapur. The huge Vijayanagara army was simply too large for 'Ain-ul-mulk to face, and he hence fled to his old employer, the Nizam Shahs of Ahmadnagar, without even properly entering the battlefield. But this in turn proved to be a costly miscalculation, as Couto recounts it, for many in the Nizam Shahi court were deeply suspicious of him. Husain Nizam Shah was hence persuaded by a certain Qasim Beg to have 'Ain-ul-mulk (as well as Salabat Khan) killed immediately, and only his wife and children managed to flee to Berar. Meale himself, and one of his sons, were then allegedly saved from certain death by Husain Nizam Shah's aged mother, who reminded her son that "Mealecan was the son of Çufocan [Yusuf Khan], with whom they had close ties of kinship." Instead, they were sent to the fortress of Bahula, southwest of Nasik, where they remained for a time.[60] The Portuguese for their part were obliged to order a rapid and humiliating withdrawal from all the territories and fortresses they had recently occupied, returning to their possessions in the island of Goa, Bardes, and Salcete.

Now, even a year after Lucas's letter, in December 1556, the matter of Meale had not been resolved. The prince and Khwaja Shams-ud-Din Gilani were at this point still in the power of Husain Nizam Shah, as we learn from a letter written from Chaul by a certain Francisco Pereira de Miranda:

> Mealle and *Coje Cemacedym*, in the defeat that they were subjected to by the *Ydalcam*, of which Your Highness would have already been informed, decided in the last resort to take shelter with all their entourage with the *Nizamuluco*, in the belief that they would be well received by him as he owes it to them as vassals of Your Highness, given the friendship and peace that has been in place for so long; but they found him very different from his duties, and what they had hoped for, because not only did the *Nizamaluco* hold them prisoner for a year, but even when the Governor sent him an ambassador especially to ask him for this, he did not let them go without taking a ransom for *Coje Cemaçadim* of 60,000 *pardaos*, and for Mealle of 30,000. Now the Governor is trying to oblige the *Nyzamaluco* to return these ransoms as they were taken from vassals of Your Highness. It is not yet known what he will do in this matter, but it appears to me that he will return nothing of these ransoms, since he is inclined to war and a young man, as I have mentioned."[61]

The author of the letter now continues, in an acid tone: "And since these matters all were carried out through me in this fortress, and I had no small amount of work in extracting them from his power, I remind Your Highness that all the honors and benefices that you order should be given to Mealle here are all wasted on him, for he is weak-spirited and a poor warrior [*por ser de pouco anymo e maao homem de guera*], and since he has other [bad] qualities so that he will never be good either for himself or for anyone else, so that one could well save on all these expenses that are made on him."

We have another version of these same negotiations and their outcome, in a letter written by the Portuguese ambassador to the Nizam Shahi court, a certain Duarte Rodrigues de Bulhão, in early 1557. In his letter, Bulhão describes how the governor Francisco Barreto "instructed me to go to the *Ynizamalu-*

quo, a subject [*sic*] of Your Highness since Chaul in his lands is your fortress, and that I should ask him for the prisoners that he had detained there which is to say Meale and his two sons, and *Coja Cemaçadym*, vassals of Your Highness, who on account of the defeat that they suffered took shelter under his protection, and that he instead of sheltering and favoring them, had captured, and sacked and robbed them." The Portuguese envoy then recounts how he himself had been ill-treated at the Ahmadnagar court by Husain Nizam Shah, "who did not welcome me and treat me well as he was obliged to do as the ambassador of Your Highness, but instead did less than he did for his neighbors." Only at the end of six months of attendance, "at times using threats, at times ruses," had the ambassador brought matters to a conclusion.

> And at the end of six months that I remained there, with him being away in the war he was making against the *Ydalcam*, on which [campaign] he took me, he consented to give me *Coja Cemaçadym*, passing him over into my hands since I was present; and Meale and his two sons he had sent over to me in Chaul, as they were in a fortress far from the court, and they were brought by an ambassador whom he sent back with me to the Governor. But I did not agree to accept *Coja Cemaçadym* in any manner, saying that he had already taken 60,000 *pardaos* from him, and that he ought to set him free and not hand him over to me. He [Husain Nizam Shah] responded that for love of the Governor he had reduced 40,000 *pardaos* from the 100,000 he was supposed to receive, and he would be glad if I would agree to the 60,000 *pardaos*. I replied that I had not been sent there to ransom them but to take them away for free, and that would be because they were vassals of Your Majesty. Finally, they were handed over, with *Coja Cemaçady* at once naming guarantors [*fiadores*] for the 45,000 *pardaus* that he had to give in [Portuguese] India, as he had already handed over only 15,000; we left and arrived in Chaul, where I waited some days for Meale and his sons, and as soon as they arrived, I set off with all of them toward Goa where I handed them over to the Governor, who was delighted and contented, as if he were in Portugal, in the grace of Your Highness.[62]

The return to the "interior" had failed miserably, and Meale was now "home" again in Goa, save that Goa was scarcely what he thought of as his home.

THE FADING YEARS

After this unfortunate expedition, Meale seems to disappear for a time from the official archives of the *Estado da Índia* (though any researcher who has

Public display of the ambassador of the ruler of Bijapur in Goa. In Jan Huyghen van Linschoten, *Itinerario. Voyage ofte schipvaert . . . naer Oost ofte Portugaels Indien . . .* (Amsterdam: Cornelis Claesz, 1596). *Author's collection*

spent time in the Torre do Tombo cannot be foolhardy enough to claim that the documents have been exhaustively studied).[63] Official projects for the conquest of Bijapur and the Konkan equally seem to disappear, and not only because Meale came to be seen as "weak-spirited and a poor warrior, and since he has other [bad] qualities so that he will never be good either for himself or for anyone else." Rather, it was because at the end of the 1550s and the beginning of the 1560s, relations between Goa and Bijapur passed through a phase of curious cordiality, and the Portuguese even sent an embassy of sorts to the court of Ibrahim's successor 'Ali 'Adil Shah, in the hope of constructing an alliance with him against the Ottomans.[64] This young and new sultan was described as "most liberal and magnanimous," of "great status" and a "kind person," the very opposite of the image that the sultans of Bijapur as the very incarnations of tyranny had had in the first half of the sixteenth century. In this situation, the person of Meale came to lose its political significance for a time, as a pawn that could simply not be "queened." The focus shifted instead to Gujarat, where the acquisition of Daman seemed to open new possibilities of a conquest, as well as to Sri Lanka.

We do know however that Meale spent the remaining years of his life in Goa, where he came eventually to be acquainted with the chronicler Diogo do Couto, with whom he conversed (whether directly in Portuguese or using interpreters) about the history of the Bahamanis and the sultans of Bijapur. Some of the confused outcomes of these conversations may be found in Couto's *Década IV da Ásia*, where the chronicler explicitly claims that he discussed the career of Yusuf 'Adil Khan with "his son Meale (being in Goa, as we shall describe below), with whom we spoke of all these things."[65] It is clear from a close inspection of Couto's text though that he used Meale more as a source to give his own text authority and to validate his history of India, than as a real historical informant. There is no other way to explain the many errors regarding the chronology and history of the Deccan (as well as the numerous false etymologies) in his *Década IV*, as well as in other sections of his *Décadas da Ásia*. Even so, Couto's version is still somewhat more rigorous than the always fanciful text of the other chronicler Gaspar Correia. For instance, Correia presents Meale as the son of Isma'il 'Adil Shah (rather than his brother), and also asserts with easy authority that he was a close relative of Asad Khan Lari ("the son of one of his nieces"). According to this text, after the death of Isma'il 'Adil Shah in 1534, Meale fled to Mecca and the Red Sea from where he returned in 1538, since at the time he found himself in the port of Jiddah when the Ottoman fleet of Hadim Süleyman Pasha passed through there on its way to Diu.[66] These "legends" transmitted by Correa suggest that in the mid-sixteenth century, Meale was something of an object of curiosity, about whom many rumors and myths circulated even among his contemporaries.

At the same time that he disappears more or less from the official records of the *Estado*, we have seen that the figure of Meale continued to be present in another archive, that of the Society of Jesus. Here, however, he is less a weighty political figure and more an object of contempt and hostility, as we have observed in the incident of late 1557 involving his daughter. For he continued to live as a Muslim with prestige and resources in a house in the very heart of Goa, next door to the main church and college of the Jesuits themselves. However, as time went on, it grew more and more difficult to protect his family from the continuous pressures of the Counter-Reformation. Several references in the Jesuit documents show us the ever more constricted space that he could occupy in around 1560. An example comes to us from 1562 (in the form of a letter from the Jesuit Baltasar da Costa), and is connected once more to Meale's children.

> In this city [of Goa], some days ago there still lived a Moor who was married to a Mooress, who had four children; among whom was a girl who was already grown up, and she was asked for by Meale who is a Moor who claims to be or says he is the king of the mainland by right, in order to marry one of his sons, since the father of the girl was an honorable man who had already in past times been a captain on the mainland, and as the girl was appropriate for this, and the son greatly desired to marry her. The mother [of the girl], either unable to bear the loss of her daughter, or because Our Lord wanted it thus, decided to turn Christian along with the children she had who were very young, and also persuaded the girl to do so; however, her father took her from the house and handed her over to Meale, to whom he had promised her.[67]

The mother then went to complain to the Jesuits, and the archbishop of Goa, Gaspar de Leão Pereira, was consulted; he for his part "at once sent for her [the girl], and asked her questions." Five years after the episode of the conversion and carrying away of his daughter, we may imagine the sentiment of déjà vu that would have struck Meale. According to the Jesuit letter, "he at once got on his horse . . . and rode after the girl to the house of the Lord Archbishop." Initially, in the presence of her prospective father-in-law, the girl reportedly "said that she wanted to remain a Mooress," thus refusing the proposition of her mother. The Jesuit source however claims that "it is very likely [that it was so] because he [Meale] has the reputation of being a great wizard [*grande feitiseyro*], as all the kings of this land commonly are"! But the triumph of the thaumaturgical prince Meale did not endure. Under the insistent pressure of the archbishop, he was obliged to return home, and once he had left, the girl (with her mother still present) was asked once more, "and once she was sure, she said that she wanted to become Christian." The rules of the game fixed by the Counter-Reformation and its institutional apparatus did not really permit any other outcome, though we know that Meale "at once went to the house of the viceroy to complain of the injury that they had done him by taking away his [future] daughter-in-law." The response of the viceroy Dom Francisco Coutinho, Count of Redondo, was unequivocal: "in such cases, nothing else could be done than what had been done." Goa in 1560 was not Goa in 1540, and we note that the Jesuit letter even half-doubts the royal status of Meale. Instead of being "the Moor to whom the kingdom of *Balagate* belongs by right," he was now only a Moor "who claims to be or says he is the king of the mainland by right."

Meale seems to have died in around 1567, as we see from a letter written by one of his sons, Yusuf Khan (perhaps the third son, who had been left behind in Goa during the expedition of 1555–56), to the new king of Portugal, Philip II, on 3 December 1581. He wrote:

> My father *Mealleção*, son of the first *Idalxaa*, came to this city forty years ago with his wife and household to take shelter and live under the protection of the Kings of Portugal, and their Viceroys always gave him many grants and honors because they always saw in my father much fidelity and loyalty for all of the service of the Kings of Portugal until his death, and he died in this city some fourteen years ago. And I was born here and was brought up here with nothing lacking for me to be a native except that I was of another law [*sem me faltar nada pera natural mais que ser doutra ley*] and always, both in matters of war and of peace, the viceroys and governors found me possessed of all the loyalty that a true vassal should have, and I accompanied them by sea and by land.[68]

Here we see the subtle movement from a father of Turko-Persian cultural heritage to a son who is far more Lusitanized, but still "of another law"—that is to say still a Muslim. We are aware that Yusuf Khan, shortly after writing this letter, entered into contact with a certain Diogo Lopes Baião, a Portuguese who "traded in horses in the *Balagate*, a man who was suspect both before God and the Crown" (to cite Diogo do Couto), but who "managed to persuade" Yusuf Khan that he ought to return to Bijapur, where he had hopes of being acclaimed king. Already in his letter cited above we get the sense that Yusuf Khan had some dreams along such lines.

> From letters written by the Count Viceroy Dom Francisco Mascarenhas Your Highness will have come to know of the events in this Kingdom of *Ballaguate*, and in what state its affairs are; and how ambassadors of the *Nizamalluxaa* [Nizam Shah] and *Cutuxaa* [Qutb Shah] came to this city and have insistently asked the viceroy that he makes me the King of the *Ballaguate Idalxaa* as the Kingdom belongs to me by right, and that they would be willing to help in this matter with all their power. And that first I would offer homage and fealty and be a true vassal of Your Majesty, and render up the service of all of the Konkan which will yield 70,000 *cruzados* more or less, just as my father had done in a contract with the viceroy Dom Pedro Mascarenhas (who is with God) when he in his time raised him up to be King, as Your Majesty will know of in far greater detail. And I ask that Your Majesty should cast his eyes on me and make me great, because with your favor I hope to become King of the Kingdom of my

> grandfathers which has been usurped from me, and you will always have in me a true vassal, different from all the others who have ruled or might rule over the said Kingdom. And thus I remain praying to God that he lengthens the life of Your Majesty in his kingdoms for His great service.

The reference is to the turbulence following the murder of 'Ali 'Adil Shah, and the troubled succession of Ibrahim 'Adil Shah II, seen here as yet another opportunity. However, if we follow Diogo do Couto, when Yusuf Khan eventually decided to leave Goa with the horse trader Baião, and arrived at "a village called Perio that was a league from Benastari," he found himself in a trap. He was taken prisoner by a captain who had been sent there for that very purpose by the Bijapur regent Dilawar Khan Habshi; "and he was taken to where he was, and together they set out over the Ghat; and arriving at a fortress called Morigi [Miraj], they found a message from the King [Ibrahim 'Adil Shah II] that they should at once put out his eyes, for he feared that if he continued with them there might be some shift, which Marutachão [the captain] at once did, and the poor Çufo [Yusuf] was greatly deceived."[69]

Of another son of Meale, we know something, and this is Muhammad Khan, described by Couto as a "bastard son" of Meale, who accompanied him on his expedition in 1555. The Portuguese chronicler tells us that he too, like his half brother Yusuf, was contacted some years later by two prominent figures from the Bijapur court who once more were mounting a conspiracy to get rid of the sultan. This son of Meale proved more wise, and refused the offer. An official document from the 1580s notes however that a certain Dom Henrique, a notable of Moluccan origin who held the post of *bendahara* of the city of Melaka, had recently married a Christian daughter of Muhammad Khan, and by way of dowry from the Crown was to receive an annual revenue of 60,000 *réis*.[70] The gradual and inexorable Christianization of the family thus continued, which would take another son of Muhammad Khan to convert to Christianity at the end of the sixteenth century, and take up the name João de Meneses. By turning Christian, he was able in the seventeenth century to have the Portuguese title of Dom, and enter the prestigious Order of Christ. In a letter from the viceroy Dom Francisco da Gama (dated March 1627), we find a reference then to the recent death of Dom João Meale, "grandson of Mealecão," to whom the Crown had granted the captaincies of Nagapattinam and Honawar as dowries for two of his daughters.[71] Or again we find the case of a certain Dom Fernando Meale, knight of the Order of Christ, who had participated in a rather brutal attack on a magistrate (*ouvidor*) in Cochin in the early 1620s, but managed to be released as a knight of a prestigious military order.[72] For these men, the name "Meale" — as well as in some instances "Xá" — was transformed from the name of an ancestor to a surname, transmitted from generation to generation.

For their part, the historians and chroniclers located in seventeenth-century Bijapur do not seem to have retained much of a memory of 'Ali bin Yusuf 'Adil Khan. Even his attempt to raise himself as sultan in 1555–56 does not merit a mention in the Persian chronicle of Muhammad Qasim Firishta, *Gulshan-i Ibrāhīmī* (written in the early seventeenth century under the patronage of Ibrahim 'Adil Shah II). In one of the rare passages where he treats the relations between the Portuguese and Bijapur, he notes the following — with reference to the 1510s. "He [the regent Kamal Khan Dakhni] also concluded a peace treaty with the Franks, who, after the return of Yusuf 'Adil Shah, had besieged Goa and retaken possession [of the city] with large bribes to the governor. This event occurred at the time of the accession of the young Sultan, and it was finally decided that the Franks could remain in control of Goa under the condition that they did not attack the other cities and regions of the coast. So, from that day, the Portuguese remained in control of Goa and in observance of this treaty, did not advance any further into the territory of the 'Adil Shahis."[73] To put it mildly, this was something of a radical simplification, which suggests that the longer-term 'Adil Shahi strategy was to claim that, like so many other pretenders, Meale simply did not exist. This seems quite often to have been the case elsewhere in the sixteenth century, when the

Portuguese attempted to create and deploy a "reserve army" of Asian princes coming from a wide swathe of territories across the Indian Ocean: the Moluccas, Sri Lanka, Munhumutapa, Badakhshan, and even Arakan in northern Burma (in the seventeenth century).[74] Eventually, the *Estado da Índia* would even be moved to promote marriages between these princes and princesses, when they found themselves in Goa or in Lisbon, whether in a convent or in the middle of a military career. Even if they rarely or ever were placed back in their kingdoms of origin, they did play the role of informants or pseudoinformants, nourishing the dreams and illusions of conquest that were a part of the quotidian ideology of the early modern *Estado da Índia*.

Yet, as the instance of Meale, and indeed of Yusuf Khan, shows, these individuals also came to be profoundly isolated and alienated, allowed to retain their religious identity and "another law" to be sure, but under rather stringent conditions. In effect, despite his many attempts and pleas, 'Ali bin Yusuf Khan was never a free man from the moment he set foot in Goa in late

1543 to when he died there in around 1567, save for the brief period when he crossed the Ghats in 1555. First a closely guarded prisoner, then a prisoner to the extent of not being able to leave the town, it is unclear what he eventually gained by leaving the relatively comfortable existence he had briefly enjoyed as a guest of the sultans of Gujarat. In this he reminds us of a celebrated figure from the previous century, the Ottoman prince Sultan Cem (1459–95), not an inappropriate comparison in view of the fantasies in Bijapur that their own founder Yusuf was an Ottoman prince.[75] Cem, as we know, unsuccessfully competed with his brother Bayezid for the Ottoman throne, and then fled first to Mamluk Egypt and then to Rhodes, where he was treacherously taken prisoner by the Hospitallers in 1482. In the remaining thirteen years of his life, he passed between the eastern Mediterranean, France, and Italy. On the one hand, his brother was interested in his not returning to the Ottoman domains; on the other, the Papacy pressed him both to convert and to lead a new Crusade — in neither matter evoking any great enthusiasm from the Ottoman prince. As a recent commentator puts it, "rather than being in command, Cem seems to have been an instrument for different parties," adding that "he was also an ideal instrument for the disunified and squabbling European states which in the face of growing Ottoman power, were dangerously incapable of defending themselves effectively."[76]

Here the parallels cease. What emerges from the career of Meale is the relative weakness of the Bijapur sultanate, which was riven by internal tensions and difficulties, as well as under severe and near-constant pressure from Vijayanagara and Ahmadanagar. These were the problems that the Portuguese in Goa were able to exploit in order to hold on to Goa, and when — as in 1555–56 — Bijapur and Vijayanagara made a successful alliance, the Portuguese were obliged to retreat posthaste to the safety of the limits of Goa. But the parallels between Cem and Meale are also inexact in another respect. For we are reminded that Cem "was not a figure of great strangeness to those at the Papal court, where he was treated by the notables as one of them." Historians of the episode thus tend to view the problem as a political one, rather than having cultural significance. It is here, I would argue, that the case of Meale differs considerably. For despite centuries of proximity and cohabitation with Islam in Iberia, the Portuguese who found themselves in sixteenth-century India were for the most part quite bewildered by it.[77] Added to this was their relative unfamiliarity with the sort of Turko-Persian culture from which Meale came, even as he was clearly nonplussed by the manner in which he was treated at Goa. If dealing with the likes of Martim Afonso de Sousa and Dom João de Castro was difficult enough, it is clear that Goa by the late 1550s was an even harder place for a Muslim prince to find himself. The only solution was assimilation, and the great highway to assimilation passed not only through language, but also through religious conversion. It was a lesson that the grandchildren and great-grandchildren of Meale may have understood well enough, but that he could not — or did not wish to — grasp.

3 The Perils of Realpolitik

Wee cannot limitt Scenes, for the whole Land
It selfe, appeard too narrow to with-stand
Competitors for Kingdomes: nor is heere
Unnecessary mirth forc't, to indeere
A multitude; on these two, rest's the Fate
Of worthy expectation: Truth and State.

—John Ford, *Perkin Warbeck*, prologue (1634)

IN PRAISE OF EXILE

At the turn of the nineteenth century, a minor Mughal prince by the name of Mirza ʻAli Bakht Azfari wrote his memoirs, in which he detailed a life in two parts: a first half of about thirty years when he was a prisoner in Delhi in a sort of gilded cage (or *qa'id-i salātīnī*); and a second half when he wandered through much of the Indian subcontinent in search of political support before eventually settling in the region of Chennai (Madras). Reflecting on the difference between these two experiences, Azfari came to a rather paradoxical conclusion: the real wonders and marvels he had seen were in Delhi as a prisoner and not "on the road" during the rest of his life.[1] It seems in general that there is nothing like a long spell of imprisonment to bring out certain forms of both lucid and morbid reflection; never having had the experience myself, I cannot testify one way or another. Still, the sheer number of significant works that owe their origins to the incarceration of their authors is legion; one is even a little disappointed to encounter a case such as that of Meale, where such enforced immobility does not produce a more elaborate set of writings or reflections. Perhaps an amanuensis is needed—a Rustichello of Pisa to each Marco Polo—or perhaps just the guarantee of an eventual audience. Certainly Cem Sultan—whom we encountered briefly at the close of the last chapter—is known to have composed poetry, including some in a state of exile (*ghurbat* or *hijrat*), which in his case coincided in good part with imprisonment.[2]

Literary legend also often wishes to attribute writings to celebrated figures in exile or prison. A notorious case is that of the last Mughal emperor, Bahadur Shah "Zafar" (1775–1862), who was exiled by the British to Rangoon (in Burma) in the very last years of his life, after the bloody and unsuccessful rebellion against colonial rule in India in 1857–58. A popular verse that bears his name and poetic "signature" runs as follows.

Having asked for a long life,
We managed to get four days.
But two were spent in longing,
And two passed in expectation.

Unfortunately, there is no trace of these verses in any reliable version of the emperor's *dīwāns,* or collections of verse; the verse in fact appears to have been composed considerably later by a poet, Sayyid 'Ashiq Husain (1880–1951), known as Simab Akbarabadi. But the temptation to attribute it to the nostalgic figure of the last Mughal has obviously been too great to be resisted.

Imprisonment (*qa'id*) was not merely a periodic reality but also a preferred literary trope in the world of the Ottomans, Safavids, and Mughals. Princes often thought of themselves as enclosed in gilded cages, and the practice that eventually emerged in all three imperial instances of bringing up members of the family in the confines of the palace — while awaiting an eventual succession struggle — could only have exacerbated matters further. But exile (or *ghurbat*) and wanderings were also quite familiar situations. To Sultan Cem we can easily add other figures such as the Safavid prince Alqas Mirza, or the Mughal dynast Babur himself and his son Humayun (exiled for a time to Iran), to say nothing of later more-or-less fraudulent Mughal claimants such as the versions of Sultan Bulaqi. Imprisonment and exile were thus seen quite rightly as being two sides of the same coin of alienation.[3] Nor was this an experience limited to the Islamic world alone. A celebrated late fifteenth-century instance is that of Perkin Warbeck (d. 1499), a wandering impostor of Flemish extraction, who challenged Henry VII of England on more than one occasion by claiming to be one of the imprisoned "Princes in the Tower" — namely Richard, Duke of York. His eventual capture and execution did not quell the rumors and even seem to have fanned them in some quarters. The continuing fascination exercised by this figure can be seen in the composition of a seventeenth-century play by John Ford, *The Chronicle Historie of Perkin Warbeck: A Strange Truth* (1634), which enjoyed a certain success both in its own time and later, as well as in Mary Shelley's far later novel, *The Fortunes of Perkin Warbeck, a Romance* (1830).[4]

The themes of wandering (and exile) as well as incarceration lie at the heart of the experiences dealt with in this chapter as much as in the previous one. However, history is manifestly more than simple chronology, and it may appear that there is no pressing reason why the reflections in this chapter—which deal with an extended episode from the late sixteenth and early seventeenth century—should not have appeared before the previous chapter dealing with the mid-sixteenth century. But, as we shall see below, there was a significant shift in the intellectual context of encounters and interactions between the time when Miyan 'Ali bin Yusuf 'Adil Khan arrived in Goa from Gujarat in the 1540s and the end of the sixteenth century. It may be useful to outline the two central elements of this shift before entering into the details of the instance that this chapter seeks to explore, that of Sir Anthony Sherley. For the explanatory framework that we shall use to pose the activities and writings of Sherley depends on the tension between two attitudes and procedures—namely realpolitik and ethnography—that each suffered important changes in the passage between the moment of the Portuguese irruption into the Indian Ocean and the Spanish conquest of America, on the one hand, and the foundation of the Dutch and English East India Companies a century later, on the other.

AGENCY AND FORTUNE

What form of political theory did the Portuguese and Spaniards carry with them in their projects of conquest to the two Indies? Clearly, there was a strong medieval Iberian heritage linked to texts such as the *Siete Partidas* of Alfonso X in the Spanish case; there was also a heavy dose of Christian crusading zeal, as well as a more particular millenarian edge deriving from Joachim of Fiore and the fifteenth-century Joachites. But these ideological elements were not equally shared by all participants in the enterprise; obviously, Columbus was more under the direct sway of Franciscan apocalyptic thinking than Hernán Cortés (though the latter too felt the influence of that order), and the same contrast can be made—albeit with the chronological order reversed—between Afonso de Albuquerque and Vasco da Gama in the Portuguese case. What place then can we find for realpolitik, or "reason of State" in some form, either as an implicit attitude, or even as an avowed position in all of this? It turns out that the Spanish conquistadores have been read more closely by historians in this respect than their Portuguese counterparts. A prime example is Cortés, whose *Cartas de relación* have been examined with a view to their potential relationship with the writings of that celebrated exile Machiavelli.[5] The conclusion is ambiguous: Cortés obviously had not read Machiavelli, and even if he used the ends as justifying the means, it is clear that he stopped short of avowing the degree of cold-bloodedness (or shall we say lucidity) that the Florentine espoused. However, Cortés did have a certain Machiavellian view of human agency, and its place in relation to the dictates of Fortune (*fortuna* or *ventura*). As John Elliott has reminded us, the conquistador gave signs on more than one occasion that for him "the wheel [of Fortune] could be stopped in its revolution by hammering in a nail," and that in effect "Fortune could, after all, be mastered by man" even if some form of facilitating divine intervention were needed for this purpose.[6]

The discursive baggage that Portuguese aristocrats carried in their heads to Asia in the sixteenth century is harder to discern in the current state of play. Both millenarian and somewhat more general providentialist notions were clearly present, but analysts of the extensive letters of Afonso de Albuquerque (which one is often tempted to compare to Cortés's *Cartas de relación*) have sometimes been inclined to see a broadly Machiavellian streak there too. Still, the problem remains of how to reconcile the manner in which individuals were inclined to articulate and justify their actions as individuals, and their larger sense of the momentum of a grand structure such as a state or a nascent empire. Variants of such a question are posed time and again by writers of those curious and hybrid sixteenth-century Portuguese texts, the subimperial chronicles, which center on a single heroic figure (or a small clutch of them) in order to distill the essence of lived realities in Portuguese Asia and give them a human visage. Who is Afonso de Albuquerque to his son, Brás, author of the *Comentários*? Clearly he is to an extent a victim, both of the machinations of jealous actors on a petty scale, as well as of the grander problem of royal ingratitude, as indeed of the vagaries of Fortune. But he is also portrayed as a powerful actor of singular genius, who effectively invents the Portuguese *Estado da Índia* from the whole cloth.[7] Who is someone such as Dom João de Castro, whom we encountered in the previous chapter as Meale's ambiguous benefactor, when we view him through the lenses of his personal chronicler Leonardo Nunes? Here again is an actor seen by his chronicler/hagiographer as rising above the common multitude, and possessed of both virtue and will-power, but one whose thoughts in relation to his actions are hardly "theorized" for us convincingly in Nunes's pell-mell prose.

Again as with Cortés, we could of course turn to Castro's extensive letters for help. In the affair of Meale, we find Dom João de Castro much preoccupied with notions of "credit" (*crédito*) and "honor" (*honra*); the Municipal Council of Goa, he notes in September 1545, would not consent to hand over Meale to his nephew the sultan, "on account of the great dishonor and little credit [*grande deshonra e pouco crédito*] that would follow from such a thing to us." In his own subsequent letter to Ibrahim 'Adil Shah, Castro returns insistently to these themes: his charge from his own master is "to fully maintain justice for everyone [*guardar inteiramente justiça as partes*]," and the laws that he follows (*nossa lei* — here perhaps used in the sense of the Christian religion) will simply not permit him to perjure himself (*que não sejamos perjuros*). In a later letter to his own lord and master Dom João III, he notes that when he arrived there, he "already found that in all of India there was not one king or lord who trusted in the Portuguese to the extent of a straw, the more so when it became notorious to all that we were selling Miale and his sons to the *Idalcão*."[8] It is the same vocabulary and set of phrases — honor, credit, trust — that Meale would effectively turn against him and the other Portuguese.

Analysts of the seventeenth-century situation in Portuguese Asia have discerned something of a shift by that time. Writing of the world of the "service nobleman" in the 1620s and 1630s, Anthony Disney argues that their effort was in general to conjugate the demands — both complementary and contradictory — imposed on them by the ideas of *fama do valor* (reputation for courage) and *fama do cabedal* (reputation for wealth). The latter corresponded closely to the idea of *honra* evoked by Castro a century earlier, but was not entirely congruent with it; as for the latter, it centered on the fact that "a nobleman of rank needed to sustain a certain lifestyle, to support his followers and dependents in reasonable comfort, and to maintain a reputation for generosity."[9] But it is not entirely clear that such ideas of honor and valor extended to those who did not belong to one's own civility or political system; rather, with such actors other, more ruthless notions came into play because they were perceived not to play by the same "rules of the game." The great difficulty was however in arriving at a clear comprehension of the boundaries of a political system, beyond defining it simply through received ideas regarding monarchy and constituted kingdoms. Many of the great political thinkers of the later sixteenth and seventeenth centuries, whether Shaikh Abu'l Fazl in Mughal India or Thomas Hobbes in England, assumed that the natural domain over which their theories would extend was the unitary sovereign state, rather than a state that existed explicitly in a world of competing states. Their central problem was in understanding how sovereignty came to be what it was in such a unitary state, what the relations were between rulers and ruled, and — in the final analysis — why the monarchical state was superior to the alternative, namely a society with dispersed and competing powers that might end in chaos. But the life experience of many aristocrats in the sixteenth and seventeenth centuries was not limited to a single state, or even a single empire. It was hence essential to understand how one conceptualized power not simply as the relation between rulers and ruled but as the relationship between different, and irreducible, poles that were destined to coexist. Here, the passage from the sixteenth century to the century that followed was of some significance. For a variety of reasons that have been explored elsewhere, there was a widespread belief among intellectuals in the sixteenth century that a single monarchy would come to dominate the entire world. The prime candidates for this role were the Spanish Habsburgs (in particular Charles V and Philip II), and the Ottoman sultans. In 1531, Erasmus had claimed for example that it was public knowledge that "the Turk will invade Germany with all his forces, in a contest for the greatest of prizes, to see whether Charles will be the monarch of the whole world, or the Turk. For the world can no longer bear two suns in the sky."[10]

But the century itself brought about no tidy denouement. Neither of the two great sunlike empires referred to above was able to beat the other into submission, although both made substantial inroads into a variety of territories extending both east and west. The Habsburgs came to control swaths of disconnected territory in Europe, added to this an empire in America and the Philippines, and eventually — after 1580 — came to be masters of the Portuguese Empire through the devious medium of the Union of the Crowns. In comparison to this, the Ottomans remained masters of a more compact space extending west to east from Morocco to Basra, with territories that for a time were to be found in both East Africa and eastern Europe. But the brute reality of the sixteenth century was that the imperial spectrum did not collapse; rather, it expanded quite considerably. The Mughals, who had been a rather minor power as late as 1560, had emerged by 1600 as major players in Asia with pretensions that extended over all the Indian subcontinent and spilled over into Central Asia. For a time, the Burmese Toungoo dynasty threatened to create a considerable state in mainland Southeast Asia by pushing into neighboring Thailand and the Malay Peninsula. The Russian state made steady advances to the east over the course of the century, into both Siberia and Central Asia. To the northwest of Europe, two rather petty states—England and the Netherlands—began in the last quarter of the sixteenth century to carve out maritime empires for themselves both in the Atlantic and eventually in the Indian Ocean. By 1590, the world that Dom João de Castro had inhabited was no longer quite recognizable, and one may well suspect that he might have been rather uncomfortable with it. The millenarian conjuncture that had operated in such a powerful manner during much of the sixteenth century between the Tagus and the Ganges began to dissolve, for neither the year 960 H nor the Islamic millennial turning-point itself in 1000 H (or 1591–92 CE) brought with them anything of great import. To be sure, there were comets and shooting stars aplenty, and a few natural disasters to accompany them. By the 1610s, Sir Walter Raleigh was beginning to sound like a relic of another time when he insisted that politics on a world scale could still be comprehended in terms of the tension between Habsburg and Turk, a battle that either the one or other would win: "there hath been no state fearful in the east but that of the Turk, nor in the west any prince that hath spread his wings far over his nest but the Spaniard."[11] Other actors, including his contemporaries, began to understand matters in a somewhat different way. Some were Iberian, others Italian, but they also included the odd Englishman, especially the ones who had traveled far beyond the limits of their native isle.

IRAN AND EUROPE

In 1888, a year before his death at the age of seventy-five, the Reverend Scott Frederick Surtees of Dinsdale-on-Tees was moved to publish a pamphlet at private expense in Hertford. Twenty-eight pages in length, the work was titled *William Shakespere of Stratford-on-Avon, his epitaph unearthed, and the Author of his Plays run to Ground.*[12] A member of the north Yorkshire gentry, the reverend had earlier published such works as *Julius Caesar: showing beyond reasonable doubt, that he never crossed the Channel,* and had also shown some previous published interest in the Bard of Avon. The fact that he thought that Shakespeare was not the author of the plays attributed to him is not particularly surprising. Rather, the surprise lies in his choice of candidate: not Marlowe, not Francis Bacon, not even the Earl of Oxford, but rather a relative unknown: "Anthony Sherley and no other" (declares Surtees) "was he who wrote these plays."[13]

This important discovery has, alas, largely passed unnoticed and finds no mention in the writings of recent authors such as Stephen Greenblatt.[14] The reverend's rather disjointed and rambling style, and elliptical mode of reasoning (largely having to do with the recurrence of characters named Antonio in Shakespeare's plays), would probably appeal anyway rather more to radical postmodernists than New Historicists. But the man he chose to honor thus, even if more obscure than Bacon or Marlowe, was not entirely unknown to historians. In fact, he even enjoyed a certain celebrity in the early seventeenth century, for reasons not wholly unrelated to his own talent for self-publicity. Sir Anthony Sherley (1565–1633) first came to public attention with the appearance of an anonymous pamphlet titled *A True Report of Sir Anthony Shierlies Journey Overland to Venice, from thence by sea to Antioch, Aleppo, and Babilon, and soe to Casbine in Persia,* in October 1600, the year of the foundation of the English East India Company on the basis of a charter from Queen Elizabeth. The text of the *True Report* was allegedly "reported by two Gentlemen who have followed him in the same the whole time of his travaile," and its significance emerges already from the second part of its extended title. For the brief narrative claimed to deal with "his entertainment there [in Persia] by the great Sophie: his Oration: his letters of Credence to the Christian Princes: and the Priviledg obtained of the great Sophie, for the quiet passage and trafique of all Christian Marchants, throughout his whole Dominions."[15] We will turn presently to who Sherley was (to the extent that we can actually pin down this slippery figure); but first it may be worth our while to devote some attention to the "great Sophie" himself.

The Safavid dynasty came to gain control over much of Iran from 1501, as a result of the defeat of the Aqqoyunlu armies by Shah Isma'il at the battle of Sharur in that year. Isma'il then entered Tabriz in the summer of that year, and was raised to the throne; his name was increasingly heard from that time on in European elite circles, notably those of Venice, which took a great interest in the affairs of Iran. The Venetian merchant Andrea Morosini, resident in Aleppo, was a major source of rumors, which he used to fan enthusiasm in such figures as Marino Sanuto. Isma'il was himself descended on his mother's side from Uzun Hasan Aqqoyunlu (r. 1453–78), but his prestige largely lay in the fact that he was the head of a Sufi order, the Safaviyya, whose members and supporters comprised the human core on the basis of which his early rule was consolidated. The elite among these followers were often termed the "old Sufis of Lahijan" (*sūfiyān-i qadīm-i Lāhijān*), and while their relations with the dynasty veered uncertainly from one extreme to another, they helped give

Shah Isma'il a certain mystical and even messianic aura both within Iran and outside it.[16] From the first decade of the sixteenth century, it was common enough for Italians and Portuguese to refer to the Safavid shah as the "Sufi" or the "Great Sufi," an epithet that was then carried over to his descendants, notably his long-reigning son Shah Tahmasp.

Though their initial political strength was concentrated to the northwest, the Safavids quickly recentered their enterprise within a decade, and by the time the Portuguese came definitively to occupy Hormuz in 1515, they were in control of the mainland territories that looked out on the Persian Gulf. The aggressive character of Portuguese actions certainly did not make a positive impression on the Safavids, and the governor Afonso de Albuquerque was thus obliged to send an emissary under a certain Fernão Gomes de Lemos to the Safavid court camp near Tabriz to ensure that a rupture did not take place in relations. By the time of this embassy, the shine was somewhat off the image of Shah Isma'il, in view of the heavy loss he had suffered to the Ottoman sultan Selim at Chaldiran in August 1514. Still, rumors persisted regarding the shah and his attitude toward Christianity. Some, such as the Portuguese apothecary and diplomat Tomé Pires (whose *Suma Oriental* dates to about 1515), insisted that he had a particular proximity to and fondness for Christians, even if Pires realized that he was "a circumcised Moor and a follower of Ali, although many Moors say that he is a Christian." The explanation that was provided for this was that Isma'il allegedly had Christian relatives on his mother's side, and these "Christians [had] fed him and taught him, and he took from them what seemed to him good, and he was always obedient to them." Indeed, Pires went so far as to see this as a recurrent combat between "the sect of Ali" and "Mohammed's doctrine," and claimed that Isma'il "reforms our churches, destroys the houses of all Moors who follow Mohammed [i.e., Sunnis] and never spares the life of any Jew."[17]

It seems that despite Pires's positive rhetoric, and the view that the twelve Imams of the Shi'is might somehow be a version of the Christian apostles, the Portuguese *Estado da Índia* never really counted on the possibility of a proper alliance with the Safavids against the Ottomans. The embassy of 1523, which we are aware of through the detailed account of António Tenreiro, does not appear to have had any major strategic purposes in mind. However, Tenreiro does eventually seem — in the course of various difficulties he confronted in the passage between Iran and the Mediterranean — to have encountered a diplomatic mission that had as its purpose the building of an alliance between Safavid Iran and a European power. This was a complex mission sent out by Charles V in 1529, partly in response to a letter that he had received from Shah Isma'il in 1523 where the latter proposed an alliance against the common Ottoman enemy. Unaware that Isma'il had died in 1524, the letter from the Habsburg ruler still addressed him as sovereign, and was the first significant attempt to involve Safavid Iran in an alliance with the western European states. The chief envoy, Jean de Balbi, a Knight of Rhodes, seems to have arrived in Baghdad (at that time still under Safavid control) in May 1530, but was manifestly unable to make a great deal of his mission before being killed in a skirmish. The other personage involved in the affair was an intriguing one, namely the Englishman Robert Brancetour (or Bransetur), who continued to serve Charles V later in the 1530s and thus incurred the wrath of the court of Henry VIII.[18]

We learn more of Brancetour from the reports sent by the English diplomat and poet Sir Thomas Wyatt, who was with Charles V in January 1540. Wyatt informed Charles that Brancetour was considered by the English monarchy to be a rebel and traitor, as he had tried to persuade some Englishmen in Spain to revolt against Henry VIII. As a consequence, Wyatt asserted, his conspiracies had made him "convainquysht in hole Parliament." The account continues with this exchange between Charles V and Wyatt, as reported by the latter to his king Henry.

> Ah, quod he, Robert? That same Sir, quod I. I shall tell you, quod he, Monsieur l'Embassadour, it is he that hath been in Perse. As he saith, quod I. Na, quod he, I know it by good tokens; for when I sent the knight of the Rhodes, he of Piemont [Jean de Balbi], with charge to the Sophi, through Turkey, he fell sick, and this man, for the love he knew between the King and me, helped him; and in conclusion, when he saw he should die he opened his charge unto this man and told him what service he should do to me and to all Christendom, if he would undertake it. And he did so and it seemed true, for the King of Perse the same time did invade, and he went about the tother way by the sailing of the Portygalles and brought me sure tokens of the man, as well what money I gave him as other things. And this was no small service that he did; and I have had him follow me this 10 or 12 years in all my voyages, in Africa, in Province, in Italy, and now here; and since that time I know not that he hath been in England, whereby he hath done offence to the King, unless it be for going with Cardinal [Reginald] Pole that asked me leave for him by cause of the language.[19]

Charles V had intended through this mission, which has retrospectively been termed the Balbi-Brancetour mission, to build a relationship with distant and mysterious Safavid Iran. Brancetour, apparently an English cloth merchant, who seized the opportunity to curry favor at the Habsburg court and launch a career in diplomacy, had initially attempted after the death of Balbi to return via the Mediterranean. But since his route was blocked, he was obliged to take refuge with the Portuguese at Hormuz, and eventually was sent back in a ship by the Cape route, returning to Portugal in 1532. The following brief letter from Shah Tahmasp to Charles V, of which only a Spanish version survives, was the concrete result of this mission.

> God is pure and great. Powerful King of the world, fortunate, resourceful, just and famous Lion of the Sea, great lord and Emperor Don Carlos, may God grant you what you wish. After making infinite wishes [for your well-being], I make it known how Roberto Bransetor your servant came to me with a message and his arrival greatly helped settle our friendship. He is a noble person. He let me know what you had written and sent so that it was shown that we were united, and I have driven away from me those who were not [a part of this], and each day our friendship will grow and its opponents will weaken. At the time they arrived, I was making war in Coraçon [Khorasan] and with God's help I was able to defeat, kill and destroy all of the kings and great captains who were more than two hundred thousand men, and I settled the government as I wanted. After this, I returned to Tabriz. Concerning what you wrote and sent me, your messenger carries back the reply and may it please God that its sign will soon become clear. For the sake of friendship, we should always write and send messengers and may it be such that the Moors are kept in their place, and you should keep me advised of all the news there may be. May the honor of the world ever accompany you.[20]

The Spanish text seems to have been finessed somewhat, to the extent of suggesting that "Moor" was a category reserved for the Ottomans. Still, the letter in fact led nowhere, beyond indirectly causing the public execution of the unfortunate Andrea Morosini by the Ottomans, who denounced him as a spy. No real alliance was to be had with the Safavids, and the idea of the encirclement of the Ottomans remained a chimera. But the Habsburgs did revive the project again in the 1560s, both through Philip II and through the central European branch of their family (Ferdinand I and Maximilian II).[21] There was again a curious English flavor to the affair. Thus, in 1562, when Philip thought to send an envoy to Iran to revive the project that his father had begun some three decades earlier, his choice as ambassador was Sir Richard Shelley, a Catholic who had been a Tudor diplomat and spent time in Istanbul, Spain, and Italy without ever quite renouncing his relationship to the English Crown.

Though Shelley eventually received the rather reluctant support of the Portuguese, it was decided by his principals that he should proceed by the overland route via Astrakhan recently explored by other English merchants such as Anthony Jenkinson. The idea of this mission was abandoned soon though, when it seemed that Habsburg relations with the Ottomans might be on the mend. However, Maximilian II revived the matter again in 1566–67, this time proposing as an envoy Jacob Drapper, a merchant from Pera, who was to be sent on this occasion via the Cape route to the Persian Gulf. But this project too was stillborn, on account of the lack of enthusiasm shown by a number of key parties (notably the Portuguese), as well as the far more attractive option of making peace with the new Ottoman sultan Selim II (r. 1566–74).

Thus, in the course of the first seven decades of the sixteenth century, not much had advanced in terms of political or diplomatic dealings between the chief western European states and Safavid Iran. The ideas and ambitions remained roughly the same on the part of the Venetians and later the Habsburgs, and were based on the conception of an inveterate opposition between Sunni Ottomans and Shi'i Safavids that could be exploited for the benefit of the European opponents of the House of Osman. The gradual but perceptible evolution between a heterodox and charismatic style of Safavid kingship such as that of Shah Isma'il, and the move to a more orthodox Shi'ism under his son Tahmasp, was not a matter that greatly attracted the attention of the Western visitors who occasionally left accounts of Iran, even if the intelligent reader of the account of Michele Membré (Venetian envoy to Iran in the 1540s) could have gathered some evidence for this.[22] At the same time, it is clear that the extent of commercial traffic between the Mediterranean and Safavid Iran was not inconsiderable in these years. Merchants in Istanbul and Aleppo had a fair sense of the Iranian market, and networks of commerce run by Italians, Armenians, and Sephardic Jews also doubled as webs of espionage at the service of a number of the major powers of the time. Even the English Muscovy Company had had a short-lived glimpse of success in the 1560s, in the aftermath of the visit of the merchant Jenkinson to Qazwin in 1562. Jenkinson had carried a rather strange letter from Queen Elizabeth in English, with copies in Hebrew and Italian, to the "Great Sophie of Persia," treating him as the "Emperour of the Persian, Medes, Parthians, Hyrcanes, Carmanarians, Margians, of the people on this side, and beyond the River of Tygris, and of all men, and nations, between the Caspian sea, and the gulph of Persia." The letter ended with the sentiment that "neither the earth, the seas, nor the heavens, have so much force to separate us, as the godly disposition of naturall humanitie, and mutuall benevolence, have to joyne us strongly together."[23] But Jenkinson's experience in Iran turned out to be a somewhat fraught one. He arrived at a moment when the Safavids and the Ottomans were preparing to make peace, leading to the execution in July 1562 of the rebel Ottoman prince Bayezid, who had fled to the Safavid domains. He was deeply disturbed when he was treated with the Persian term *gāwur,* which he himself paraphrased as "unbeliever, and uncleane: [they] esteeming all to bee infidels and Pagans which doe not believe as they doe, in their false filthie prophets Mahomet and Murtezallie." His description of a rather disastrous interview with Shah Tahmasp in late November is worth revisiting, even if briefly. Jenkinson began by delivering the queen's letter and announcing that he "was of the famous Citie of London within the noble realme of England"; his declared purpose was "to repaire and traffique within his [Tahmasp's] dominions . . . to the honour of both princes, the mutual commoditie of both realms, and wealth of the subjects." The fact that the letter was in three unfamiliar languages apparently did not please the shah. The exchange then continued as follows.

> Then he questioned with me of the state of our countries, and of the power of the Emperour of Almaine, King Philip, and the great Turke, and which of them was of most power: whom I answered to his contentation, not dispraysing the great Turke, their late concluded friendship considered. Then he reasoned with me much of religion, demaunding whether I were a *Gower,* that is to say, an unbeleever, or a *Muselman,* that is of Mahomets lawe. Unto whom I answered, that I was neither unbeleever nor Mahometan, but a Christian. What is that, sayd hee unto the king of Georgians sonne, who being a Christian was fled unto the sayd Sophie, and hee answered that a Christian was he that beleeveth in Jesus Christus, affirming him to bee the sonne of God, and the greatest prophet: Doest thou believe so sayd the Sophie unto mee: Yea that I doe sayd I: Oh thou unbeleever sayd he, we have no neede to have friendship with the unbeleevers, and so willed mee to depart. I being glad thereof did reverence and went my way.[24]

Eventually, in March 1563, Jenkinson was allowed to depart from Qazwin after the intervention of some of the influential members of the court—who were favorable to trade and afraid that "there would few straungers resort into his countrey"—had ensured that he was at least treated with some minimal courtesy. This then led to further English trade missions in the 1560s, notably those of Arthur Edwards and Thomas Bannister, which eventually resulted in a partial thawing and the grant by Shah Tahmasp of some *farmāns* for trade, "all written in Azure and gold letters, and delivered unto the Lord

Keeper of the Sophie his great seale." Still, none of these ventures resulted in profits of any significance, and the death of Shah Tahmasp in 1576 seems to have dampened English enthusiasm altogether. A letter written by Queen Elizabeth to Shah Muhammad Khudabanda in 1579 apparently could not even be delivered.

Seen from the Iranian point of view, the negotiations over the course of the first eight decades of the sixteenth century with the European powers must have appeared complex. There was, first of all, the diversity of parties to be contended with: the Habsburgs in Spain, as well as their counterparts in central Europe; Venice, the old opponent of the Ottomans; various other central and eastern European interests as well as the Russian monarchy; the Tudors in England; and not least of all the Papacy itself. It was the Papacy that remained persistent after the death of Shah Tahmasp, in particular using the skills of the Florentine savant Giambattista Vecchietti, who visited Shah Muhammad Khudabanda at Tabriz in June 1586, and claimed to have been received with much pleasure (*con molto piacere udita*) by the Safavid court.[25] Vecchietti eventually returned to Italy in 1589 via the Cape route, carrying a letter from the Safavid monarch, who had in fact died in the meantime. In sum, at the moment of accession of the sixteen-year-old Shah 'Abbas I in October 1587 (following the deposition of his father), nothing of much concrete significance had been either achieved or consolidated in terms of Safavid dealings with European powers other than the Portuguese, who for their part continued to maintain a significant presence above all at their fortress in Hormuz, but also in respect of some other islands of the Persian Gulf, as well as at Kamaran (or Gombroon) on the mainland.

This is surely not the place to offer a comprehensive reinterpretation of the external policy of Shah 'Abbas, even if that task is now increasingly a pressing one.[26] His reign we know was extremely complex, but then it lasted four decades, and these were decades full of political twists and turns of the greatest complexity in respect of the larger politics of Eurasia. A couple of generations ago, Vladimir Minorsky's view of him still focused largely on his "curious blend of unconscious bloodthirstiness, joviality, and love of novelty, pageantry, and carousal."[27] More recent historians focus instead on "the vast scale and multi-layered nature of [the] achievements over Abbas's reign," as well as "the demarcation of a politically stable, physically larger and economically more vibrant polity whose makeup was significantly more complex than it had been when Ismail I entered Tabriz over a century before."[28] For much of the sixteenth century, as we have seen above, Safavid Iran did not play a central role in larger Eurasian shifts, with the possible exception of Shah Tahmasp's crucial intervention in the 1540s to support the exiled Mughal ruler Humayun (d. 1556), and bring him back to power in Delhi — a decision that the Safavids may well have later regretted. But this was to change in the early seventeenth century, a moment when Iran (and the Persian Gulf) began to appear — at least in some contemporary geopolitical conceptions — to be the center of an emerging interimperial world order.

Still, the early years of Shah 'Abbas's rule were manifestly less about external matters than setting his own house in order. An early treaty with the Ottomans signed at Istanbul in March 1590 accepted rather humiliating conditions as the price for external peace, and ceded extensive territories that the Ottomans had occupied over the previous twelve years (including the prestigious center of Tabriz). The shah then set about consolidating his rule against rival internal centers of power, including some of those who had supported his own bid for the throne. By the mid-1590s, he had managed to rid himself of the erstwhile kingmaker Murshid Quli Khan Ustajlu as well as the troublesome Ya'qub Khan Zu'l-qadr, and also surmounted a series of challenges that his court astrologers had suggested might pose serious problems to him in the context of the Islamic millennium of 1000 Hijri (1591–92 CE). His eastern neighbors, the Mughals, kept a nervous eye on his doings, and we have extensive reports on his activities sent to the Mughal court from agents in the Deccan, where Iranian migrants arrived on a regular basis carrying rumors and scandals from Iran. These reports suggest an image of a headstrong and vigorous young ruler, given to dangerous sports on horseback, but also characterized by a certain whimsy in his functioning.[29] There might have been a certain irony in all this for Mughal observers: after all, their emperor Akbar had assumed the throne at fourteen, had been given to rather vigorous physical activity in his own youth, and had also had his own share of problems with his tutors and would-be protectors in the early years of his reign, disposing of some of them with a certain expeditiousness. But the Mughals were equally aware that within a few years of assuming rule, Shah 'Abbas had begun to affirm the place of an increasingly orthodox Shi'ism in his kingdom, further exacerbated by the conflict in the Khorasan region with the Sunni Shaibanid dynasty from Transoxiana and its ruler 'Abdullah Khan. This then was the larger context for the diplomatic intervention of Anthony Sherley, which in turn produced a most curious and original global view of geopolitics.

ENTER ANTHONY SHERLEY

In 1607, a certain Anthony Nixon published a text titled *The Three English Brothers*, and dedicated it to the Earl of Suffolk, the Lord Chamberlain of James I's household.[30] The work begins with an account of the oldest of the Sherley brothers, Sir Thomas, and "his Travailes, together with his three yeares imprisonment in Turkie, his Inlargement by his Maiesties Letters to the great Turke: and lastly, his safe returne into England this present yeare, 1607." But it is the second section, titled "Sir Anthony Sherley his Adventures, and Voyage into Persia," that is of central concern for us. It begins thus.

> Mankind doeth unjustly, and without cause complaine of the State and condition of his life, for that it is fraile, subject to infirmities, of a short continuance, and governed rather by Fortune, than by Vertue. But if we shall consider what excellent sparks of ornament there are yet left in man's nature, notwithstanding the soyle of some, which by the corruption of Adam, is universally contractyed unto all: and that we would but descend into our mindes, to see what matter of worth there is, or might be lodged there, both for the life, Active, and Contemplative: we should not find Mankinde so wholly depraved in his degenerate nature: but that we may observe some signes and tokens yet left in him, of the notable light and resplendant beautie of his first creation, which by the two principall parts whereon the mind consisteth, viz. Understanding and Will, and the faculties belonging unto them, may easily be made manifest, what notable memorials both of their studies, and travels, have been recorded to the world, and worthy to bee continued to all ages, untill the end of time, and the beginning of eternitie, by the naturall instinct, and industrious labours of the mind, to checke and controll the dull and sluggish conditions of such men, as in their home-bred affections consume their time in base humor, and the delights of idle pleasure. And when I think upon the circumstance of the subject I am to intreat of, I am drawne into an admiration, that Sir Anthony Sherley, having so slender beginnings, should neverthelesse continue that state, countenance and reckoning, as hee hath done ever since his departure out of England, even in the Courts of the greatest princes, in, and out of Christendome: so farre exceeding Stukeley, that I am afraid to bee taxed of an impartiall [*sic*], and rash judgement.[31]

The reference here is to the popular and tragic figure of Thomas Stukeley (c. 1525–78) from Devon, who after serving in France and Ireland, eventually played a significant role in the Battle of Lepanto, before embarking with the Portuguese king Dom Sebastião in his disastrous North African expedition of 1578 against Sultan Abu Marwan 'Abd al-Malik al-Sa'di.[32] Here Stukeley — who remained a staunch Catholic until his death — was eventually killed along with the Portuguese king in early August in the celebrated Battle of Alcácer-Quibir while commanding the center of the Portuguese battle formation. By the 1590s, he had emerged as a tragic hero in England, and been represented onstage in a popular play written by — or at least attributed to — his fellow Devonshireman George Peele (1556–96) titled *The Battell of Alcazar and the Death of Captain Stukely.*[33] A slightly later play, *The Famous History of the Life and Death of Captain Thomas Stukeley*, from 1605, was also possibly on Nixon's mind at the time of his writing. In any event, he is not tender on Stukeley or his posthumous reputation. For, he continues, his purpose is not

> to intimate a comparison between them [Sherley and Stukeley], there being so great difference, both in the manner of their travels, the nature of their imployments, and the ende of the intendments. The one having his desire upon a luxurious, and libidinous life: The other having principally before him, the prospect of honour: which, not in treacherous designes (as Stukeley attempted in the behalfe of the Pope, against his Countrie) he hath impaired, or crazed: But contrariwise hath so inlarged, and enhaunsed the same, that his fame and renowne is knowne, and made glorious to the world, by his honourable plots and imployments, against the enemie of Christendome: which, according to the instructions I have received, I will briefly relate unto you.

Nixon then proceeds with an account of the second Sherley brother, already aged in his thirties, preparing an expedition from England to the Continent, without however being particularly clear regarding the circumstances thereof. He writes:

> After Sir Anthony his departure out of England, he landed in a short time at Vlishing [Vlissingen], where beeing honorably entertained, and feasted by the Lord [Robert] Sidney, Lord Governor of the Garrison, hee held on his journey towards the Hague, as well to visit his Excellentie, as to receive his passe for his better convoy through the Countrey. From thence he past along by many parts of Germanie, as Franckford, Noremberge, and so to Augusta [Augsburg], and from thence passed the Alpes, and within 10 days after came to Venice, having a purpose from thence, to take his course to Ferrara, in aydance of the Duke against the Pope. But the matter being before compounded, and agreed betweene them, that journey was stayed.[34]

Nixon is both obscure and disingenuous here, a quality that will characterize the rest of his account as well. As he tells it, Sherley and his companions then simply found their way into the eastern Mediterranean, drifting by stages via Crete (Candia), Cyprus, Tripoli (in Syria), and Aleppo to Baghdad. It is only hinted that this might have had some relationship with Sherley's dealings with "some Persians that were likewise in the shippe" with him when he left Venice, and with whom he had had rather friendly relations. It may therefore be necessary to take leave here for a time of Nixon's account to gain a better sense of Sherley's career and its trajectory, using the abundant source materials on him that can be found in the diplomatic archives of the time.

As we have already noted, Anthony Sherley was born in 1565, second son of Anne Kemp and Sir Thomas Sherley of Wiston in Sussex, who served as treasurer of war for the English Crown in the Low Countries from 1587.[35] Anthony like his older brother Thomas was educated from about 1579 in Oxford, at Hart Hall (later Hertford College) and All Souls College. He then participated from 1586 with some distinction in wars in the Low Countries, although he later tended to prevaricate somewhat regarding his precise role there. These campaigns brought him close to another active participant there, Robert Devereux, second Earl of Essex (1565–1601), and he thus became rather intimate with that controversial aristocratic figure. In his autobiographical *Relation*, published in 1613, Sherley was to make a great deal of this relationship.

> In my first yeares, my friends bestowed on mee those learnings which were fit for a Gentlemans ornament, without directing them to an occupation; and when they were fit for agible things, they bestowed them and me on my Princes service, in which I ran many courses, of divers fortunes, according to the condition of the warres, in which as I was most exercised, so was I most subject to accidents: With what opinion I carried my selfe (since the causes of good or ill must be in my selfe, and that a thing without my selfe) I leave it to them to speake; my places yet in authority, in those occasions were ever of the best; in which if I committed errour it was contrary to my will, and a weaknesse in my iudgement; which, notwithstanding, I ever industriated my selfe to make perfect, correcting my owne over-sights by the most vertuous examples I could make choise of: Amongst which, as there was not a Subject of more worthinesse and vertue, for such examples to grow from, than the ever-living in honour, and condigne estimation the Earle of Essex, as my reverence and regard to his rare qualities was exceeding; so I desired (as much as my humility might answere, with such an eminency) to make him the patterne of my civill life, and from him to draw

> a worthy modell for all my actions. And as my true love to him, did transforme me from my many imperfections, to bee, as it were, an imitator of his vertues; so his affection was such to mee, that hee was not onely contented, I should do so, but in the true Noblenesse of his minde gave me liberally the best treasure of his mind in counselling mee; his fortune to helpe mee forward; and his very care to beare mee up in all those courses, which might give honour to my selfe, and in worthy the name of his friend.[36]

These were not mere words, though Sherley had not always been on the good side of Essex. As a gentleman of modest fortune, he had clearly had his difficulties with the *grand seigneur* who Essex was, and had even once complained in the 1590s of being "afflicted for the opinion of my lord of Essex his couldness towards me," which had apparently had effects "nott only heavy to my minde but to my fortune."[37] Still, Sherley had proceeded to accompany Essex in campaigns from 1591 to help Henri IV of France, who rewarded him in 1593 with the Ordre de St. Michel; in accepting investiture into this order, Sherley possibly swore to defend the Catholic faith, an oath that incurred Queen Elizabeth's marked displeasure (and resulted in a brief spell in prison for Sherley). Returning to England, Sherley then contracted an ill-conceived marriage in 1594 with Essex's cousin, Frances Vernon, so that Essex sometimes then referred to him too as his "cousin." He also participated in an expedition mounted by Essex against the Spanish possessions at Jamaica and elsewhere in the Caribbean in 1596–97, with additional engagements against the Portuguese at the Cape Verdes. Late in 1597 (possibly on New Year's Eve), he made his way to Italy as part of a project (still under the patronage of the Earl of Essex) to help the exiled Cesare d'Este to retake Ferrara. But since this expedition was stillborn, Sherley eventually found his way to Venice, opportunely offering his services there to the republic; he was already noticed there by spies and informers in March 1598, and we have access to a letter written by one such anonymous letter writer to a correspondent in Frankfurt at that time. The letter is worth quoting at length for a sense of the ambiguous impression that Sherley frequently made, something that would characterize him during the rest of his career as well.

> Here, one finds a gentleman named Shurley, accompanied by about twenty-five men in his group, and he says that he has left the same number again or even more in Germany, and he spends a very large amount, and those in his entourage are for the most part captains and gentlemen. When he arrived, the rumour went

> around that he had come to take part in the war at Ferrara, which he found was already over; nevertheless, he has been sustained over here, and is thinking of spending time in this place. He has been in France, and has been captain of the English light cavalry [there]; still he speaks French very badly [*il parle fort mal franchois*], and he says that very soon [France] will be in a much worse state than it has been on account of a new party that will come up, and he says he is well-informed on all this; and also how he passed through Holland while on his way here, and that he was (or so he says) well-regarded and received there. Nevertheless, he hardly speaks better of the States [-General than of France] and, on the contrary, he unceasingly extols the greatness of Spain and even more that of the Pope, and says that he has received great offers from the one and the other, and that (if he finds nothing better elsewhere), he will see what he decides to do. It would be good if the States [*Messrs. les Estats*] were informed of his behavior so that if he passes through or deals with their country they are on their guard, for he says that no matter where [the support] comes from, that he would rather wind up ruined than spend less. If he were wise and of good counsel, he would talk less and would be more to be feared. He has married a close relative of Monsieur le Conte d'Essex and says that he is his great favorite, and that he had received eight thousand pounds sterling to make this voyage over here. But since he is a spendthrift who has spent all his means, and those of his father who he has ruined, and he lives here on what he has borrowed, one cannot believe that he was sent by the said Count. And all the more because he states he has great enemies and spies everywhere, it would be good to keep an eye on his actions. For if he has received the sort of offers he says, it must be on such terms that if he carries them out he will cause prejudice and damage to the good side.[38]

By late April, a copy of this letter had fallen into English hands and was forwarded by an agent in the Netherlands to the Earl of Essex with the following dry commentary: "Your lordship knoweth Sir Anthony thoroughly, and I do not send it [the letter] as a thing whereunto I give any great credit, nor have I any other feeling of the gentleman than as of one whom your lordship affecteth greatly, but if things be written or said to the hurt of the gentleman, or hindrance of the service on which your Honour may employ him, the same may be so considered of as shall be to your liking."[39] During his stay in Venice, Sherley was himself apparently an assiduous letter writer, keeping up a correspondence across his wide network of friends and acquaintances. In particular, he seems to have corresponded directly both with Essex and with Anthony Bacon, an important figure in intelligence networks of the time, and older brother of the far more celebrated Francis Bacon. By these means, he seems to have come to know of one of Essex's new projects, namely to support and invest in a Dutch enterprise to open direct trade with Asia via the Cape of Good Hope. This was part of a reorientation in the Earl's view of the world, for as a recent biographer has remarked, until 1595 Essex had "been associated mainly with those who advocated the primary importance of war on land."[40] Extending his network of patronage from Drake and Hawkins to consummate men of the sea such as William Monson and John Davis, Essex now set about defining a "new combined arms strategy" aimed at decimating Spanish power and replacing it with a combination of English and French might. In this, the Dutch were meant to play a tertiary but nevertheless helpful role.

In April 1595, the first Dutch expedition of four ships had been sent out to Asia under Cornelis de Houtman. It had made its way to the Javanese port of Banten, and returned in 1597 with a cargo that was not of the greatest significance but which nevertheless encouraged new investors to participate in the Asian enterprise. Among these was a wealthy Dutch merchant of Breton origin, Balthazar de Moucheron, who set about creating the so-called Veerse Compagnie for trade with Asia, and promptly reemployed Houtman to this end. The scale of matters remained small, with only two ships being fitted out; but Essex persuaded Moucheron to accept his protégé, the English navigator John Davis, as chief pilot on the expedition.[41] This fleet eventually set sail from the Netherlands on 15 March 1598, at much the same time as the anonymous letter from Venice cited above was written. Its experience was to prove something of a disaster. After reaching Saldanha Bay in southern Africa in November, Houtman made for Madagascar, despite the fact that he had already had unfortunate experiences there on his previous voyage. He then crossed the width of the Indian Ocean to reach Aceh in northern Sumatra in June 1599, hoping to benefit from the extensive trade of that center, which had developed over the second half of the sixteenth century as a focus of resistance to Portuguese trade in the region. Instead, what followed was a series of misunderstandings and maneuvers exacerbated by the Dutch commander's maladroit manner of dealing, culminating in an armed conflict in early September, in which Houtman and many of his party were killed, and his brother taken prisoner by the Acehnese.[42] John Davis and others managed to flee with the two ships, and eventually limped home to Middleburg in July 1600 having accomplished little of consequence.

To Sherley, attempting to piece together a master strategy while resident in Venice in the spring of 1598, news of this planned expedition must have appeared very promising indeed. He may or may not have known that the Dutch in fact had no plans of visiting the ports of West Asia at the time. In view of Essex's absolute opposition to Spain and the Habsburgs, it also seems unlikely that Sherley would have really hoped for much aid from that end; but it is possible that he had dealings with the entourage of Pope Clement VIII (1592–1605), who was particularly interested both in overseas missionary activity and in constructing an anti-Ottoman alliance on some scale.[43] We can gather a sense of his plans from a letter written from Lyons by the naturalist Thomas Chaloner to Anthony Bacon in June 1598. Chaloner had just returned from Venice and had encountered Sherley there before the latter's departure for Constantinople and parts farther east in late May 1598. Sherley and Chaloner were both clearly aware that this eastern enterprise was a risky one, undertaken "without especial order" and potentially treasonable. Chaloner thus begins his letter with expressions of the loyalty of Sherley, "whose love and zealous affection to my Lord Marshal [Essex] and yourself [Bacon] is so well known that it were vain for me to make any long protestation thereof." He then proceeds to explain Sherley's strategy as follows. Sherley, he notes, had "left no stone unmoved or means untried to find employment in the state of Venice, which is so far from entertaining new actions or new instruments for war, that they hardly vouchsafe those few which they have either good grace or large pension." Nor were there other promising wars in Italy for the employment of a footloose gentleman-soldier, or at least one interested in "any matter of great consideration." Sherley's other option, Chaloner notes, would have been to return to France and seek employment with the Huguenot forces of the Duc de Lesdiguières, constable of France, but this seemed less than promising since in France "there are already almost as many captains as there are soldiers." So, he had had to make the best of a bad job.

> In conclusion, finding all projects answer his expectation weakly save only that of the Levant, he imparted it unto the Grand Duke [Doge] and Signor Foscarini. The former named by letters urged it as a matter most necessary and of weighty consequence, promising to signify his allowance and opinion thereof to my Lord Marshal. The second in my presence gave him the greatest encouragement possible, affirming the undertaking of such an exploit to be beneficial to all Christendom and in particular to Venice, which by the traffic overland from thence was mightily enriched before the Portugales were lords of those parts. And for the facility thereof he held it so manageable that none but God only by miracle could

> give disturbance thereto. To prove that it stood with the grounds of Christianity he used many reasons, as the transporting of war from our homes, as it were, into another world, the overwhelming of ambition and dispersing of those wares and merchants to all traffickers, which to the empoverishing of all estates are now only made private to the Spaniard. In sum he held him happy that should by this good and lawful means immortalize his name for ever.[44]

What precisely this project "of the Levant" consisted of remains quite unclear in this long passage. But it is clear enough that it was directed broadly at the revival of the "traffic overland" against the Cape route, a prospect that Chaloner claimed had already worried the Portuguese king Dom Sebastião so much that he had written to Pope Pius V of this threat "against which he despaired to be able to prevail." Further, Chaloner noted that there was an advantage to the fact that Sherley was striking out on his own and not following orders: for "if it seem not good to the highest in our isle to give an open applause to this action, yet it is no new thing for princes to wink at private men's actions, which they will never commend till the event succeed fortunately." Besides, he assured Bacon that from now on Sherley's "intent is to attempt nothing without warrant from England."

As this letter intimates, while at Venice, Sherley had sought the advice of Giacomo Foscarini, an important diplomat and administrator who had served in Crete, and knew the politics and trade patterns of the eastern Mediterranean well. He had also had contacts with eastern Christian merchants such as a certain Angelo Corrai, possibly an Aleppo merchant with considerable experience of trade in the Ottoman domains.[45] It was along with Corrai, Sherley's younger brother Robert, and a sizable party of about twenty-five persons then, that Anthony Sherley set sail from the port of Malamocco near Venice on 24 May 1598. On board the ship were Iranian merchants, from whom it is possible that Sherley and his party gained fresh information regarding the current situation in the Safavid territories. But things turned sour very quickly, and following a violent altercation with Italian merchants on the same ship, the English group was summarily set ashore on the island of Zakynthos (Zante). From there, Sherley sent a letter to Henry Lello, English envoy at Istanbul, claiming that "he was sent by Her Highnes [Elizabeth] towards the Red Sea, to meet with a fleet of Holanders that are gone thither under color of traffick," an evident reference to the Moucheron-Houtman expedition. He also requested Lello "for his more safety to send him the Grand Signor his commandment or pass through his Dominions." Lello obliged and obtained an Ottoman passport or *laissez-passer*, but reported the matter to Sir Robert Cecil and eventually realized that he (like many others) had in fact been duped with regard both to the official nature of the mission and to its eventual destination.

From Zakynthos, the English party made its way slowly to Crete, then to the port of Tripoli (in the Levant), and eventually arrived in Aleppo, dogged throughout by difficulties and misadventures, including the arrest of Corrai. In Aleppo, Sherley entered into contact with Levant Company merchants, whom he once again assured of his intention to make contact with John Davis and the Houtman expedition. However, he announced his next destination now as Baghdad (which was accurate), and also persuaded the merchants to make him a sizable loan "to be repaid the treasurer [of the Company] in England by the Earl of Essex." Sherley and his party then left Aleppo on 2 September 1598, making their way to Bira on the banks of the Euphrates, and then to Fallujah and eventually to Baghdad. Again, an altercation broke out on this leg, with Sherley this time denouncing two of the Englishmen in his party for treasonable conduct and sending them back to Aleppo (from where they were deported to England and imprisoned). Nor did things go much better in Baghdad, where the Ottoman governor Hasan Pasha grew quite suspicious as to the size of the English party (who claimed they were mere merchants) in comparison to the modest amount of merchandise they carried. Sherley and his party eventually departed the city under circumstances that are unclear, left the Ottoman domains as quickly as they could, and reached the Safavid city of Qazwin on 1 December 1598, more than six months from the time they had departed from Venice. Everywhere, Sherley had left rumors and doubts swirling in his wake. William Clark, one of the English merchants in Aleppo, summed matters up thus: "It was reported at his being here that he was sent upon Her Majesty's affairs. If it be so no doubt but good payment will be made, but some think he goeth upon his own business, which I fear will prove too true."[46]

We have thus far accompanied Sherley's party as far as Qazwin, from where they eventually attained Isfahan in late January 1599, and remained there for four or five months. What exactly transpired in this relatively brief Safavid sojourn still remains something of a mystery. Sherley first encountered Shah 'Abbas while at Qazwin, in the company of the important Safavid notable Marjan Beg. Sherley describes their first meeting in his *Relation* (of 1613) as occurring while the shah was still in his encampment, so that Sherley's party had to make their way to him "through all those Troupes. . . . When we came to the King, we alighted, and kissed his Stirrop: my speech was short unto him; the time being fit for no other: That the fame of his Royall vertues, had brought me from a farre Countrey, to be a present spectator of them; as I had beene a wonderer at the report of them a farre off: if there were any thing of worth in mee, I presented it with my selfe, to his Maiesties service. Of what I was, I submitted the consideration to his Maiesties judgement; which he should make upon the length, the danger, and the expence of my voyage, onely to see him, of whom I had received such magnificent and glorious relations."[47]

If indeed Sherley did make such a speech, all this must clearly have been conveyed through the Christian go-between Corrai, who served throughout as interpreter. Sherley had no great talent even for the Romance languages, and it is clear that he made little progress with Turkish and Persian as well. Other contemporary reports by those in Sherley's company suggest that this address was in fact a polite fiction, and that no real words were exchanged at the stirrup kissing. Still, it is notable that even in Sherley's own optimistic account, no mention was seemingly made here of the fact he might be an ambassador, or that he might possess official letters of accreditation from any European monarch. Rather, he seems to have presented himself as a man of considerable cultural and diplomatic means who could serve the shah well in view of his connections into the courtly world of Europe; one contemporary writer states that he might have claimed a familial relationship to James VI of Scotland in his dealings with 'Abbas, but this need not necessarily have been more than a vague reference to a distant kingdom.

Sherley's Iranian dealings of the years 1598–1601 represent the ultimate paradox in matters of early modern diplomatic history. They are extremely richly documented, and yet deeply mysterious. The best-known corpus of materials includes the account of William Parry in the form of his *New and Large Discourse* (published in 1601); the *True Discourse* of George Mainwaring; the French *Relation* of Abel Pinçon, who served as Sherley's steward, eventually published in 1651; and the account of a certain Ulugh Beg, later converted to Christianity and known as Don Juan de Persia.[48] To these we can add a large body of diverse diplomatic materials in a variety of languages, which accumulated over the course of Sherley's complex wanderings of the next couple of years. While one can reconcile these materials with regard to a certain basic sequence of events and encounters, they diverge in very large measure on many matters, some of which are questions of mere detail but others issues of a far greater importance. The greatest problems that these materials refuse to resolve are two in number. First, it remains impossible to comprehend the basis on which Sherley built his credibility at the Safavid court, or indeed to discern what precisely he was taken for by Shah 'Abbas and his entourage. Second, it proves equally impossible to understand what exactly his charge was when he left that court in May 1599 in order to return to Europe by way of a complex itinerary. With regard to the first of these questions, none of the contemporary European accounts is of much help beyond suggesting that Sherley's personal charm was irresistible; the Safavid chronicles for their part are characteristically silent on the whole matter. Mainwaring declares for instance that very soon after the first ever meeting, the shah "came and embraced Sir Anthony and his brother, kissing them both three or four times over, and taking Sir Anthony by the hand, swearing a great oath that he should be his sworn brother, and so did he call him always."[49] The reference is apparently to the address or title of "Mirza," which Anthony Sherley was given by the Safavid monarch. Parry for his part describes a scene where in an early meeting the shah and his entourage were seated on the ground, but ordered "stools to be brought for Sir Anthony and his brother"; after an impassioned discussion regarding war with the Ottomans, Parry informs us that the exchange of views "made the King instantly to conceive so exceeding well and grew more and more into such liking of Sir Anthony that once a day at the least he would send for him to confer, and compliment with him; yea, sometimes he must be sent for to come to his bed-chamber at midnight, accompanied with his brother, for that purpose."[50]

In a valiant attempt to give some pragmatic meaning to these dealings, some modern historians have proposed that Sherley's main source of credit was the fact that he was a military expert, someone who was au courant with the modern manner of making war in western Europe. Sherley, in his *Relation*, suggests a version of this reading; already in Qazwin, he notes that 'Abbas "had divers discourses with mee, not of our apparrell, building, beauty of our woemen, or such vanities; but of our proceeding in our warres, of our usual Armes, of the commodity and discommodity of Fortresses, of the use of Artillary, and of the orders of our government." Sherley remarks further that he had with him "certaine Models of Fortification in some bookes at my lodging," and that the day after these discussions 'Abbas and some of his chief nobles visited him and "spent, at least, three howers in perusing them, and not unproperly speaking of the reasons of those things himselfe."[51] This may indeed have been the case, though it can only be a matter of speculation what these treatises on the art of fortification were and how they escaped the Ottoman inspection of Sherley's effects in Baghdad.[52] Still, one is inclined to take the importance given to Sherley's intervention in such matters as another example of his deft mythmaking, and agree with the overall judgment that in view of the brief duration of his stay, "the time available for army reform to be effected by a man who never knew Persian or the Turkish dialect of court was negligible."[53] Rather, it does seem that European military influence at the time on the Safavids was more plausibly exercised by those of Sherley's party who remained behind after his own departure, learned Persian properly, and invested to a great extent in Safavid court culture.

Sherley's own *Relation* is equally difficult to interpret with regard to the exact nature of his mission when he returned to Europe. He informs his readers that he had put before the Safavid court a comprehensive proposal for an alliance between the Safavids and the Christian powers against the Ottomans, using both moral arguments and pragmatic ones. On the moral side, there was the issue of "the extreme tyranny of the Turke" and the miserable state of 'Abbas's erstwhile subjects, who "were throwne out of their possessions." On the pragmatic side was the favorable balance between the state of the Iranian "*Militia* which was fresh and uncorrupted," compared to the Ottomans with their "corruptions of government, want of obedience, sundry rebellions, and distractions from any possibility of being able to make any potent resistance against his Maiesties proceedings."[54] All that was needed to tilt the balance would be to divide the Ottoman forces across two fronts, drawing some of them into Hungary as well into other fronts to the west, and this was where the alliance with the Christian powers would prove essential. Sherley's narrative takes the form here of a classic debate, dividing the Safavid court into those who supported his view and those who opposed it, with each side being given the occasion in the text to make long and rather windy speeches. On Sherley's side, if we are to believe him, were the two *ghulāms* or royal slaves of distinction, Allah Virdi Khan and Tahmasp Quli Khan, while the opposition was apparently centered on the figure of a certain Haidar Beg, the *wazīr.*[55]

Whether such debates really took place, or were merely a rhetorical flight of fancy, we are aware in any event that by the early summer, Shah 'Abbas had determined to send an embassy led by a notable from the corps of Qurchis, a certain Husain 'Ali Beg Bayat, together with Anthony Sherley, to a whole host of European powers, proposing a generalized and potentially quite complex alliance against the Ottomans. Sherley later made the most determined efforts to discredit Husain 'Ali Beg, using a variety of arguments: that he was merely an improvised last-minute substitute for the real envoy, a certain

Hasan Khan; or that he had been sent "in the forme onely of a testimonie, though honoured with some good words in the letters, for the better reputation of the businesse."[56] Eventually, a rather curious Augustinian, Frei Nicolau de Melo, was also added to the group with somewhat unspecified tasks as well. Robert Sherley was left behind in Isfahan, as a hostage of sorts, as were a number of other Englishmen from Sherley's original party. The group made its way north from Isfahan to the Caspian Sea, where they boarded a vessel that took them to the estuary of the Volga and from there to Astrakhan. Here, they joined another Safavid embassy to Moscow, this one led by a certain Pir Quli Beg. Step by step, dissensions grew within this motley party, first between Sherley and Melo, then between the Englishmen and the Iranians, and finally even within Sherley's own group. On arriving in the Moscow of Czar Boris Godunov, the quarrelsome party was therefore subjected to close examination by the Russians, and more mutual recriminations were exchanged. Parry reports that Sherley on one such occasion lost his temper with Melo, and "gave the fat friar such a sound box on the face . . . that down falls the friar, as if he had been struck by a thunderbolt." The suspicions all these quarrels evoked ensured that the party was then placed under a form of house arrest, which endured several months, until shortly after Easter of 1600.

It was during this period that Sherley wrote an important letter to Anthony Bacon, dated 12 February 1600.[57] In the missive, Sherley mentions his "many letters" sent in previous months and years, and writes of the "infinite labour as must accompany so great an Enterprise as this was." He fears that his reputation has been damaged in England on account of "all the persecutions that malice and the spite of idle tongues" have caused to him. Nevertheless, after complaining at length about the Portuguese friar Melo, he attempts to lay out a justification for his recent actions, and a broad (if rather improbable) new geopolitical scheme.

> Now from this evil preface, I will enter into the matter of what I have done. I have opened the Indies for our merchants in that sort that only excepting the outward show of power, they shall have more power than the Portuguese, through Persia they may bring as secure as between London and St Albones, the hatred which the whole Indian body beareth to the Portuguese being such that let only another trader enter, they will rather lose by him than sell to the Portuguese. This is one service which I have done for our state, and hereinclosed for the encouraging your belief, I have sent you the copy of the Patent given me for all merchants by the King of Persia, and I judge that my deserving is not ill,

> to have effected that which hath been so often attempted and were hopeless; which besides brings with it two mighty profits, our own wealth and the enemy's impoverishing.

To be sure, Sherley is aware of the objections that might be raised to the effect that the English and the Ottomans have a trade partnership; for him, trading with the Safavids will give the queen "a richer, greater and an infinite more honourable trade than that." The key to the next step now follows.

> The King of Tabur [Lahore] is the mightiest king of the Indies. With him I have so well fitted my credit that I have received two messages from him: in one he hath desired of me, some man which knows the wars to discipline his men, which I would not promise him, but have left with my brother, a gentleman, one Powell, ready to move upon the first commandment, and upon his coming unto him he will make war upon those forts of the Portuguese which are upon some parts of his dominions. In the other we have spoken of a thing of much mightier importance, if any of Don Antonio's sons will come into his country he shall be assisted with money and men, for the recovering of the rest of the Indies. For the better hope of which occasion he shall also find eight thousand banished Portuguese in Bengula and Syndy which will join for any such innovation, though for anything I can gather, being one there, he will have no great use of force, where the people's affection is so great to his house.

Later in the same letter, Sherley reiterates the project, adding that "if Her Majesty please to send any of those two [Portuguese] princes, only let her please to write to this King of Muscovya for his passage, and then upon my life, I will put him safe in La Hur and in an exceeding great fortune for a prince that is so far from any." While he does not mention the Mughal emperor Jalal-ud-Din Muhammad Akbar by name, it is he who is referred to here as "the King of Tabur [Lahore] . . . the mightiest king of the Indies." We cannot be in the least certain that Sherley in fact entertained any real correspondence with him during the brief period of his Iranian sojourn, nor is there any evidence that Captain Thomas Powell was ever sent as a military specialist to the Mughal domains. But it was certainly astute to have picked up on the notion that anti-Spanish sentiment still existed in the Portuguese *Estado da Índia*. In this context Sherley mentions the figure of Dom António, prior of Crato (1531–95), the illegitimate son of the Portuguese prince Infante Dom Luís, who had emerged in 1580–81 as a pretender to the throne and an opponent of the ambitions of Philip II over Portugal.[58] We are aware that Dom António spent time in both England and France, and participated in attempts to resist the Habsburgs both in the Azores and then by way of an attack on Portugal itself. He died in Paris in 1595, and it is not impossible that Sherley had met him on one or the other occasion. The sons he referred to were Dom Manuel de Portugal and Dom Cristóvão de Portugal, of whom the former enjoyed some success in European court circles, marrying into the House of Orange. Sherley's project here was therefore to hive off the *Estado da Índia* as an independent entity, using a somewhat improbable alliance of discontented Portuguese, renegades resident in Bengal and Sind, and the Mughals themselves. This was a notion to which he would return not long afterward, and a measure of the amplitude of his alliance-building conceptions.

By June 1600, Sherley and his party had arrived in Arkhangelsk, where they made contact with the merchants of the English Muscovy Company. It would appear that here a strange transaction took place by which he persuaded the Iranian emissaries to hand over thirty-two cases containing gifts from Shah 'Abbas to various European princes to him. These cases subsequently disappeared, and Sherley was accused of robbing them, while he for his part insisted that the goods had been largely worthless and he had merely disposed of them to avoid embarrassment. From Arkhangelsk, the party then embarked on a ship around Norway, to arrive at the port of Stade in Germany. En route, William Parry left the party to carry news of Sherley's adventures into England, thus becoming the source for the first publications about him. The main body of the party made its way via Emden to Prague, court of Rudolph II, where they arrived on 20 October 1600. They would remain there slightly over three months, running up considerable expenses, but also providing Sherley with an opportunity to once more take the measure of political affairs in Europe.

However, the arrival of this embassy by its rather complex northern route had already been preceded by other contacts between Iran and Italy using the more direct passage via the Ottoman domains.[59] Sherley had dispatched Angelo Corrai with letters to Venice, where he arrived via Tabriz, Erzurum, Trabzon, and Istanbul on 28 November 1599. Described by his Venetian interlocutors as "a man of small stature [*un uomo di statura piccola*], with a black beard, olive complexion, robed in a black camlet, of about forty years," Corrai declared that "he came from the King of Persia, sent by the Englishman Antonio Sherley, who had lately spent some time in this city [Venice], and was now in Persia, held in great esteem by that king."[60] The letter he carried from Sherley was dated in Gilan, on 24 May, and contained largely gener-

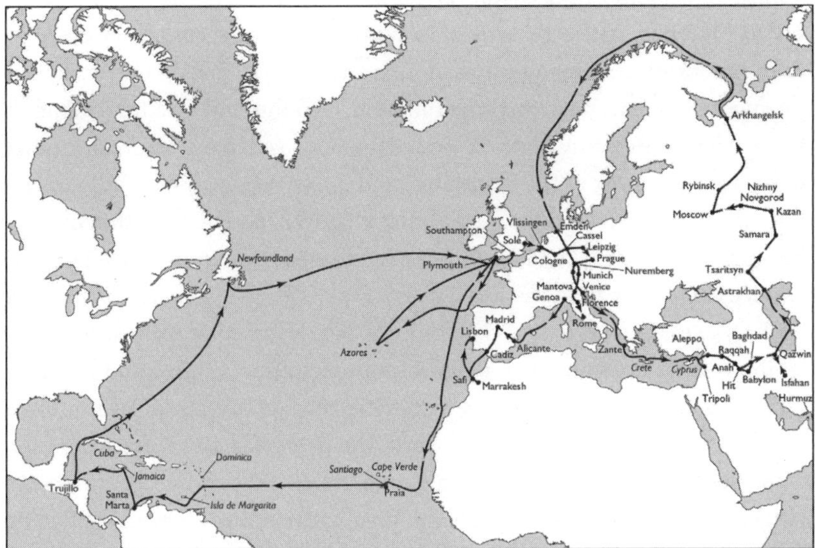

Anthony Sherley's travels

alities, save for the claim that he now had the entire "faith and trust [*fede e credito*]" of the Sofi, that is, Shah 'Abbas. After being questioned at some length and painting a rosy picture for the prospects of Christianity in Iran, Corrai left Venice, apparently to join the Duke of Mantua. Other letters carried by him from Sherley and Frei Nicolau de Melo seem to have reached the Spanish court as well.

Though the Venetians and the Spaniards were thus somewhat ahead of the curve, as it were, by the last few months of 1600, most of the major European powers were aware of Sherley's activities, and Henri IV of France had already written to his ambassador at Istanbul warning him about the implications of this mission. In part, this was the result of Sherley's great talent for self-publicity and the splash that he deliberately made while entering Prague, for instance. However, in the period of his stay at Prague, things also became extremely complicated for Sherley, as he multiplied his contacts and his correspondents. The news from England was somewhat disquieting. In late 1599, the Earl of Essex had fallen into disgrace on account of his dealings in Ireland; in June 1600, he was tried and convicted of various offenses at the instance of his nemesis Sir Robert Cecil, and though he was released in August, his star was clearly on the wane.[61] At the same time, Sherley's relations with Husain 'Ali Beg continually deteriorated, and various counter-efforts were mounted by Sherley to discredit the Iranian. From Prague, Sherley made his way to Florence, where he arrived in March 1601, to receive news via Venice of the imprisonment and trial of his patron Essex. Enea Vaini, an Italian notable of the time, described the moment. "To this ambassador [Sherley], through letters from England via Venice there arrived today, so he says, news of the imprisonment of the Constable, and of his two brothers, and of many other principal men, and the best of that kingdom, and he fears that by now they may well be dead, on account of which he has turned the most afflicted and disconsolate man in the world [*resta il più afflitto e sconsolato huomo del mondo*], so that I feel compassion for him." Sherley had not made a good initial impression on Vaini, who found him possessed of an unsound physiognomy, and an air of moneygrubbing, besides the fact that he spoke a "jumble of Italian and Spanish."[62] By early April, the news of Essex's execution was confirmed, and Sherley went on to Rome, by now quarreling continuously with Husain 'Ali and the other Iranians. Finally, the embassy was obliged to be divided into two, since it was decided that it was the Iranian who represented the true core of the mission. Husain 'Ali was thus sent on to Valladolid and the Habsburg court, while the Papacy offered Sherley a consolation prize of sorts, suggesting that he return to Asia with letters for the viceroy in Goa and other Portuguese officials.

THE MASTERLESS SHERLEY

The first half of 1601 thus represented a turning point of sorts for Sherley. The perspicacious Antonio Fernández de Córdoba, fifth Duque de Sessa and Habsburg ambassador in Rome, thus wrote to his master Philip III on 10 April 1601, with the following evaluation.

> And here I will only point out that the Englishman was very much bound to the Count of Essex, and since the latter's imprisonment and death, he has become disillusioned and is completely without hope of ever again being admitted to the presence of the Queen, who has also been greatly displeased that he undertook this embassy on account of the friendship she has with the Turk; and also because the said Don Antonio has publicly declared himself a Catholic, which he had begun to do in secret in Prague, but he is determined to serve Your Majesty if Your Majesty should so desire. He is a very practical man and a good soldier on sea and on land; he has much news of the Portuguese Indies where he has been, and of Persia and of other places and he offers to give Your Majesty information which would be very important for your royal service.[63]

Portrait of Anthony Sherley (1601), possibly by Egidius Sadeler.

Sherley's religion had already been a matter of some interest and an object of curiosity. In some letters, including that sent from Gilan through Corrai, he had spoken of the need to spread the Catholic faith as if he were himself one. But a secret evaluation from the Papal nuncio in Paris, probably written in late 1600 or early 1601, had stated the following: "This cavalier is of great spirit and of much value in matters of war and fortification. Of his religion, nothing certain is known, but his mother had considerable affection for the Catholic religion. His father and his older brother are heretics, but he has always held himself to be a moderate man and indifferent in this matter, and it is believed that he became a Catholic in Venice in 1598."[64]

But Sherley proved incapable now of making stable decisions, rather turning this way and that, and playing one card after another. By early June, the Duque de Sessa, now growing somewhat exasperated, had modified his opinion of him: "The Englishman without doubt is a man of inventions and inconstant, though he is very practical and has a good understanding."[65] As his prospects with the embassy evaporated, Sherley went on from Rome to Venice, then Ancona, and then across the Adriatic to Ragusa, where he was apparently to be found in July 1601, awaiting Dom Manuel de Portugal (older son of Dom António), once again with a view to organize a revolt against Spain in the *Estado da Índia* with Dutch and Portuguese help, as well as some disaffected elements from the erstwhile entourage of Essex. But the Portuguese prince did not appear, and this project soon fell through, so that Sherley returned to Venice in early September, where he began rapidly to accumulate debts leading to an incident, possibly in May 1602, where he was thrown off a bridge in that city, probably by the agents of his indignant debtors. At about this time, in late 1601 and 1602, Sherley also began to entertain a quite regular secret correspondence with James VI of Scotland, persuading him to seek Habsburg help to sustain his claims in England, and also having him write directly to Shah 'Abbas.

For a time then, Sherley appears to have been prepared to pass information to almost any party if the price were right, but also to mount a series of projects and alliances such that contemporaries struggled to find a coherent pattern to his activity. Though they were disgruntled with him in late 1601, the Habsburgs for example obviously paid him regular sums of money from late 1602 onward, but they eventually could not protect him from being arrested in March 1603 in Venice on multiple charges: for having insulted an important Iranian merchant, Fathi Beg, and for trumped-up charges of complicity with the corsair activities of his older brother Sir Thomas, still incarcerated by the Ottomans. The Spanish *Consejo de Estado* eventually suggested that Sherley be asked to move to Spain or Flanders, but for the time being he showed no great desire to do so. Further, with the death of Elizabeth on 24 March 1603, Sherley found another powerful protector that he could now openly deal with: James VI of Scotland (now also James I of England), who showed a desire to intervene vigorously on his behalf with the Venetian authorities. This both secured his release and bought him more time from the increasingly exasperated Signoria, so that Sherley continued through 1603 and much of 1604 to reside in Venice, hatching plans, gathering information, and bombarding the Spanish monarchy with one proposal after another (to some of which we shall return below, often sent using the code name of "Flaminio"). In these letters and proposals, usually written in a macaronic Italo-Spanish, he noted the deteriorating state of relations between the Safavids and the Portuguese in the Persian Gulf, with the Safavid annexation of the semiautonomous region of Lar in 1601 and the capture of Bahrein in 1602 (both accomplished under Allah Virdi Khan and his son Imam Quli Khan), and wondered somewhat disingenuously whether the shah might have been motivated by the opportunity of an alliance with England and Dom Cristóvão de Portugal. He commented on the Dutch capture of the vessel *Santa Catarina* in Southeast Asia, as well as Dutch activities in the Moluccas, and proposed measures to be taken against them before they came to threaten the Philippines. He laid out rather elaborate plans for the invasion of Cyprus by the Spaniards, using a fleet of galleys in order to strike at the Ottomans.

At the same time, Sherley seems through much of 1604 also to have received money from the emperor Rudolph II's court in Prague to pass on information regarding the Ottoman Empire. This information involved the potential and actual wars of the Ottomans both on the Hungarian front and that with the Safavids, and derived in part from Sherley's connections with English diplomats in Istanbul, but also from periodic letters he received from his brother Robert — still resident with Shah 'Abbas. In one of his letters to Rudolph dated September 1604, Sherley noted that "all points towards the aggrandisement of your kingdom and continued good fortune, which Your Majesty truly deserves having fought for so many years for Christianity, and against the innundation of the Turks." In a slightly earlier letter, he had assured the emperor that "two years will not pass before Your Majesty will be Emperor of the East and the West," adding that "if my life and my blood can play the smallest part they shall be given with the same readiness as heretofore."[66] Whether or not they actually intercepted these letters, the Venetian authorities apparently came to know of them; and eventually, possibly under pressure from Ottoman diplomats, they decided in early December 1604 to issue a final and irrevocable decree expelling Sherley from Venice, under pain of death if he returned. He thus passed on to Ferrara, and then made his way some months later to Prague.

While at Venice, Sherley had spent time not only corresponding with Rudolph II but also in dealings with his ambassador to the Serenissima, François Perrenot de Granvelle, Comte de Cantecroix. He had thus been consulted on the arrival in Prague of two new Safavid envoys, Zain al-Din Khan Shamlu and Mahdi Quli Beg. Eventually, in May 1605, it was decided that he could play a useful role in the negotiations, and he therefore arrived in Prague on 10 June. He remained there barely a month, but this was time enough for him to set in motion a new scheme. We have seen that Sherley had for long been preoccupied with a strategy for encircling the Ottomans, using the Iranian front on the one hand and the Hungarian one on the other. Additionally, he had also thought of creating other irritations, as with his scheme for an attack on Cyprus. Now, he had a new proposition to make. The Moroccan sultan Ahmad al-Mansur al-Saʿdi, who had reigned since the time of Dom Sebastião's disastrous expedition of 1578, died in 1603. His three sons now disputed the succession, and Sherley came to the view that one or the other of them could be persuaded to open a new front against the Ottomans, still further dividing the resources of the Sublime Porte. He managed to bring together a curious alliance to support this enterprise: James I, whose motives are not entirely clear; Philip III of Spain, whose role was to be largely maritime in nature; and Rudolph II, who for his part was sufficiently persuaded of Sherley's competence to invest some real finances in the affair. Departing from Genoa, Sherley and his party made their way to Alicante and Madrid, and then set sail again from Cadiz and arrived in Safi in early October 1605. Here, Sherley set about the complicated process of negotiating with one of the weakened Saʿdi claimants, Sultan Mulay Abu Faris, in a mission that lasted slightly less than a year, divided between Safi and Marrakesh.[67] Sherley did not make much headway in his anti-Ottoman proposals; indeed, the only real success he had there was negotiating the release of some Portuguese captives, including the son of the former viceroy at Goa, Aires de Saldanha, after which Sherley may be found in Lisbon in September 1606. By this time, Sherley had clearly lost interest in Prague and its possibilities, and his main purpose was to play the Spanish Habsburg card. In early October, he therefore appeared in Madrid accompanied by an entourage of thirty persons, and took up residence in the Jesuit college. Here, possibly with the help of an English Jesuit, Joseph Arthur Creswell, he began to craft a series of propositions that he sent at a sustained rhythm to the *Consejo de Estado*, assuming the position now of an *arbitrista* — a writer of projects for the reform and renewal of the Habsburg dominions.[68]

A first substantial project among these addressed the possibility of the "just and licit conquest" by Spain of Morocco.[69] Here, Sherley suggested that Spain was wrong in spending so much energy and resources in quelling the Dutch revolt, for "one gains a far different reputation by conquering a province outright than what one gains by putting down a rebellion." He added that the three princes who disputed the rule over Morocco were weak, sensual, and dissipated, and would be easy to defeat. Once this was done, the Spaniards could gain control of the trans-Saharan gold caravans, bringing together maritime trade through the ports of Senegal with a form of control over Timbuktu, whose present governor Sherley claimed was a Spanish renegade, who would be easy enough to bring around. On a quite different front, Sherley proposed (and here he returned to a proposition he had formulated earlier, in 1602) that the *Estado da Índia* should be divided into two parts, one governed from Goa and the other from Ceylon. He also proposed fresh fortifications in the Straits of Singapore, as well as the settlement and considerable fortification of the island of Saint Helena in the Atlantic. A new division of trading centers manned by royal factors was proposed in Spanish America. Plans for new fleets, some using the most up-to-date ships built in England, were laid out. Fresh diplomatic dealings with Moscow and the Sweden of Charles IX were mentioned. There was a proposal for the marriage of a Stuart princess with a Habsburg prince from central Europe. The projects were incredibly wide-ranging and almost dizzying in their implications.

Interestingly enough, these projects caught the eye of Philip III, as we see from a series of orders and instructions in which he ordered them looked into with care. The idea of engaging in a North African adventure was laid aside, but one of Sherley's ideas that came to be debated was of creating a corsair squadron under his command, manned with Dutch and English sailors and soldiers, and to be used to attack both Ottoman shipping and the Dutch ships that were now increasingly to be found in the Mediterranean. In this way, heretic would ingeniously be set against heretic. Overruling the advice of some of his advisers, the Spanish king granted Sherley this command on 19 February 1607. He was named "General of the said tall ships [*General de los dichos navíos de alto borde*]," which were to operate out of the kingdom of Naples, with a personal payment of two hundred ducats a month. Armed with this document, Sherley departed from Madrid, via Genoa, and made his way to Naples, where he arrived in May or June.

But Sherley proved in no great hurry to constitute this fleet. Rather he left Italy and found his way to Prague in early October, ostensibly to report on his Moroccan mission, but in fact to receive the title of count of the empire from Rudolph II, so that from that time on he would inevitably refer to himself as "El Conde Don Anthony Sherley." This title was really a mere formality, as a contemporary Spanish diplomat observed: "The title of Count of the Empire is one that the Emperor only gives to some knights when they ask for it, and it is worth no more than the dignity of the title without implying any other preeminence or authority in the Empire, unlike the other Counts who are born and confirmed in Germany." Sherley made further financial claims at Prague and also made the habitual anti-Ottoman proposals, but all this came to nothing. He then returned to Italy, where he based himself for several months in Ferrara, while attempting to attract English mariners in the ports of the Veneto for his projected fleet. It was during this period that Sherley seems, for the first time since 1598, to have reconsidered the central basis of his interstate and interimperial strategy until then. What if the Ottomans were not the great enemy in reality? Were there not things to be gained from making peace with them? In this he claimed to have been encouraged by his recent and fortuitous contacts with a Sephardic Jew called Gabriel de Buenaventura, who affirmed that he had been the go-between in secret peace negotiations between Philip II and the Ottoman sultan Mehmed III (1595–1603), but had been imprisoned and thus unable to bring the terms of the agreement to light. Sherley forwarded the supposed Ottoman-Habsburg treaty to the Jesuit Creswell, and rather uncharacteristically added a verse at the end, which he attributed to "a certain author [*un autor discreto*]," but which in fact derived from the celebrated Spanish translation of Ariosto's *Orlando Furioso*.

> To conquer always is a glorious thing,
> 'Tis true, indeed, a bloody victory
> Is to a chief less honour wont to bring,
> And that fair field is famed eternally,
> And he who wins it merits worshipping,
> Who, saving from all harm his own, without
> Loss to his followers, puts the foe to rout.[70]

In sum, the best victories were bloodless ones, gained by cunning negotiation and diplomatic practice rather than acts of war and bloodletting on the battlefield. There was obviously a deep contradiction between this idea and the project of constructing and leading a corsair fleet into the Mediterranean against the Ottomans and Dutch merchantmen. But the management of contradictions had after all ever been Sherley's long suit.

It would seem however that Sherley's somewhat changed attitude toward the Ottomans had one significant consequence: it drove a wedge between him and his longtime secretary and right-hand man, Giovanni Tommaso Pagliarini, with whom he had become associated while at Prague in late 1600, a knight of the Order of St. Lazarus who had been the cupbearer of the Papal nuncio at Prague. In April 1608, Pagliarini decided to break with Sherley, contacted the Spanish ambassador in Venice, and through him denounced Sherley in no uncertain terms. The chief document of denunciation is dated mid-May, and its terms are particularly interesting: Sherley, according to Pagliarini, was a "man of no religion [*huomo di nissuna relligione*]" who "arranged his conscience like a water-mill in keeping with the material to be ground [*secondo la materia per macinare*]."[71] It is a type of metaphor to which we shall have occasion to return. Further, wrote Pagliarini, his former master was a creature entirely devoted to the pursuit of political power and financial gain. Sherley was "a man who comes running whenever there is an offer of money [*corre dove è il dinaro offerto*]" but at the same time wholly incompetent in the management of his financial affairs so that he was "overwhelmed by debt, owing money in every part of the world," to all sorts of creditors, be they "Turks, Persians, Armenians, Moroccans, Jews, and many poor German merchants." Sherley was moreover "fickle and corrupt," as well as "mendacious by nature," the sort of man who "thinks all night of new enterprises, but without any basis [*tutta la notte pensa nuovi imprese, ma senza fundamento*]." So perfidious was he that while in the service of Rudolph II, he had opened secret dealings with rebels in Hungary and — worst of all — had considered visiting Istanbul to "encourage the Turk in new damages against the Emperor [*per solevare il Turco a nuovi danni dell'Imperatore*]." This was a curious return to an old accusation that had been floated in England at the moment when Sherley had just embarked on his Iranian mission; it had been claimed then that while Sherley had given out that "he would serve th'emperor against the Turke, [it is] . . . nowe sett downe that he dothe serve the Turke against th'emperor, and so he is torned from a Christian to a Turke, which is most monstrus. No dowt, yf ytt be so, the Lord will punish the same."[72]

Though Pagliarini's denunciation reached high state circles in Spain, no action was taken on it. For his part, Sherley returned, accompanied by his usual pomp and circumstance, from Ferrara to Madrid toward the early part of August 1608, and remained there for almost half a year. Rumors abounded that he was rounding up a set of disreputable English and Dutch auxiliaries to help him with his fleet. Eventually, in late February 1609, he left Spain for Sicily, and arrived in Palermo toward the latter half of March. There now followed a series of minor activities and maneuvers, which leave us with the impression that Sherley was simply treading water. His relations with the Spanish viceroy in Sicily, Don Juan Fernández Portocarrero, Duque de Escalona, while initially cordial, began to deteriorate with the passage of months. The viceroy was manifestly irritated with Sherley's tendency to invent new schemes while not executing those that he had been already charged with. He more or less accused him besides of wanting to usurp viceregal authority over all of Sicily. The constitution of the fleet that Sherley was supposed to head took an inordinate amount of time, and — contrary to Sherley's initial claims that it would finance itself — began to act as a drain on the treasury. In late August, Sherley wrote to Philip III claiming (with considerable exaggeration) that he had a fleet of eighteen vessels and four thousand soldiers ready to leave port within the space of ten days. At roughly the same time, he wrote to Madrid requesting that he be admitted into the prestigious Order of Santiago, adding that he should be forgiven "for any errors of his youth, before he had been informed of Our Holy Faith, which should not prevent him from receiving any of the honours that were due to a Catholic knight, above all since it was not his personal fault but rather because he had been born in a kingdom that was separated from the obedience of the Church, despite its subjects, on account of the tyranny of its Kings."[73] He also wrote from Palermo to his father in England in early September, claiming to be caught up in a whirlwind of frantic activity: "Sr. Captain Peper will tell you in what a labyrynth of business I am, that I have not time to eat much less to write. I am going hence with 23 ships, 7000 men to land, and 12 pieces of cannon. . . . [F]or my part I know by God's grace that I will not fail to accomplish what I owe to my quality and your honour, and if I die, I will die well."[74]

It soon became clear that Sherley was in no great hurry to die. In October, the viceroy ordered him to set sail, and he made his way from Palermo to Syracuse. There he remained until early February, and his one attempt to sail out in January caused him to nearly lose his flagship in a storm. Eventually, the fleet did venture out, and after returning briefly to Zakynthos, made an attack on the island of Skiathos in late March. As there were some Ottoman troops on the island, there were losses on the two sides, and Sherley's party retreated to its ships. After a few other minor pillaging raids, the fleet returned to Palermo in mid-May 1610 with very little accomplished. The viceroy was furious and made this plain in his letters to Madrid. Sherley's fleet, he noted, "employs men of various nations who lack military discipline." There then followed a swingeing attack on the person of Sherley himself, whom Escalona now considered to be a time waster and an incompetent commander. "[The fleet] is under the command of a person who is not one of Your Majesty's subjects, and therefore not too punctilious about carrying out your orders. The result has been that instead of the seas being cleared of corsairs, thus enabling merchant shipping to operate freely, the pirates are more numerous than ever. Under the guise of carrying out Your Majesty's orders, many excesses have been committed which are unworthy of Your Majesty, contrary to your gracious desires, and the welfare of your subjects."[75]

Sherley mounted a desperate counterattack of his own. The viceroy, he complained, had subjected him on more than one occasion to "public ignominy." Striking a dramatic tone, he wrote to the king: "I beseech you that if I have failed in any matter regarding your service, you should cut off my head. But if the greed and rapine of this man [Viceroy Escalona] and his servants, who have destroyed this poor kingdom worse than [Roman magistrate Gaius] Verres, have brought me to this unfortunate state, then Your Majesty as King, and a just and Catholic King at that, should take the trouble to have justice rendered to me, for this is not just an affront to my fortune, but to my reputation, and in such a degree that I can on no account cease to seek out its restitution, which I am confident that God will grant to me." Far from being a failure, he claimed, his cruising expedition in the eastern Mediterranean had been a thundering success.

> I brought all of Turkey to a state of terror, so that it is known that they fortified themselves in Constantinople and the trade of the Levant was suspended for all these months, so that not a boat was to be found in all those seas. And with the suspension in trade, the Turk was damaged to the extent of more than a million and a half in his customs-revenues, and others say it was twice that amount. The Venetians have never shown greater respect to a general of Your Majesty; and in recompense for all this work and expense that I have incurred to serve the King, our lord, and to serve him as he deserves to be served, the Viceroy with false words recalled me to Palermo. I went there overland, and he seized the prizes and took away the fleet, and ordered the captains not to obey my orders. I have either committed a fault or not, and in either event, there should be a trial and sentence before ordering punishment.[76]

But this was a battle that Sherley finally could not win. Escalona's reports on him merely confirmed what had already been decided as early as February 1610, when it had become quite clear that Sherley's projected fleet was not going to have any great effect. At this time, the *Consejo de Estado* had already opined that the fleet should be suppressed and Sherley himself recalled. "Considering the mode of life of this man," they wrote, "his status and qualities, one is led to the conclusion that little more could be expected of him than what the Duque de Escalona reports." By late June, Sherley had been obliged to quit Palermo for Naples, and from there made his way reluctantly to the Iberian Peninsula, arriving in Barcelona in early January 1611. From there, he made his way to Madrid, to plead his cause with those in power and in particular to ask for relief from his many debtors.

By 1611, Sherley's public career had finally ground to a halt. In September that year, aged forty-six, he eventually retired to Granada, where he was given a modest pension, and where he spent most of the remaining two decades of his life. In Madrid, in February, Anthony Sherley had had occasion to meet his younger brother Robert again, after a gap of over a decade. Robert, now married to a Christian Circassian woman, Teresa, was sent out by Shah 'Abbas on a mission to Europe in February 1608, and his voyage paralleled that of his older brother in a curious way. Making his way through the Caspian Sea and the Volga to Moscow, he set out from there to Cracow and then Prague. In Prague, Robert Sherley too was granted the title of count, and generously paid off his brother's outstanding debts to merchants in the city before going on to Milan and Florence. In September 1609, while Anthony Sherley was in Palermo, his brother was received by Pope Paul V in Rome, who treated him with honor and great consideration. He then departed for Spain, and arriving there in January 1610, presented a letter from Shah 'Abbas to Philip III. Everywhere, Robert Sherley seems to have made a rather different impression than Anthony, and the English ambassador in Madrid, Francis Cottington, noted that he did not have "those vanities which so much govern his brother Anthony."

Though they had maintained a correspondence over the years that Robert remained in Iran, there seems to be little doubt that the relationship between the two brothers grew distinctly cool over the decade of their separation, with Robert Sherley reproaching Anthony more than once for his unreliability. Thus, in a letter of 1605, he writes: "I am soe besids myself with the travailes and wants I am in, and in the little hope I have of yor retorne or of anie man from yow, that I am almost distracted from the thought of anie helpe for my delivry out of this Contrey, I doe not altogether blame yow becawse I knowe you have likwyse suffered discomodytie in those parts yow live in, thoughe they cannot be compared unto myne." A further letter, dated September 1606, takes a less pathetic and sterner tone: "I restt mightyly confused, insomuche as I can have no tru advise from you. . . . Your often promisinge to send presents, artifissers, and Sigr Angele, and I know not howe many els, hathe made me be estimed a common lyar; brother for Gods sake, eather performe, or not promis any thinge, because in this fashion you make me discredditt myselfe, by reportinge things which you care not to effecte." Accusing Anthony Sherley of no more than "desembling complaments," the letter notes bitterly that "there is no more frindshippe, nor brother, truthe, honnor, and conscience, being bannisht from the earthe; deere brother pardon me if I be plane with you, the loosars have free lyberty to speake what they leestt, by which I am autorrised, havinge lostt my time, and am in hazzarde to loose my selfe also."[77] Yet, in February 1611, when Anthony Sherley arrived in Madrid in disgrace from Palermo and harried by his debtors, it was to Robert's residence that he went, and in which he came to be lodged for a time. Cottington reports that things went well at first between them, and that Anthony Sherley "talks sometimes of going for England, and sometimes of a journey into Persia with his brother." However, before Robert Sherley's departure from Madrid in June, the relationship turned very sour, when he discovered that his brother was secretly advising Spanish officials on how to prevent him from proceeding to England.

After Robert Sherley's departure from Spain, it was reported that Anthony continued for some months in Madrid in a state of ostentatious poverty with "scarce any [clothes] to put on his back." It was reported too that "he hath scarce money to buy him bread and is lodged in a Bodegon, which is little worse than an English ale house." In December 1619, Francis Cottington noted that he was still "a very poor man, and much neglected, sometimes like to starve for want of bread." He added that "the poor man [Anthony Sherley] sometimes comes to my house, and is as full of vanity as ever he was, making himself believe that he shall one day be a great Prince, when for the present he wants shoes to wear. The two brothers are much fallen out, and both by word and writing do all the harm they can, in defaming each other, but I must needs confess that the Ambassador [Robert] is the discreeter of the two."[78] Two years earlier, Anthony Sherley had been consulted by the *Consejo de Estado* on rumors regarding Sir Walter Raleigh's projects in Guiana, and had offered not merely a counterplan, but his own "life and labour for it, or alternatively I will serve in Poland, Milan, or in any duty that His Majesty may command." There were no takers for this generous offer. Further, his project to exploit a copper mine in Baeza in 1613—which had sustained him reasonably for a time—had also clearly fallen down by then.

Practically the last archival trace to be found of Anthony Sherley dates to 1626, when he proposed that he and his son Don Diego (of whom we know very little) be given rights over the island of Fadala, and Mogador (Essaouira) in Morocco. Here, he proposed to make fortifications, trade in wheat and other goods, develop fisheries, and act as a responsible vassal of the Spanish Crown. He also agreed to maintain a fleet of ships there, for his own use and that of the Crown. Though the proposal was given a sympathetic hearing, nothing eventually came of it, because Sherley was unable to raise the financial resources required.[79] A local chronicle of Granada reports the following concerning the end of his life. "In this year [1633], there died in this city of Granada the valorous knight, the Conde de Leste, the Englishman who sacked the city of Cadiz in the time of the king Philip II, though he did so against his will; for later he took refuge in Spain and His Majesty aided him with some revenues on silk in this said city of Granada, where he lived not very prosperously [*no muy sobradamente*]. His body was buried in the parish church of St. Peter and St. Paul in this city. He left a son with good qualities [*de grandes partes*] who His Majesty will [surely] take into his service, for he is so capable in all matters."[80]

Robert Sherley had died at Qazwin some years earlier in July 1628, while negotiating unsuccessfully in Iran between the English and Shah 'Abbas, and his bones were eventually laid to rest by his wife in Rome. The two brothers ended their lives far apart then, but both in a state of exile.

"THE MACHINE OF THE WORLD"

The Sherley brothers, and in particular Anthony Sherley, have certainly attracted a great deal of popular and scholarly attention since the seventeenth century. The orientalist Edward Denison Ross, the author of a biography of Anthony Sherley published in 1933, described him as "an inveterate and unscrupulous intriguer, a sententious hypocrite devoid of all real sentiment, being incapable of single-minded devotion to any person or cause." On the positive side, he counted his "great physical courage and a reckless love of adventure," his "rare insight into the Oriental mind, keen powers of observation, and . . . retentive memory," and finally suggested that "he must have possessed an almost hypnotic power in personal intercourse."[81] Boies Penrose, writing five years later in 1938, was even more condemnatory and noted that Anthony "was a self-seeking adventurer pure and simple, a born intriguer, a complete opportunist, a man whose word could never be relied on and whose personal dishonesty leaves us gasping." His only gift, he added, was "of leading men by the nose," but for the rest he was "a completely sinister person, to be avoided by all who valued their reputations or their fortunes."[82] Three decades later, by the late 1960s, the judgments had softened somewhat. Thus, Anthony Sherley was described by D. W. Davies as "the epitome of the Spanish adventurer," even though he was English. Rather than seeing him as an extraordinary character, or a larger-than-life scoundrel (whether endearing or not), he argued besides that "there were hordes of men in Europe who gained a livelihood, as did Anthony, by serving as minor diplomats and spies for one European monarch after another, their knowledge of the secrets of a number of courts making them valuable if dangerous servitors."[83] More recently, it has been argued that the main interest of Sherley lies in the fact that "his diplomatic career constitutes a flagrant example of the versatility of intelligence agents at the beginning of the seventeenth century."[84]

A quite different reading of Anthony Sherley's career was proposed, however, a few years after Davies's book, which we have cited above. This was by the Danish historian Niels Steensgaard, whose focus was neither on the picaresque nor the adventurous, but rather on issues of international political economy. Steensgaard developed a close examination of the circumstances surrounding the fall of Hormuz in early May 1622 to a joint force of Iranians and the English East India Company, and thus turned to the question of the geopolitical context of this event. He argued that the event was far from trivial, but encapsulated the resolution of a "structural crisis . . . a confrontation of fundamentally different institutional complexes." Concluding his book, Steensgaard then went on to make a somewhat startling claim. He suggested that his own "solution" to the conundrum of the significance of the fall of Hormuz was wholly defensible, but at the same time "alien to the sources, in the sense that only a few of the persons involved suspected and none of them was able to survey such a correlation of facts as the one presented [in his book]." He then went on to add: "The one who came closest to understanding this correlation was in fact the visionary, Anthony Sherley." He referred specifically to Sherley's proposal, put forward already in January 1607, of "diverting one of the most important commodities of international trade, Persian raw silk, from the usual trade routes through the Ottoman Empire to the route via Hormuz, Goa and Lisbon."[85] It may be thought that Steensgaard, like so many others, had fallen victim somewhat to Sherley's gifts for self-promotion when he wrote of how the Englishman "became the catalyst that set off further attempts to establish contact and precipitated intensive efforts to create the great alliance with Persia." But his main analytical thrust here was, I believe, somewhat different: he suggested we might for a time turn our gaze away from Anthony Sherley the rambunctious actor, to Sherley the manipulator of concepts and schemes (however exaggerated the term "visionary" may be here).

We have already made some use of his 1613 text, *Sir Antony Sherley his relation of his trauels into Persia,* and we shall return to it briefly below.[86] It is a somewhat mysterious work, published while Sherley was resident in Spain, and we have no clear idea of how it came to be communicated to its printer in London, Nicholas Okes. But it is merely the tip of the iceberg, for Sherley was a prodigious writer, certainly from the late 1590s onward, of letters, reports, memoranda, and the like. Many of these were purely functional, or *pièces d'occasion,* but others were more polished works, some involving collaborators in view of Sherley's limited rhetorical (and even syntactical) skills in languages other than English. The central work in this corpus was completed by him, ironically enough, some six months after the fall of Hormuz (though he was unaware of it), in early November 1622, while Sherley was resident in Granada. It is a work immodestly titled *Peso político de todo el mundo por el Conde Don Antonio Xerley,* and at least four manuscript copies of it are known, suggesting a certain diffusion.[87] It was opportunely dedicated to "the Most Excellent Lord Conde-Duque de Olivares of the Council of Majesty," the new royal favorite or *valido.* Sherley was clearly aware that with the death of Philip III (with whom he had had long relations), and the succession of his sixteen-year-old son as Philip IV in March 1621, there was potential for change at the court. The face of this change was that of Don Gaspar de Guzmán, the Conde-Duque of the dedication, a powerful and ambitious nobleman who was at that time in his midthirties.[88]

Texts of *arbitrío* and reform were not exactly in short supply in Iberia during the decades of the Union of the Crowns (1580–1640). They might have titles such as *Restauración política de España,* or *Restauración de la abundancia de España,* with the term *restauración* taking its place with *conservación* against the enemy: decline or *declinación.*[89] In Portugal under Habsburg rule, a not untypical text of this type that comes to us from 1599 is titled *Reformação da milícia e governo do Estado da Índia Oriental* (Reformation of the militia and government of the State of the East Indies).[90] These were often patriotic texts, even verging on the xenophobic in their condemnation of the role played by foreign elements. It has equally been remarked that such texts frequently treated the polity as a diseased body that needed a physician to effect a cure, or at least to check the rapid spread of the disease. Such a conception was shared, as it happened, both by internal proponents of reform and by external observers, more or less gleefully rubbing their hands. Thus the Venetian representative in Spain in about 1620, Pietro Contarini, wrote of the imperial polity as "this machine that is so great in kingdoms and riches [*questa macchina così grande di regni e richezza*]," but went on to add that it was "like a body racked by many indispositions, with have weakened its vigor [*è come corpo aggravato da molte indisposizioni, che tiene indebolito il suo vigore*]."[91]

Such texts of reform and regeneration might vary considerably in terms of theme, focusing on money and finances, agriculture, the military, or trade and manufacture. But the variation could also be in scale, some focusing narrowly on local or provincial problems, and others casting their net far wider. What might a text called *Peso político de todo el mundo* (The political balance of the entire world), in fact set out to do then? Sherley's survey of the world is an impressive one, written as usual in a somewhat Italian-inflected Spanish, and begins with a vast geographical tour that carries him from Spain to France and Germany, then to the Italian states (including Venice, which he detested), Bohemia, Poland, and Muscovy, with brief stops in Cathay, Sweden, and Denmark, presented somewhat pell-mell in that order. England and Holland receive an extended treatment, and after dealing with North Africa, Sherley moves at length to the Ottomans ("el Turco"), and following a detour through sub-Saharan Africa, naturally develops a quite elaborate section on the Persia of the Safavids. Mughal India and the rest of South Asia merit some mention, and there is even a rapid reflection on China, Japan, the Philippines, and the Moluccas, the whole concluding with a long section titled "the places that English and the Rebels [Dutch] can capture in the southern seas, besides those that they already have, passing the Straits of Magellan, through the entire coast of Brazil and in the archipelago of the West Indies to the Bay of Bahama and the mainland of Florida." What we have here is a work of geopolitics, inflected with considerations of political economy in the sense above all of policies toward trade.

In his *Relation* of 1613, Sherley had already made it clear that he had certain preferences with regard to the sorts of things he liked to observe and analyze. Here is the relevant passage, written with respect to the Ottoman Empire. "It will not bee amisse, to use so fit an opportunity to discourse of the Turkes whole government of those parts, which I did not behold with the eies of a common Pilgrime, or Merchant; which passing onely by goodly Citties and Territories, make their judgement upon the superficiall appearance of what they see: but as a Gentleman bred up in such experience, which hath made me somewhat capable to penetrate into the perfection and imperfection of the forme of the State, and into the good and ill Orders by which it is governed."[92] There are two contrasts being drawn here, one explicit and the other less so: the first sets the gentleman against the pilgrim or merchant, making the former a deep observer and the latter a superficial one; and the second implies that the gentleman is uniquely equipped "to penetrate . . . the forme of the State." If this be the case, then it is clear why someone like Sherley would disdain forms of ethnographic observation on a more or less systematic basis. His primary and declared angle of vision would take him time and again to consider the state as an object, and thus make him concentrate his intelligence on the practice of politics. It also helps us to understand the stance of a slightly later traveler, the "*gentilhomme angevin*" François le Gouz de la Boullaye (1623–68), who deliberately sought to emphasize the ethnographic role  of the traveler, and thus presented himself precisely as a pilgrim.[93]

It is then as an analyst of the state that Sherley's text dedicated to Olivares presents the Englishman. The long introductory section of the text may be cited at length for us to get a sense of Sherley's tone, and the form of rhetoric he wishes to deploy. This is how it runs.

> Most Excellent Sir:
> Since our Lord [*nuestro Señor*, God or the King] has seen fit that for the restoration of this Monarchy [*esta Monarquía*], the valor and supreme qualities of Your Excellency might serve as master and captain in order to guide and govern this voyage and the movements made therein by the great vessel of his Empire, and since this movement is suspect to all other nations or envied by some, or simply dangerous to certain others, since it [the empire] is the most powerful of all not simply in terms of its armaments but in its materials and in the very stuff with which it is fabricated; so that the navigation might be secure and the movements might be stable, as might its goals, and so that they [the movements] might serve to carry it to its goals, I supplicate Your Excellency that you might give yourself some trouble by opening wide your hand and taking in it the measure of all of the world [*todo el mundo en pesso*], and having taken its measure consider with the clarity of your great understanding the substance that this Monarchy possesses and the point up to which this greatest Monarchy can and must have the capacity to aim; and the substance that all the other nations can employ to divert its aim; and whether this substance is natural or acquired; or whether it is neither natural nor acquired but simply a question of opinion; and how and where they possess it, and the intentions that all the kingdoms in the world have with respect to this Monarchy, and the aspects in which they reflect her, for her qualities and disposition and the goals that follow from her disposition and qualities are so general and universal that it is impossible in any other manner to arrive firmly at a sound judgment regarding what is required for her conservation, authority

> and growth, or for her proper administration, without being aware of the sorts of opposition that impede her and distract her from her aim; and the opportunities that these forms of opposition have to be able to impede her, and whether these blockages are long-lasting in themselves or have grown on account of the carelessness of the Government over here, whether they are made up of a single body or are a patchwork of many pieces, and if these patchworks are joint in a single piece or are divided into disparate intentions with each one following its own path. In fine, what each of them can do and is worth, and what this Monarchy can and should do to all of them and against all of them by disposing of and applying all that it can and is capable of.[94]

Three distinct aspects of this opening passage can be noted. The first is the familiar *topos* of the ship of the state, of which Olivares is to be the "master and captain," determining the direction of its navigation. A second idea is that both the Spanish monarchy and those who oppose it are each made up of a "substance [*sustancia*]" but nevertheless may be either unitary or a "patchwork [*remiendos de muchas pieças*]." The third and, to my mind, most singular idea is that the only way in which Olivares can sensibly address the problems facing the Spanish monarchy is by taking "the measure of all of the world [*todo el mundo en pesso*]." This was Sherley's great gambit, and it probably did not fall on deaf ears. As John Elliott has written, "the Count-Duke [of Olivares] was probably the first ruler of the Spanish Monarchy to think in genuinely global terms, and it is no accident that he should have felt at home with that bold adventurer Anthony Sherley, who would spin the globe with confidence and offer to reveal the secret strengths and weaknesses of every kingdom and sultanate between the Danish Sound and the coast of Malabar."[95] Sherley then of course proceeded with the familiar tactics of *captatio benevolentiae*.

> I confess, most Excellent Sir, that such an enterprise is most arrogant [*es muy soberbia*], requires much work, and is very difficult to the point that it is almost impossible to arrive at a safe haven with it, because with the experience of a single man acquired in the days of a mere lifetime which is so limited in its extent, it seems impossible to be able to attain such a well-founded course in so large a matter; and it is vanity to present Your Excellency with relations of what has been said and written, for what people say and write is itself for the greater part [based on] the accounts of others still. And besides such accounts, there are still others which are content to describe cities, and costumes, and monstrosities that have never been seen, to which each pilgrim or merchant refers as payment

> for his travails or in order to raise up the price of his merchandise, and even if such accounts do not have more depth, rare are those which could or can say with a sure science [*cierta ciencia*] that what they describe is a certain thing; and it would be very daring for me to speak as an eyewitness [*como testigo de vista*] of such an immense universality and dare to present Your Excellency with aspects, subjects and discourses regarding all the nations and their substance, which is a matter that is really worthy of the great place and value of Your Excellency, ever uncaring of matters of fantasy, and [instead] engaged in the conservation and growth of the authority of His Majesty and the service of this great Monarchy. I do so because I am sure of being able to do so, and if the work is of some great use to Your Excellency it might serve as a romance to amuse you when you feel tired from [dealing with] affairs of greater significance.

This is the Sherley we are familiar with by now, opposing mere pilgrims and merchants to genuine men of the world like himself, who have no great interest in "costumes, and monstrosities that have never been seen." Yet, it is obviously his conviction that he has a grasp of the world based not on mere hearsay but on a form of direct understanding, as something indeed approaching an "eyewitness [*testigo de vista*] of such an immense universality."

His survey of the world begins naturally with Spain, by which he means the two Iberian monarchies and their empires. Regarding Spain proper, he is rather cautious, indeed preferring to err on the side of flattery.

> Spain in past times was the Indies of the ancients because of the great export they had from her of gold and silver, and she is still the Indies of the moderns because of the many and rich goods that they export from her besides gold and silver and jewels, and it is the substance on the basis of which they [the moderns] can accomplish all that they are able to do. The gentlemen [*los señores*] here are serious and sober in their courtesy; the knights are affable, and the populace [*el bulgo*] is peaceable and well-inclined, and they are self-respecting people, and on that account its militia is the best of the whole world in terms of valor and obedience. The vassals are most faithful, and the most devoted to the service of their kings among all nations. It is a great pity and brings a bad reputation to the Government that there are so many vacant offices in such a good land, and on that account personal services are lacking in a place where there are such good and loyal vassals.[96]

The last is an obvious dig at Sherley's own lack of employment by the state when there are so many offices available. The larger geopolitical problem, as

Sherley sees it, is however the imperfect integration of Portugal into the Catholic Monarchy. "Portugal is opposed," he writes, "and hence turns against the rule of Castile; and as she is different in language, differentiates herself as much as possible in costumes and customs and everything else. She is an ancient enemy and an uncertain vassal, and changeable in her faith, with facility, for even though in a state of submission, she can hardly conceal her hatred [*encubrir su odio*]."[97] Some twenty years before the rebellion and Braganza restoration of 1640, these words have a somewhat prophetic ring to them. Nevertheless, Sherley is optimistic overall in concluding his evaluation of the Iberian empires under the Catholic Monarchy.

> These kingdoms have a most robust constitution, a most strong complexion, and the most powerful nature to be able to conserve themselves and grow if they apply the great means that they possess to this end, with activity, vigilance and care; and the unique quality that no other State possesses is that all the necessary materials and substance for these means is native to them and is a part of this Monarchy, which does not need to acquire anything [from outside]. The ills and weaknesses that the usual discourses claim that it has are more the result of outside lack of care [*el descuydo ageno*] or distraction in not wanting or not being able to take of them, than on account of their own disposition; and these ills can be cured easily by cleansing these kingdoms of some intrinsic humors, and from bringing them around to proper application and use, through which one can profit from what is so abundantly available; and by cutting off the power of extrinsic humors, which can be done with great facility once one has knowledge of the substances [*las sustancias*] of all the other nations and potentates, and one is certain of one's own substance.[98]

We return here to the notion of "substances" that make up states, but also to two other ideas, the one banal, the other less so. The first of these is the deploying of humoral language to speak of reform, in the pseudomedical discourse of state we have referred to above. The second is Sherley's notion that the Iberian empires taken together can, if need be, constitute an autarchic space that in fact "does not need to acquire anything" from the outside world. He repeats this a few pages later in his evaluation of France, which he argues has a different nature: "this kingdom is not entirely self-sufficient [*este reyno no tiene subsistencia entera de por sí*]." This leaves France considerably weaker than the Catholic Monarchy; however, the French attempt to compensate for this by their deviousness. "The nature of the Frenchman is to be false in his love and poor at concealing his hatred; this is in general, but their ministers are the most possessed of artifice, and the best at concealment, and the most sagacious negotiators that exist among the nations."

Sherley is thus not above deploying cultural stereotypes in a strategic manner, far from it, but this is the only extent to which any form of ethnography appears to interest him. Further, the occasions when he uses it are somewhat unpredictable, for example when reflecting on the central European Habsburgs, his erstwhile employers. In the Palatinate, he notes, the aristocracy "have the title of princes, though in reality they are merchants." They are, moreover, "the capital enemies of this Monarchy [Spain], [but] enemies only in opinion, being loudmouths [*bocingleros*] with no more or greater effect." Nor is the population in general worthy of any greater consideration. "The people are not far removed from barbarians. All their trade and contracts and any negotiation are soaked in wine, but only for their advantage, as they think themselves more dexterous in this business [trade] than any other nation. From one day to another, they forget what is not to their advantage. They are malicious and suspect that others are the same too. The Germans who have spent some time in Italy or Spain, and have drunk up the dregs of their wine under the sun of those lands, are particularly able and clever in all negotiations."[99] On the other hand, one can well understand that his short Russian sojourn and imprisonment had not left Sherley with a particularly good impression of either the polity or the people. It is only matched, probably, by his contempt for Venice, which has "a very malevolent aspect with regard to this Monarchy," and "calls itself a Republic, but under the name of liberty is really the most tyrannical State there is or has been [*el más tiránico Estado que ay o a sido*], and keeps up [the name] as an artifice in order to mislead all princes." The fortunate thing, he notes, is that the Venetians in the final analysis count for little on their own; they are thus obliged to busy themselves constantly in constructing alliances. Muscovy, on the other hand, is a far more sizable and important state, but hardly worthy of great respect either.

> Their religion is Greek but very adulterated, and despite not being well-inclined to any other sect than their own, they do get along with heretics [Protestants]. Foodstuff of all sorts abound, and they have it extremely cheap. The Prince is the absolute and despotic lord of all lives and goods. Their militia is made of cavalry and infantry. The cavalry uses the same arms as the Tartars: bows, scimitars, and maces, but few lances and leather shields. The infantry is more or less made up of bowmen, with a few harquebuses that are three palms and less. They are a false people, with neither law nor word [*sin ley ni palabra*], malicious, suspicious and

so given to drinking that from nine in the morning to the next day, one cannot have trade or dealings with them; lying and most cruel, but so subject to their Princes that they could be called bestially obedient.[100]

We begin to comprehend then that Sherley's intentions in the text are a good deal more complex than those of many of his contemporaries. He does not locate "tyranny" or "despotism" in the Islamic states, or those of the East, but is willing to admit quite freely that they might exist in the very heart of Europe. With regard to Ming China, he notes that it "is a very great empire extended over an enormous territory and so plentiful in everything that is necessary for life and its enjoyment that it could with a liberal hand share it with the whole world"; the sole serious problem is that its military is made up of uninterested peasants and that it has no access to horses of good quality. He notes that the Ottomans, while showing some weaknesses in terms of "their natural constitution and lack of application," are nevertheless in a situation such that they can be reformed. It is also of great importance to look to the cold-eyed judgment he brings to the Safavids in the early 1620s, hardly touched by any vestige of sentimentality on account of his past dealings with Shah 'Abbas.

The Persian is a powerful potentate, but most unequal to the Turk, and though his militia is good it cannot compare to the Turkish one. The war he makes on the Turk is not a war of equal power [*igual poderío*], but rather of periodic attacks, laying waste to whole provinces to deprive the Turkish army of all sorts of supplies. So that the victories they have had against the Turk have resulted more from the necessities into which the latter's armies have fallen on account of these devastations, and from the fatigue of the long and rigorous route they must take to arrive at the Persian frontier, than from the valor and power of [Persian] arms. Nor can the Persian retain what he has won from the Turk for any more time than is needed for the general government of the Turkish empire [*imperio turquesco*] to recover from its infirmities, and for its militia — along with the improved health of the rest of the body — to recover its spirit and brio and to have a leader to rule it well. . . . Finally, this kingdom [Persia] though it has much in abundance, lacks an even greater number of things, and it has one of the greatest weaknesses [*las mayores faltas*] that an empire can have: and that is that it has a seafront, and no force on the sea, nor does it possess the possibility of having any such force for lack of wood.[101]

The purpose of these sections of the text, which I have deliberately cited at some length, was naturally twofold: first, to demonstrate that Sherley possessed direct knowledge and a rich empirical experience of many of these areas, unlike most other armchair writers or *abitristas*; and second, to argue powerfully and cogently that the whole world was to be conceived of as a single machine (*máquina*), which operated through certain levers and points of pressure.

Here then, following the empirical exposition, is a significant passage in which Sherley's political realism and global vision is laid bare.

> Now that Your Excellency has taken the measure of this great machine of the world [*esta gran máquina del mundo*] and has seen all the objects, aspects and dispositions that all of its parts, given to the use of the potentates who possess them, have toward this Monarchy, and that some of them assume a bad aspect on account of opinion, others because of pretensions, others because of suspicion, others since they have been offended, and others for they think themselves aggrieved, and if they aid or appear to aid this Monarchy, they do it because they need her, which need will not last if other nations can take care of them with a larger and more generous hand than this Monarchy does. And on gazing everywhere, Your Excellency will have seen very few [states] that are attached to this Monarchy, and that this attachment is fragile, and extremely so in some cases. I beseech Your Excellency not to lose patience, and to spend a little more effort, and look to it that all these parts do not act against this Monarchy with bad dispositions for these said reasons alone, and for the sole cause of particular motives, but because of the collective interest that stems from the eternal repugnance that smaller states have toward larger ones.[102]

There is perhaps an unconscious resonance here of a text directed in 1601 by Richard Hakluyt to Sir Robert Cecil, namely his dedication to the English translation of António Galvão's *The Discoveries of the World, from their first originall unto the yeere of our Lord 1555*. Hakluyt had advised Cecil to read Galvão's work with attention, and "to take a sea card or a mappe of the world, and carrie your eie upon the coast of Africa from Cape de Non . . . and follow the shore about the Cape of Buona Sperança till you come to the mouth of the Redde Sea . . . crosse over to India, and doubling Cape Comory compasse the gulfe of Bengala, and shooting by the citie of Malacca through the Streite of Cincapura, coast al [all] the south of Asia to the northeast part of China, and comprehend in this view all the islands from the Açores and Madera in the West, to the Malucos, the Phillipines, and Japan in the East." He added: "you shall heere finde by order, who were the first discoverours, conquerours and planters in every place: as also the natures and commodities of the soyles, togither with the forces, qualities, and conditions of the inhabitants. And that which I mention of the Orient, is likewise to be understood of the Occident."[103]

But where Hakluyt provided a conspectus combined, at best, with an account of origins, Sherley proposed much more. What then was "this great machine of the world [*esta gran máquina del mundo*]" as he saw it? It seems highly unlikely that Sherley was unaware of the medieval usage of the term *machina mundialis,* given that it was at the heart of a number of arguments in the later sixteenth century. A widespread usage was to deploy it not in relation to the material world (or globe), but rather to the larger notion of the cosmos and the cosmic order.[104] But there was also a tradition of use in a political context, and here the central text was the *Summa de potestate ecclesiastica* (1326) of Augustinus Triumphus, the monk and political theorist from Ancona, who had famously set out the proposition: "In the entire functioning of the world, there is only one government, for it is fitting that there be only one [*Tota machina mundialis non est nisi unus principatus scilicet quia non debet esse nisi unus principatus*]."[105] This was at the time intended as a defense of the Papacy and its supremacy over all Christian states. Writing in the early 1620s, Sherley naturally had a wholly other notion of what the Papacy was. "The Pope," he wrote, "is sole, absolute and supreme monarch in the spiritual domain, and in the universal and temporal domain, but so far as his own usage is concerned, he is a very limited prince." He noted that the Papacy had "its aspect fixed against heretics, Turks and infidels," but that it was otherwise a rather unstable political entity in view of the nature of Papal succession, which was not that of a regular monarchy. He concluded by stating that "the Pope endows any side that he inclines toward with great authority, because of his supreme dignity, even if as a temporal prince in reality he has no substance [*sustancia*]."[106]

One begins at moments such as these to understand the vast distance that separates Sherley's vision from that of an author such as the cleric and theorist Giovanni Botero, despite the existence of certain superficial resemblances between the two. This distance arises on account of not one but several deep differences. To begin with, the accusation made against Sherley by Pagliarini in 1608, that he was a "man of no religion [*huomo di nissuna relligione*]" may be worth taking somewhat seriously. The violent and even vituperative attitude toward Islam and Muslim societies that characterizes the thought of so many of his contemporaries (such as Bodin and Botero) is scarcely to be found in the pages of the *Peso político* or elsewhere in Sherley's writings.[107] Indeed, his whole notion of the Ottoman Empire as a structure is that its political organs correspond closely to those of Habsburg Spain: the *chief defterdār* "is the same as the *presidente de hazienda*"; the Ottoman Divan is roughly the same as the Spanish *Consejo de Estado* and may even be better in its workings, since it is centralized and thus avoids "confusion among Councils." The serious problem he identifies with the Ottomans (and which he claims was conveyed to him by the former grand vizier, Serdar Ferhat Pasha, "an old man of valor and much experience who lived in Aleppo"), is that since the time of Sultan Süleyman, women have come to exercise too great an influence over Ottoman court politics. Yet, on the other hand, he argues that where the Portuguese and Spaniards have been so hasty and foolish as to expel the Jews and the Moriscos from their territories, the Ottomans "brought much good to Turkey through their many skills [*muchos oficios*]."[108] Here then is Sherley's vision of the Habsburg-Ottoman axis, hardly opposed as black and white.

> And I find it certain, most excellent Sir, that the two greatest powers that there are today in the world are those of this Monarchy and of the Turk, with which the kingdom of England along with the rest of its [Protestant] sect might to some extent be able to hold its own place if only what England possessed to do so was it own native substance [*substancia suya natural*]. But since all the power that this kingdom [England] has of its own is limited by the size of the kingdom, and all the remaining breadth that it has acquired is through exchange, and since on its own it does not have the substance to carry out or sustain those exchanges, once one knows their secret they can be cut off or at least restricted with the application of a little care to do so. And once this is done the rest of its body of its power will collapse, so that it seems to me that effectively there are only two great planets in the matter of domination, of which this Monarchy as the larger one is the sun, and the Turk's empire is the moon. And as it is inevitable that the sun of this Monarchy, on account of the passage of time, will make its way through many [zodiac] signs, some of which will heat it up more than others, it is the wisest course to arrange everything in such a way that it is not eclipsed through opposition with the moon, from which many evils and perilous and pernicious effects will always follow.[109]

In this triangulated conception of Protestants-Habsburgs-Ottomans, there are naturally a number of subsidiary elements also in play, such as the Safavids or Muscovy. But there is a clear relationship here between Sherley's view and the line of development regarding notions of balance of power that came through Francesco Guicciardini and Francis Bacon. Guicciardini was of course a popular writer in the court of Philip IV, and his works were well known to Olivares as well; as for Bacon, Sherley certainly knew him and his thought, even if his closer personal relations were (as we have seen) with the older brother, Anthony Bacon. In a celebrated passage of his essay "Of Empire," the younger Bacon had written: "During that triumvirate of kings, King Henry the Eighth of England, Francis the First King of France, and Charles the Fifth Emperor, there was such a watch kept, that none of the three could win a palm of ground, but the other two would straightways balance it, either by confederation, or, if need were, by a war; and would not in any wise take up peace at interest." He then had gone on to refer to the earlier work of Guicciardini on Italy, and the balance "between Ferdinando King of Naples, Lorenzius Medici, and Ludovicus Sforza, potentates, the one of Florence, the other of Milan."[110] It thus appears pretty clear that Sherley creatively developed the Italian usage of the time regarding the concept of *la bilancia*, and then applied it over a far more grandiose canvas than either Guicciardini or even Bacon could have dared. Behind both of these writers lay, to be sure, the ever-present shadow of Machiavelli, but Sherley contemptuously — and no doubt tactically — dismisses him as follows. "Others take out a poultice of rules from Machiavelli's pouch, not realizing that he was only the secretary of the tiny republic of Florence, and as his science was born within such narrow walls, and since in his time there was an equality of powers among the greatest states of Christendom, and the superiority of this Monarchy was only just beginning to emerge," his blinkered vision could not carry the early seventeenth-century theorist of world affairs very far.[111]

Enough of the key elements are now in place for us firmly to grasp where Sherley intended to lead Olivares. In effect, by the first half of the 1620s, he had gone back to the position that he had briefly assumed around 1608 regarding the nature of the essential alliances that the Habsburgs should seek in the complex world panorama he described. Where once he had appeared dramatically in Europe in order to propose a grand alliance with the ruler of Iran, seen by him then as a counterweight to the Ottomans, his position by the time he wrote the *Peso político* was rather different. He argued instead that peace with the Ottomans was the pressing need of the day, in order to allow the Habsburgs to concentrate on their real rivals, namely the Protestant powers to the north. A series of smaller alliances within Europe would help in this matter. Safavid Iran could not be considered a meaningful or effective counterweight to the Ottomans, and therefore was to be seen as a less-than-pressing priority.

The news of the fall of Hormuz to Shah 'Abbas and the English East India

Company in May 1622 seems if anything to have made Sherley's view on the matter all the more firm. As a global strategy, Sherley now pressed for a series of actions in which the interests of Spain and Portugal would be closely linked, with the Portuguese naturally being held to a subordinate role. Still, the advantage of a peace with the Ottomans would be to draw the Safavids' attention westward, and thus aid in attempts to recover Hormuz for the Portuguese *Estado da Índia*. Sherley's grand scheme now carried other significant elements to it, many of them harking back to the proposals he had put to Philip III in 1608. The advantage of his mechanical view of world politics, and his relentless deploying of realpolitik, was that there was no place for sentimental attachment to alliances.[112] Thus, if the circumstances warranted it, some elements in a strategy could be radically inverted while others could be held constant. We see this in an elaborate summary document addressed by his agent in Madrid, Juan Nicolás, to Olivares in January 1623, after news of the Hormuz fiasco had come in. In this Sherley proposed the following concrete actions.

1. The creation of a new trading company in Mexico to trade in Moluccan spices across the Pacific, using the route of the Manila galleon.
2. The reorganization of the pepper and spice trade from Asia, to undercut the Dutch East India Company and its trade.
3. The urgent need to seal off the Straits of Gibraltar, to ensure that Dutch and English shipping could no longer gain access to the Mediterranean.
4. The urgent need to make peace with the Ottomans, but in such a way that it would appear that the initiative came from Istanbul rather than Madrid; the central European Habsburgs and the king of Poland should be included in the peace.
5. The need for a friendship with Christian IV, ruler of Denmark, in order to divide the Protestant camp and obtain access to cheap shipbuilding materials.

In all this, Sherley insisted, it was necessary to set aside the outdated thinking of the sixteenth century, represented precisely by men such as Botero (though he did not name him), who saw Ottoman-Habsburg rivalry as the central oppositional axis around which the world was defined. Sherley asked rhetorically: "Who wishes to destroy the Catholic church: the Turk or the heretic? I have to respond that between the two of them, it is clearly the heretic, for the Turk does not make war on Christendom, and if he does so it is not with the same vehemence as the heretic."[113] Yet, in the final analysis, what interested him was not even the ideological opposition between Catholic and Protestant, but the underlying clash of interests between the dominance of Spain and the rising powers of England and the Netherlands.

SHERLEY, THE ALIEN

Was Sherley anything other than a voice in the wilderness by the time he wrote in the 1620s, with his credibility eroded by his incessant past adventurism and uncertain loyalties? Historians of Habsburg Spain have puzzled over this matter, and concluded in the last generation or so that he was perhaps of greater significance in the early years of Philip IV's rule than had once been thought. We know that his proposals, both those in the *Peso político* and the subsequent summary text by Nicolás, were in fact considered in a junta in Olivares's chambers in February 1623, and subsequent proposals were again taken up by the count-duke in August-September 1626. Robert Stradling has even argued that "in the first decade of his [Olivares's] government . . . two characters, Antony Sherley and Baltasar Álamos de Barrientos, enjoyed Don Gaspar's receptive attention."[114] Álamos de Barrientos was the author of the *Tácito Español* (1614), and may have been the object of Sherley's following snide remark in the *Peso político*: "Others, one might well think, will settle for showing off with the phrases and aphorisms of Cornelius Tacitus. . . . And although these are excellent and come from an eminent personage who was born in the greatest monarchy that has ever been, whose government and Senate he participated in, nevertheless if one takes them on the fly without applying oneself to the mind of their author and the issues on which he pronounced the aphorism, one kills their light, stumbles and falls."[115]

In the final analysis, however, it would appear that though presenting himself too as an adherent to the current fashion of *razón de Estado*, Sherley's greatest stumbling block would have been the persistent influence in Spain of men like Botero. Botero's *Relazioni universali* of the 1590s displayed a veritable obsession with the idea of "despotic government [*governo despotico*]," located by him in a variety of Muslim, Gentile, and Eastern Christian states, from Mughal India and Muscovy to the Ottoman Empire. He reserved a particular scorn for the Ottomans, arguing that "Ottoman government is completely despotic [*affatto despotico*], for the Grand Turk is so absolute a master of all things within the bounds of his dominion, that the inhabitants are called his slaves, not his subjects . . . and there is no single person, however important, whose life is safe."[116] Elsewhere, he contrasted this situation with that of "the kingdoms of Spain, Portugal, and France, the principalities of Germany and the other states of Christendom . . . [which have] fewer wars and rebellions than among these barbarous peoples; this is because cruel laws and customs make men cruel, while humane ones make them humane."[117] Sherley's vision of the world, while drawing periodically (as we have seen) on cultural stereotypes, was nevertheless dominated by very different notions for the most part: the idea of all states as possessing a form of potential power that could be externalized and was embodied in the notion of "substance"; the crucial question of whether states were autarchic or dependent on others for their basic resources; finally, the complex articulation of the pieces of the "machine" in its entirety and how it could be manipulated by one or the other major state or empire to its advantage. As a blueprint that did not depend on the opposition of "just monarchies" and "despotic governments," and made no consequential distinction between religions (or even cultures) beyond their effects on political interests, a conception such as his might really have served any monarchy of the time.[118] To this extent, Sherley's vision thus remained true, we might say, to his life experience. Though set down on paper in the unlikely location of Granada — home to the last Muslim dynasty to rule over any part of Iberia — his perspective could have very nearly been located anywhere; perhaps for this very reason, it came to be located nowhere.

4 Unmasking the Mughals

For my part, when I enter most intimately into what I call myself, I always stumble on some particular perception or other, of heat or cold, light or shade, love or hatred, pain or pleasure. I never can catch myself at any time without a perception, and never can observe anything but the perception.

— David Hume, "Of Personal Identity" (1739–40)[1]

FROM THE OTTOMANS TO THE MUGHALS

The fall of Constantinople in late May 1453 to the forces of the Ottoman sultan Mehmed "the Conqueror" ensured that no European intellectual worth his salt could afford from that time on to ignore the existence of the "Turk," as they liked to term the scions of the House of Osman. A few weeks after this event, the rather appropriately named Aeneas Piccolomini, bishop of Siena, wrote a celebrated letter, noting that the conquering Turks were "not Persians, nor are they Trojans, as certain others think. They are a race of Scythians, come from the depths of a barbarous land."[2] The bishop's textual sources for his treatment of the Turks were dubious indeed, but would be bettered somewhat in the decades that followed, even if Europeans remained hard put for long centuries to trace the proper origins of the Ottomans. This was partly because they had paid so little attention at the very beginning of the process of the emergence of the dynasty, in the 1330s and 1340s. In contrast, Italian and other observers were almost immediately aware of the irruption of Shah Isma'il onto the Iranian political scene in the early sixteenth century. By 1504, the Venetian agent Giovanni Rotta had written the doge a report on the matter, eventually published in 1508 as *La vita, costumi et statura de Sofi re di Persia*. Rumors on these matters began to abound across the European courts, with the excitement eventually coming to be attenuated somewhat in the course of the 1510s.[3]

This excitement, we have seen in the previous chapter, was largely a consequence of the place of Iran in typical European geopolitical visions of the period: Iranian dynasties were seen as the natural enemy of the Turk, and thus equally the natural ally of European powers. The opposition between Sunni and Shi'i also facilitated such thinking. Such a binary logic could however not account for or accord a proper place to the third (of four, including the Shaibanids) great Muslim dynasty to emerge to prominence in the period, the Mughal or Timurid dynasty in India. In the very early stages of their rule over northern India, the Mughals had passed as it were under the European radar, despite the fact that the Portuguese had been in and around Gujarat ever since the early sixteenth century. It was in the 1530s that the second Mughal dynast, Humayun, came to the attention of the Portuguese on account of his conquering ambitions over Bengal and Gujarat. He thus came to occupy a place in the chronicler Fernão Lopes de Castanheda's *História*, written in those very years, and would later be dealt with by other Portuguese writers as well. But the Mughals proceeded in the 1530s and 1540s to blot their copybook in European eyes, losing significant ground to a political revival on the part of Afghan warlords in northern India, and even fleeing into exile for a time. It was only with the emergence of Humayun's son Jalal-ud-Din Akbar as ruler in the latter half of the 1550s, and especially after his conquest of Gujarat in 1572–73, that the Mughals gradually emerged full-blown into the consciousness of European intellectuals.

This was naturally aided by the fact that Akbar received Jesuits into his court from 1580, an act that ensured that his image could be transmitted wherever the Jesuits had a voice. The single most important narrative of Akbar produced at this time was probably that of the Catalan Jesuit Antoni Montserrat. While his work remained unpublished, it was the eventual basis (together with other writings) for the text of the Italian Jesuit Giovanni Battista Peruschi, *Informatione del regno et stato del Gran Rè di Mogor*.[4] In this work, Peruschi naturally made it clear to his European readers that the conversion of Akbar to Christianity might well be imminent, an idea that he in turn derived from his Jesuit sources. The contrast to the Ottoman Empire is an interesting one; in the Ottoman case, it was rarely if ever imagined that the sultan himself might convert, but it was frequently thought that access could be had to him through Christian elements among his wives, such as the celebrated Roxelane or Hürrem Sultan (d. 1558).

Anthony Sherley, ever desirous of informing himself regarding the great polities of the world in about 1620, naturally made an effort with regard to the Mughal Empire. He had of course never visited India (unlike his brother Robert), and so must have gleaned his knowledge while in Iran, as well as later in Spain. In his *Peso político*, he devoted some pages to the Mughal dynasty, and to the rule of the emperor Jahangir (1605–27), whom he does not in fact mention by name. Of this empire, he wrote:

> The Great Magor is a potentate with very extensive frontiers and extremely rich, as is usually the case with all princes who inherit the effects of their greatest vassals, who as debtors in regard to what they enjoy during their lifetimes, pay their kings back at their death, but a good part of it comes back to their sons if the services of their fathers have merited it. And although at the beginning the Magores had a huge influx of people, whom they could scarcely contain within their frontiers, they managed to build up a great reputation in all those parts of India on account of the conquest they accomplished with the first attack on the kingdom of Lahore, and then on the empire of Cambay, which after all they had lost some years earlier."[5]

Sherley felt rather ambiguous, in the final analysis, with regard to the real place of the Mughals in his worldwide scheme. He was disturbed by the singular and important place that Iranians occupied in the Mughal domains, given the fact that the Safavids were their neighbors: this he felt went against sensible principles of statecraft (*buena razón de Estado*). Besides, in his opinion, the Mughals had a number of other obvious weaknesses: they were obliged to import horses from elsewhere, especially Iran; they had no silver mines of their own so that "all the silver that they employ there either comes by way of Persia, or through Diu and Chaul, or through Surat, or through Bengal and Pegu, or through the 'Adil Khan [*Dialcán*], or through Cathay." Then there was the matter of the limited control that the Mughals had over their own seafront, where the Portuguese treated them with little more than contempt. Sherley, who had little real sympathy for the Portuguese in Asia (making a sharp distinction between them and the Spaniards), was naturally of the opinion that more reasonable dealings could be had with the Mughals, but he concluded rather cynically: "However, the good thing is that they [the Mughals] do not have the power to do harm with their innate substance [*su sustancia natural*] even if great profits are taken from their states through exchange." This was to imply that the Mughals were in the final analysis not a maritime power worth taking into account, so that the real problem was that — in view of the excessive pretensions of the Portuguese — they would gravitate to the English, "who as newly invited guests apply themselves in every way to be on good terms, and are agreeable and of profitable service to the king and his states."[6]

Sherley's prediction in this instance turned out to be more or less right. Mughal relations with the Portuguese in both Gujarat and Bengal soured progressively in the seventeenth century, with a low point being attained when the Mughals besieged the Portuguese settlement of Hughli in Bengal in 1632, and expelled them from there (also capturing a good number of them, who were carried off to Agra). Simultaneously, the presence of the English and Dutch grew from strength to strength, first in Gujarat, then in Bengal, and eventually farther south in the peninsula where Mughal southward expansion into the Deccan eventually brought them into contact with European settlements such as Masulipatnam, Vengurla, Pulicat, and Madras. As the seventeenth century wore on, materials regarding the Mughals accumulated at a great pace in Europe. The accounts produced by the curious embassy of Sir Thomas Roe to the court of Jahangir in the 1610s were read quite widely, and accorded a credence that they scarcely deserved. Roe, who was a signal failure as an ambassador, and did not manage to extract a single worthwhile concession from the Mughals at the end of a rather expensive mission, managed nevertheless to convince the court of James I that all this was because "this overgrowne [Mughal] Eliphant [would not] descend to Article or bynde himselfe reciprocally to any Prince upon terms of Equalety."[7] The 1620s then produced the Dutch account of Francisco Pelsaert, who was resident for several years in Agra, and whose writings were eventually absorbed and somewhat reframed by the humanist Johannes de Laet in his work *De Imperio Magni Mogolis* (1631). While adding considerable detail, and on occasion chronological accounts regarding Mughal rule, it may be argued that most of these works had a perverse effect when compared to Sherley's rather reasonable and even-tempered evaluation of the Mughals. De Laet, for example, strove to convince his audience that "the Emperor of India is an absolute monarch [*imperator absolutus*]; there are no written laws; the will of emperor is held to be law."[8] This tendentious view drew no doubt on Roe as well as Pelsaert; it also pursued the unfortunate line that Botero had already insisted on, which conveniently served to paper over the real and awkward dealings that traders and ambassadors frequently had, and provided them with a blanket excuse for all their failures.

REDISCOVERING MANUZZI

These then were the vicissitudes of Europeans who were actual or potential empire builders in Asia: Portuguese, Spaniards, English, and Dutch. But what of other border crossers, who represented either small states and powers, or nothing much besides their own malleable destinies? The visitor to the rather obscure Christian cemetery in Agra will find, among a vast variety of fascinating Armenian tombs such as that of Khwaja Martiros (d. 1611) and the grave of the early English visitor John Mildenhall (d. 1614), the burial places of the celebrated European mercenaries Walter Reinhardt (1725–78) (better known as *Sombre* or even *Samrū*) and Jan Willem Hessing (1740–1803). Lost among these is another tumular inscription that has been little remarked. This one, in Portuguese, runs as follows: "*Aqui jaz quondam Bernardino Mafei veneziano sirurgico del gran rei Mogol o qual delle e de toda la corte foi muito estimado por suas curas feitas. Moreo aos 11 d'agosto no ano de 1628*" (Here lies the late Bernardino Mafei, Venetian, surgeon to the great Mogol king, who was greatly esteemed by him and all his court for the cures he carried out. He died on 11 August in the Year 1628).[9] Mafei (or better Maffei) was one of a number of Italians who found their way to India at the height of Mughal rule in the seventeenth century, often to remain there for long decades. Less known than Cesare Federici or Gasparo Balbi, famed travelers from the latter half of the sixteenth century, these seventeenth-century voyagers continued a far older tradition that preceded even the Portuguese arrival in the waters of the Indian Ocean in the closing years of the fifteenth century.[10] This was a tradition that extended certainly to the most celebrated of medieval European travelers and raconteurs, Marco Polo himself in the late thirteenth century, and also included the friar Odorico da Pordenone in the fourteenth century.[11]

The Italians exercise a particular fascination not simply for their odd resonance with contemporary Indian politics, but because they were not a direct part of an imperial presence. Rather, they were often unattached, footloose, and flexible in their political orientation. They appear on first sight therefore to represent an ideal of the "go-between" or what in French has sometimes been termed the *passeur culturel*.[12] Such figures have been the object of renewed attention both for historians and for more popular writers in recent times. An example of this may be found in the celebrated early modern historian Natalie Zemon Davis's recent book titled *Trickster Travels*. It deals with the life of Hasan al-Wazzan al-Gharnati al-Fasi, a Muslim born in Granada in about 1488 and brought up in North Africa, who eventually wound up as the great informant of Christian Europe on the Muslim African world under the name of Leo Africanus, author of the *Descrittione dell'Affrica*. Davis's book is a work of considerable craft that attempts to bring a breath of fresh air to a figure that has already been studied many times over.[13] Davis's attitude is that of the sympathetic listener, who wishes to bring alive the dilemmas of a Muslim caught between two worlds in the early sixteenth century.[14] Though Hasan, or Leo, was made a prisoner by corsairs and forced by the Papacy to convert to Christianity, we still see him as full of "agency," a veritable "trickster" who managed eventually to evade the prison that had been imposed on him in order eventually to return to North Africa. It is an edifying tale, full of hope for a Mediterranean that today seems to us more epitomized by conflict and increasingly perilous crossings than positive interdenominational relations.

The early modern world too is in fact rarely full of truly edifying tales that we must return to because they "bore witness to the possibility of communication and curiosity in a world divided by violence."[15] Less optimistic than Davis, I tend to see it myself as a world where — when outright conquest and domination was not the rule (as happened in Mexico and Peru) — cultures met frequently in a situation of "contained conflict." Europeans in sixteenth- and seventeenth-century India did not rule the roost; rather they remained perched in a series of coastal enclaves, at times fortified and at times not. Occasionally, they even acquired a house for a factory inland, as happened with the Dutch East India Company in Agra. However, the lack of outright domination or of the material conditions to enable the production of a full-blown Orientalism in the Saïdian sense does not mean that we are dealing with a situation of mutual understanding or bonhomie. I have explored this at some length elsewhere while dealing with the writings of Sir Thomas Roe, the English Company's ambassador to the court of Jahangir in the 1610s.[16]

Some may wish to argue, however, that the notoriously sarcastic Roe was hardly the typical European in early modern India. What of others, who "went native," and who adopted Indian *mœurs* and ways — the sorts of characters whom William Dalrymple described with such affection in his best-selling popular book *White Mughals*?[17] Was it not the case that such men (or, very rarely, women) were those ideal *passeurs culturels*, who mediated effortlessly between one cultural complex and another? This chapter seeks to reexamine one such case, perhaps the most significant of them, namely that of Nicolò Manuzzi in seventeenth- and eighteenth-century India, a figure sufficiently attractive to have been one of the central characters in a mid-twentieth-century cult work in French called *Bourlinguer* (Knocking About).[18]

On 18 January 1712, a Venetian resident of the coastal town of Pondicherry in southeastern India, living under the protection of the French East India Company, produced a will and testament. The man in question was probably just under seventy-four years of age at that time, and described himself as "the Seigneur Nicolas Manouchy resident of the said Pondichéry, sound of spirit . . . and understanding [*sain d'esprit . . . et entendement*]," and the sum he left behind was the fairly respectable but not enormous one of 1,585 *pagodas* (a *pagoda* being reckoned at about 8 French *livres*). The main beneficiary mentioned in the will was a brother, Andrea, resident in Venice in the "quarter of St John the Evangelist and St Stin," meaning the area just north of the Frari church — which coincidentally today houses the Archivio di Stato in Venice. There were particular reasons for producing the will. For Signor Manuzzi was due at that time to embark on a mission to distant Lahore, to the court of the Mughal emperor Bahadur Shah, whom he had served at various earlier moments in his career, when the emperor had been called prince Shah 'Alam, and Manuzzi for his part had claimed to be a gifted European physician.[19] The testament thus mentions that its author was apprehensive "in case of his death during the voyage that he will carry out [*en cas de son décès au voyage qu'il va faire*]," but passes tactfully over the fact that this voyage was on behalf not of the French, but of the gentlemen of the English East India Company, at Fort St. George in Madras.[20] In any event, the mission was aborted. Bahadur Shah, who was in fact some five years younger than Manuzzi, died in February 1712 and was succeeded after a struggle by his son Jahandar Shah, who also only managed to rule very briefly. The English Company decided that the situation was hence not propitious for an embassy, and Manuzzi could thus remain in southern India where he eventually died — probably in Madras rather than Pondicherry — in about 1720. We are aware that he made a later will in Madras on 8 January 1719, with a codicil to it the next year; unfortunately, this document is now largely illegible except for its date.[21] One thing appears constant though in all these documents: Manuzzi's devotion to the Capuchins of Madras and Pondicherry clearly stated in his desire to be buried in their church with a mass and vigils ["*une grande messe avec l'office ordinaire et les bijiles de tous les pères qui se trouveront*"]. Whatever else Manuzzi was — and as we shall see presently he was many things to many people — he certainly was a devout Catholic.

Manuzzi's name is certainly not unknown to scholars of Mughal India, or even of the history of travel. Any standard work on the Mughals, such as the late John F. Richards's volume in the *New Cambridge History of India*, will inevitably yield at least a few references to the Venetian; and some early twentieth-century authors such as Jadunath Sarkar have even drawn rather extensively on his authority.[22] Of late, scholars of culture in Mughal times have also referred to his writings on such subjects as *satī* and Indian music rather more skeptically.[23] Most recently, his work has been mobilized to analyze "the position of a European narrator in an Eastern harem," and it has been argued that "in accounts such as Manucci's [Manuzzi's], shifts in the writer's voice, authority, and narrative position indicate that cultural translations of harems to European audiences imply a simultaneous translation of the narrator's personhood, cultural identity, and authorial voice." Manuzzi is portrayed here then as rather protean, a trickster of sorts too, one who "has spent a lifetime traveling from one culture to another, adopting languages, sexualities, clothes, professions, and identities in giddy succession."[24] Yet, while placing a large conceptual burden on the Venetian's back, almost all these recent works refer not to the original text of his *Storia del Mogol*, which, as we shall see, has an extremely complex publication history, but to the four-volume English translation — serviceable but somewhat imperfect — produced by William Irvine of the Indian Civil Service in 1907–8 under the hybrid title, half Italian and half Portuguese, of *Storia do Mogor*.[25] So, in recent years, I have returned to the Manuzzi manuscripts, held in Berlin, Paris, and Venice, in the conviction that there is something to be gained by posing a fresh set of questions to them beyond asking whether he told the truth or made things up. In this chapter, I present a set of reflections, oriented around the problem of Manuzzi's self-image of himself as a European, even at the end of sixty years' stay in India.

It may be useful to begin with what we can outline of the biography of the man, since this has been the subject of some confusion. Research by the Venetian historian and archivist Piero Falchetta in the 1980s has clarified much confusion regarding both Manuzzi's birth date and the year of his departure from Venice.[26] He quotes an unpublished early eighteenth-century work of the well-known intellectual Apostolo Zeno (1668–1750), which informs us of the following:

> Niccolò Manucci [Manuzzi] was born of Pasqualino Manucci and Rosa [Bellin] . . . simple people and of modest condition [*persone idiote e del popolo*] in Venice, on 19 April 1638. When he was 13 or 14 years old, he went to Corfu to visit an uncle who was there in order to trade, and from there took an English vessel, in which he met an Englishman, who attracted by the spirit of the stripling, arranged for him to pass onward in a voyage; from where through Persia, he arrived in India, where his first and longest sojourn was in the city of Dely [Delhi], where under the tutelage of the Jesuit fathers he learned the Persian language,

> and went on to dedicate himself to medicine. At the end of five or six years when his relatives in Venice had had no news of him, he wrote to them of his excellent state, and was able to send them a ring of a considerable value, with instructions that they should sell it and employ the proceeds to buy various books on medicine whose titles he specified in his letter. With the help of these [books] which certainly reached him, he advanced a great deal in his knowledge of that art, and was thus able to have himself named physician in the court of the Emperor of Mogol, and there to observe the rites, customs, government, their religion, and everything that takes place in the running of a great empire.[27]

It would thus appear that Manuzzi left Venice in November 1651, shortly before the birth of his youngest sister Pierina, first for Corfu, then for Izmir, and eventually from there for Erzurum, Yerevan, Julfa, Tabriz, and Qazwin. This was part of a long tradition of expatriation in that city, and we need not link it to speculations regarding its alleged economic "decline" in the seventeenth century.[28] Manuzzi was to claim later that he was able to attach himself to the entourage of Henry Bard, Viscount Bellomont—giving a name to the mysterious Englishman mentioned by Zeno—who in those years was in Iran as an envoy of the exiled Charles Stuart to Shah 'Abbas II (r. 1642–66).[29] This claim, given full credence by Irvine, has more recently been cast in doubt by Falchetta; the Italian scholar points out very reasonably that Manuzzi does not even mention the rather noticeable fact that Bellomont had lost an arm in the English Civil War.[30] Whatever be the case, it would seem that the young Manuzzi eventually embarked together for the Mughal port of Surat via Bandar 'Abbas sometime between 1653 and 1655, and after about 1656 came to be employed as an artilleryman by the Mughal prince Dara Shukoh. We can now trace the rest of his long Indian career in seven phases.

1. 1656–66: This is the initial phase of Manuzzi's employment under Dara and, after the latter's imprisonment and execution, of his departure for Patna and Bengal; then we see his return to Agra and Delhi, and subsequent employment with Mirza Raja Jai Singh.

2. 1666–77: There then follows his exit from Mughal service, and attempt to try his luck in the Portuguese settlements at Bassein and Goa. Manuzzi then returns to Mughal service in Lahore, as a "physician" attached to Mughal princes. He returns thereafter to Daman and Bandra with the Portuguese.

3. 1678–82: Manuzzi suffers bad financial losses from a shipwreck (estimated at 14,000 rupees), and returns to seek the patronage of the prince Shah ʿAlam in the Deccan, again as a physician.

4. 1682–84: Once more, he returns to the Portuguese, and attempts to serve as an intermediary between the Mughals and the Portuguese. The Portuguese viceroy, Dom Francisco de Távora, Conde de Alvor, makes him a member of the Order of Santiago.

5. 1684–86: Manuzzi has altercations with the Portuguese authorities in Goa, and now returns to serve the Mughals. Distrusted by the Mughals, Manuzzi spends some time in Hyderabad, and eventually takes refuge in Madras, where he marries the Catholic widow Elizabeth Hartley Clarke (who had earlier been married to the Portuguese interpreter at Madras, Thomas Clarke, who had died in 1683) on 28 October 1686 and acquires a house and garden in Madras.[31]

6. 1686–1706: Manuzzi settles in Madras, enjoying close relations with several governors such as William Gyfford and Thomas Pitt (though not with Elihu Yale or Nathaniel Higginson). He serves as an intermediary between the English Company and the Mughal administration in Arcot. He begins to write his memoirs, and sends them in 1700 to Paris, where they end up in the hands of the Jesuits. A distorted version appears in 1705 from the pen of François Catrou (1659–1737), as *Histoire générale de l'empire du Mogol depuis sa fondation, sur les mémoires portugais de M. Manouchi* (Paris, 1705). This renders Manuzzi furious with the Jesuits. Elizabeth Clarke Manuzzi dies in Madras on 15 December 1706.

7. 1707–20: Manuzzi now leaves for Pondicherry, and sells his chief Madras residence (near St. Thomas Mount) on 3 July 1709 to Pierre André de la Prévostière. In exchange, he acquires a house in Pondicherry on the Rue Neuve de la Porte de Goudelour.[32] He also enters into correspondence with the Serenissima, with a view to publishing his work there. He now alternates between Madras and Pondicherry until his death, which we may presume occurred in about 1720. We are aware that his last will (of 1719–20) was deposited in the *greffe du conseil supérieur* of Pondicherry on 23 August 1720 by the Capuchin father Thomas, and we may assume that this took place shortly after his death.

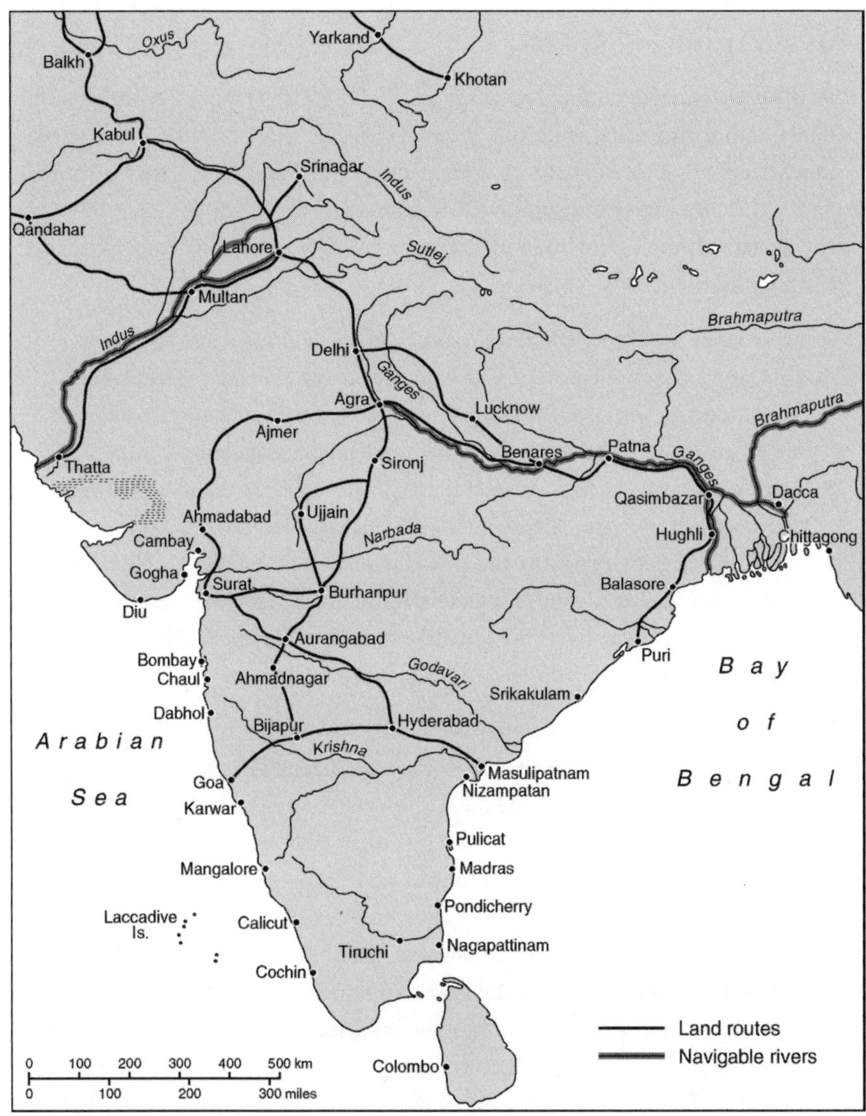

The India of Nicolò Manuzzi.

MANUZZI AND THE *STORIA*

At the heart of any examination of Manuzzi's life must lie that vast, unruly, and hence rather confusing work the *Storia del Mogol.* This is a work in five parts, in which the first three possess a certain structural coherence, with the fourth and fifth parts departing somewhat from them. Here is how he announced the initial scheme of the book in a version that was eventually transmitted to Catrou and the Jesuits.

> I will divide my history into three parts; I will divide the first into two books, [and] in the first I will recount what happened to me after my departure from Venice until my arrival in Dely; in the second, I will present a brief chronicle of the Mogol kings until the arrival of Aurangzeb on the Mogul throne with the death of his brothers. In the second [part], I will describe the conquests made by Aurangzeb, his wars and their success. In the third [part], I will say something of the politics of the Mogol, of the grandeur of the Rajas and of the other potentates of Industan, and of the revenues of this land. I will also speak of many other specific things, and in the end, I will make some remarks on the religion of the Gentiles.[33]

The work is clearly meant then to have a hero — Manuzzi himself — placed at the center of the narration.[34] It also has a second central figure, the "antihero" if one likes, which is to say the Mughal emperor Aurangzeb-'Alamgir. The bulk of the text is thus meant as a complex interplay between the fates of the two, with Aurangzeb being the older by about two decades.

But Manuzzi's aims are in the final analysis even more complicated than this schematic emplotment might suggest. There is the problem of the figure of François Bernier (1620–88), the French doctor who on his return to France in the late 1660s after a sojourn in Mughal India had emerged as a great authority on such matters.[35] Bernier, who was exceedingly well connected in France, and close to the formidable figure of the philosopher Pierre Gassendi, had managed to have his work on India published in Paris in 1670 as *Histoire de la dernière révolution des états du grand Mogol,* and Manuzzi clearly possessed and had closely read a copy of the same, as also of its continuation published the next year under the title *Suite des mémoires du sieur Bernier sur l'empire du grand Mogol dédiez au roy; Événemens particuliers, ou Ce qui s'est passé de plus considérable après la guerre, pendant cinq ans ou environ, dans les États du Grand Mogol; avec une lettre de l'étendüe de l'Hindoustan, circulation de l'or et de l'argent . . . , richesses, forces, justice et causes principales de la décadence des États*

Nicolò Manuzzi as physician. Bibliothèque nationale de France (Paris), Estampes, Réserve OD 45, fl. 2. *By permission of the Bibliothèque nationale de France*

d'Asie. It is evident however that he had little use for Bernier or his work, as we see from the following passage.

> [Bernier knew the Mughal empire] only in a fugitive manner, and superficially, and all that he recounts in his book are all relations that he has had from one or the other person, and above all acquired by him in the marketplaces [*nelle botteghe*] of India, but not believed in the courts of the princes and grandees of the kingdom. The reader will pardon me if I tell the truth and speak freely in this manner but it is true that the greater part of the relations that he recounts were heard by him from me, but as time did not permit him enough space to make the required annotations, or written memoirs, on account of the continuous

> tasks and forced service that he did for his patron Danismandkan [Danishmand Khan], who did not allow him to rest a great deal, but occupied him continuously in various matters, and among other things in comprehending Roman and Greek histories, it is likely that he did not [properly] recall the accounts that I recounted to him.[36]

We are naturally meant to contrast the figure of Bernier brutishly slaving away in Danishmand Khan's library, barely aware of what goes on in the Mughal Empire, with Manuzzi's own self-presentation as a possessor of very deep and wide knowledge. We may recall some of his initial statements in this regard. "When I left Venice, besides the Italian language, I also spoke the French language, and on the journey I learnt Turkish and Persian, and seeing myself in this land [India] I have applied myself to the Indian language. Then, desirous of knowing about the things of the Kingdom of the Mogol, I met an old doctor, a compatriot, who offered to read me the royal chronicles of the Mogol Kings and Princes."

It is on this authority then that Manuzzi claims to be able to reconstruct Mughal history from the time of Timur to that of Shahjahan, when Manuzzi's own eyewitness account can take over. This same representation of Manuzzi was then taken over and even further embellished by Catrou when he presented his own *Histoire générale*. In his preface, dedicating the work to the Duc de Bourgogne, the Jesuit noted that he had gained access to Manuzzi's work through an employee of the French Company André Boureau Deslandes, "who had exercised the highest functions in our colonies in the Indies"; he had begun reading it out of curiosity thinking that it was another adventurous travel narrative, but soon he had found "more than travels there." This was because "M. Manouchi had had access to the chronicle of the Empire of the Mogol, which he had had translated into Portuguese, and which he had inserted into the work that I had in my hands." Catrou went on to elaborate that he had "all the certainty that one can have in these matters that my chronicle of the Mogol in Portuguese has the general characteristics of the truth. M. Manouchi assures us that he had it translated from Persian with care based on the originals in the palace. It seems that the Venetian has spared nothing by way of expense in order to transmit to Europe solid monuments concerning the Empire where he resides. He has had painted at great expense, by the painters of the *serrail*, portraits of the Emperors and of the illustrious men of the Mogol [Empire]. We would have given copies to the public if we had not feared that we would thus overburden a first edition."[37]

The Jesuit thus wishes to assure the reader of the profundity of Manuzzi's knowledge, far distant from that of "traders from Europe whom commerce obliges either to pass through some countries of the Indies in haste or to reside in the ports of Indoustan, far from the capital." Rather he is a physician, long attached to the emperors themselves and their entourages, with a privileged access to the interior of the palace "which is refused to all others," over a period of some forty years. However, Catrou now enters into somewhat more slippery considerations. To be sure, Manuzzi sometimes diverges from Bernier, he states, but this is only because he wrote after him and had the benefit of hindsight. In any event, to render the text better for the public, he has mixed Manuzzi's observations with those of the Jesuit Giovanni Pietro Maffei, Pedro Teixeira, Pietro della Valle, Thomas Roe, Johannes de Laet, as well as Bernier and Tavernier![38] The personage of Manuzzi, so central to the text of the *Storia del Mogol*, now is reduced to that of a source; Manuzzi's own life story practically disappears from the text and is subsumed into a general history of the Mughals since Timur.

We shall see presently when exactly Manuzzi received news of his demotion at the hands of Catrou, who was quite well known already as the author of an *Histoire des anabaptistes*, and would go on to write works on Roman history as well as translate Virgil into French.[39] By January 1705, completely abandoning his initial intention of a three-part text, Manuzzi had in fact completed a fourth part of his *Storia*, this one written in a mix of French and Portuguese, and was even contemplating a fifth part. This went against his stated intention at the end of the third part, where he had written the following:

> I have already arrived at the end of my History, something that I so greatly desired. May God grant that just as I have had the fortune to complete these three books and narrate the things that have happened to me in these forty-eight years, so may God grant that this light that I give to the Europeans [*os Europianos*] reaches the end that I desire, for I am now preparing myself for a voyage that is far longer, while however seeking the true path and the most secure that we can hope for; and this being the true end of our desires, may Our Powerful Lord grant it both to me and to everyone with surety; meanwhile may the Reader be content to accept this work of mine and find in it the same lack that one finds in flowers, for one who has always lived among thorns cannot bring forth flowers.[40]

If we assume that these words were written in 1700, Manuzzi thus sees himself aged in his early to mid-sixties, yet practically at death's door, and preparing himself for this eventuality. It is significant that at this moment he identifies himself as a "European" bringing light to other Europeans, even if his preferred word *europiano* in fact does not exist in Portuguese (the correct usage being *europeu*).[41] A few years later, as noted, he returns to the *Storia* and begins a fourth part, justifying himself as follows, and assuming that the first three volumes have already been published in Europe.

> I made some promises to you in my last book that I would continue my History, if it pleased God to preserve my health somewhat. It appeared that my age which is already very advanced, and serious preoccupations that the consideration of the other life give rise to, could keep me from writing anything further on the subject of what is happening in the Empire of the Mogol, regarding which I have kept you abreast, dear Reader, in the first three parts of this History which I have had printed. However, notwithstanding the inclination I had to take rest, I wished to keep to my promise, and I have picked up the pen again to inform you of all the events that have taken place, and which will take place in future at the court of Aurangzeb. I will recount in this fourth part all that might have escaped me that is worthy of remark. I shall write with no passion, and with all the exactitude and sincerity possible, as I have done so far, regarding all that happens in this famous court. You, dear Reader, will find things here to instruct you, and to please you at the same time. The great and generous actions of some will seem excellent examples for you to follow, and the faults of others will be a salutary instruction to you.[42]

This rather moralizing tone suggests that the scribes that Manuzzi was using at this time were from a religious order, and the text — now in French — though not devoid of grammatical errors has a literary pretension to it that the far more lively Portuguese sections do not. It is important to recall that Manuzzi had changed scribes several times. We are aware that he began his text in Italian, but was obliged to abandon this some way into the third part. At the point of transition, into French then Portuguese, he announces the following. "Since I lack an Italian scribe [*per me mancare yl escrivano ytaliano*], I am obliged to continue my work in the French language, and even in Portuguese, which is not by preference [but] because in this land there are no curious scribes [*escrivany curiosy*], and those who are there are lacking in their letters and understanding."[43] We shall see that this eventually led him, even in his correspondence with Venice, to use Latin, since the Catholic priests with whom he maintained close contact in Pondicherry and Madras were clearly proficient in that language. To return to Manuzzi's preface to the fourth part, he continues by alerting the reader to the fact that "in Industan, everything points to some remarkable Revolutions: the advanced age of the Emperor who is over eighty-six years old, and the ambition that his sons and grandsons have always shown to mount the throne, are reason enough to fear some catastrophe, as tragic as that which occurred in the last years of Chaajahan." As long as Aurangzeb continues to live, and rules with his habitual firm hand [*avec la mesme vigueur*], things will remain under control. Thereafter, anything is possible. Manuzzi thus concludes his preface: "I hope, Dear Reader, to reap from my sleepless nights and from my application the sole fruit that I wished to have, which is your instruction and your satisfaction, and I will be all-too-happy if I could succeed in that, and I would sing the glory of God who is the sole author of all the good that men can do in this world. Adieu."

What then follows in the fourth part of the *Storia* is a rather curious confection. Beginning with the condition of the Mughal Empire in 1700, Manuzzi now gives more or less full vent to his anecdotal spirit, mixing materials regarding the Mughal court with long excursions on the curious ways of Da'ud Khan Panni, the Afghan governor of the Karnatak; these then alternate with considerations regarding the Portuguese, and close in a more or less desultory manner with the affairs of São Tomé and Madras. This part, somewhat disorganized in its pagination, together with the first three parts mentioned above, comprises the single large codex of some 469 folios that Manuzzi eventually sent to Venice in 1706. Before he did so, however, it is clear that Catrou's deception with regard to his manuscript had come to light, apparently already in August 1704, when Manuzzi claims to have received a draft of the preface to the *Histoire générale*. It is clear however that Manuzzi's indignation grew apace as he reflected on the matter. We can see this by comparing the (more or less) closing passages of part four, written in "Madrasapatnam" on 5 January 1705, with the new preface that he wrote to the whole tome (comprising most of parts I–IV), as well as a separate codex, before sending it out to the Serenissima. Here is Manuzzi in January 1705.

> The curious Reader will already have seen my four tomes, and I have sent them in the confidence that the curious Reader will have perceived their variety, and the unevenness that can be observed in the said work; the reason for this was that [lack of] time led me to it, and I continued as events happened. I went on forward thinking that the curious Reader would be content to accept the said work. If God grants me life, I will continue with the Fifth Tome [part], because seeing that I am already 68 years old, and fearful that my work will cease without appearing before this world, this was the reason to send it on. And also the fact

> that Death does not forewarn anyone, nor does it care about the affairs of one who is preoccupied in them, but carries one off against one's will, and so foreseeing this I was of the opinion that this [work] should not be left in the hands of agents, because of past experience; and I have seen a large number of such cases, in which they did not follow the orders of the testator. So I thought if I could take care of it in my own lifetime, I should not leave it to the disposition of similar people, and so I am sending it off on this occasion. And later we shall speak of the end which the government and life of this king Orangzeb will attain, for he is already 89 years old; and I will take care to send it on.[44]

There is nothing here to suggest yet that Manuzzi is greatly preoccupied by the fate of the works that he knows are in the hands of the Jesuits. Rather, he is anxious to see the fourth part appear as quickly as possible, and already talks of embarking on the fifth. By the time the preface in Italian to parts I–IV is written a few days later, his anger is manifest. The contents of this preface appear in broad summary in the Latin letter that he wrote to the Senate of Venice, and this letter at least bears a date, namely 15 January 1705.[45] However, since the Italian text was certainly composed directly by Manuzzi, it is perhaps more appropriate to turn to it. He writes:

> The curious and benign Reader will allow me to explain my discourse. It has been many years since I have begun this work of mine for the benefit of travelers, merchants and missionaries [*per benefisio dy caminanty, mercanty y missionary*], and I was also obliged to do so by many friends of the French nation from whom I have received many favors and honors, as well on account of the obligations on account of the honors that His Most Christian Majesty [Louis XIV] has been pleased to do to me, by sending me 7 medallions which I received in the year 1699: one of gold with the royal portrait and on the other side the portrait of the Dauphin with his three sons, and 6 others in silver with the indications of the victories that he has gained; and because I know that the French nation is curious to have any novelties, and also that other authors of the same nation have written some relations of this empire of the Mugole, but as I was aware that they were not well informed, nor did they even have the necessary time to know of the greatness, riches, dominion, powers, politics and so on — as can be seen in the discourses that I have sent and which I am sending again — all these reasons obliged me to send this curiosity [work] of mine to France in 1700, which I placed in the hands of one of my faithful friends, a person of consideration, and beloved and esteemed in all of India.

The pell-mell prose in Venetian dialect, full of rather odd turns of phrase and orthography, contrasts with the rather more solemn Manuzzi who appears in French, and even with the "Portuguese Manuzzi." But the picture is clear enough. Here is Manuzzi, a close friend of various French traders and missionaries, who feels obliged to let them benefit from his vast experiences. There is the irritation at Bernier and perhaps even Tavernier (though of this we are far less certain). We also come to learn of how the text was sent back to Paris via the "faithful friend," M. Deslandes. Now matters take a turn for the worse.

> This friend [Deslandes] arrived in France, and His Majesty honored him and sent him off to the West Indies to govern some lands, so that he was not able to do [publish] my work, and was obliged to hand over three interesting books, and another with 64 figures of the progeny of the great Temur Lange until this king Oranzeb with his sons, and of the kings of Visapury [Bijapur] and also those of Golconda, and their chief generals and the Gentile princes who are their vassals, with other curious things to see, to a Jesuit Father called Reverend Father Catrou Junior, a very astute person, to whom — and to other friends — the Jesuits in India wrote to do whatever was possible to take control of my work (and they managed to do what they wanted); for many of these Reverends and even other missionaries have carried out diligences to have my work, but as I know well they are fond of laying their hands on the best things in the world, which I can say as something I have experienced, as will be seen in my discourses. This Jesuit sent me a Preface to the First Book which he wanted to print: I could see that he wanted to impose his will on his work, and include fables from other authors; which [Preface] I received in the month of August 1704, and he sent me many justifications as they [the Jesuits] are in the habit of doing, none of which gave me any satisfaction, knowing that they wanted to usurp my work which I have spent years on, only for them to have the glory and the honor. I replied to him that he should not steal this effort and that he should return my work to me; but as I know them, it seems to me this will lead nowhere.

Manuzzi refers here then to three volumes in mixed French and Portuguese, today conserved in the Staatsbibliothek zu Berlin, but also to an interesting collection of portraits in the Mughal style, which he notes elsewhere he had made while he was in the service of the prince Shah 'Alam in the Deccan, through a friend called Mir Muhammad, also in that prince's service.[46] He writes:

> Before leaving the kingdom of the Mogol, I had . . . all these portraits of kings and princes, from Tamerlane to Aurangzeb, and of the sons and nephews of the last. . . . No one, so far as I know, has presented these portraits to the [European] public, or if someone has done so, they bear no relation to mine, which are authentic, while the others can only be false. In fact, to have them I spared no expense and I had to give great gifts, and all that with a thousand difficulties and subterfuges, with the promise that I would never reveal that I possessed them. I do not present portraits of queens and princesses because it is impossible to see them as they are always covered; and if anyone has made them, they are not to be believed, for they can only be of prostitutes, dancers etc., reworked according to the fancy of the painter. It should be remembered that all the figures who have a halo and parasol over the head are persons of royal blood.

This is the collection today termed the *Libro Rosso*, held at present—after complicated movements from Paris to Venice in the early eighteenth century, and then back to Paris with Napoleon in 1797—in the Bibliothèque Nationale de France (Paris); and as an inspection of the portraits suggest, they are themselves rather curious productions.[47] As many art-historian colleagues have repeatedly emphasized, they—like most other such paintings that found their way to seventeenth-century Europe—certainly cannot be considered Mughal miniatures of the first quality.[48] Some features do stand out. To begin with, the portraits of the Mughal emperors from Babur to Jahangir do bear a generic resemblance to the portraits that we know. There is, interestingly enough, no portrait of Shahjahan, though he occupies an important place in the *Storia*. Besides, the portraits are always presented using a stereotypical mise-en-scène, with soldiers carrying weapons on the borders and surrounding the central figure of the monarch who is always in movement, whether on a palanquins, an elephant, or a horse. These soldiers however at times have curious expressions, including smiles and grimaces, of a sort that would never be seen in official Mughal portraiture. On the other hand, the nobles are often presented in a courtly scene, as we can see from the case of the great Iranian *amīr* Shayista Khan. Further, the usual Mughal conventions of hierarchized presentation—where persons are presented in profile or semiprofile depending on their status, as Ebba Koch has noted—are not fully observed.[49] The strong suspicion one has is that these portraits were produced in the Deccan, probably in Aurangabad (where Shah ʻAlam had his camp), with a very loose basis in existing Mughal albums. In some instances, as with Dawar Bakhsh or Sultan Bulaqi (grandson of Jahangir), the

Emperor Jahangir on an elephant. Bibliothèque nationale de France (Paris), Estampes, Réserve OD 45, fl. 10.
By permission of the Bibliothèque nationale de France

portrait in Manuzzi's *Libro Rosso* is the only known adult portrait that exists.[50] This would cast doubt on the idea that there was in this case any prototype at all. In some instances, as with the sultans of Bijapur and Golconda, we also have the imaginary collective portrait, where all the members of a lineage appear seated side by side; this is not an original device, and one that certainly exists elsewhere in the case of Bijapur.[51]

It is clear that Manuzzi intended these portraits to accompany his text. Obviously, this could not have been in the original painted form; rather, the paintings were meant to form the basis of copperplate engravings. In point of fact, three such engravings were executed by the artist and savant Antonio Maria Zanetti (1706–78), the Younger, who prepared a catalogue of the manuscripts in the Biblioteca di San Marco in Venice where many of Manuzzi's manuscripts eventually found their way. These were the engravings of Timur (shown hunting with a gun), Aurangzeb (shown riding a horse with a Qu'ran in his hands), and of an elderly Manuzzi himself in Mughal attire taking the pulse of an Indian patient who is grimacing or smiling.[52]

THE FATE OF THE *STORIA*

In 1705, when Manuzzi wrote his Italian preface and his Latin letter to the Venetian Senate, these paintings were in Paris. However, he did manage to constitute a further set of visual materials, as he sets out again in the preface. We have already seen his skepticism regarding the prospect of ever recovering his materials from the hands of Catrou; however, besides sending a letter to the Jesuit demanding the restitution of his volumes, he notes that he has also deputed as his "agent [*percuratore*] the Reverend Father Eusebio [Eusèbe] de Bourges, a French Capuchin missionary who is leaving from this India for Europe." Manuzzi's strategy here was simple; disgusted with the Jesuits, he wished to make use of the notorious rivalry between the different Catholic missionary orders. Eusèbe de Bourges, who embarked from Pondicherry for France in February 1705, was thus handed not only the moral charge mentioned above by Manuzzi, but also a rather substantial package, as well the letter for the Venetian Senate. The contents of the package, besides parts I–IV of the *Storia* bound into a single volume, are set out by Manuzzi in his preface.

> To give satisfaction to Your Lordships [the Senate], and to show my veracity, you may see the work that I have done. I send you the true original and as a proof of this I send you the Fourth Part of my History that follows [the others] which will be carried by the above-mentioned Reverend, which the Jesuits do not have as I have not sent it to them and I am sending it here; and I will continue to make an effort to produce a Fifth tome — if God grants me enough life, I will write it to demonstrate my truth and to give ample satisfaction. And besides I send another book with 66 figures which represent the false Gentile gods, and how these Gentiles marry, their burials, penitence, sacrifices, ceremonies, with their significations, as can be seen in the [description of] the Gentile religion which is in the Third Part. And the above-mentioned curious Reverends [Jesuits] have made considerable efforts to have these two last books: and I responded to them *Nesio vos* ["I know you not"]. I believe that my Nation [*la mia nasione*] which I esteem greatly, after having read my work will be satisfied, which I [hence] humbly offer to the Most Serene Senate. And though it is written in diverse languages, the reason for this is that in these lands I could not find an Italian scribe, and if I speak

> often about my own person I tell the truth about what transpired, and I leave it to the prudence of the notary [editor] to add the Preface that the work merits. And if some modern book appears that is produced with my name or that of another author, it may be compared with my originals and the truth will be apparent. And I ask pardon if in my discourse some words or spellings are in error, the reason is that in this India I have hardly spoken my mother tongue [*la mia lingua maternale*], save on this occasion which I offer myself.

The tone has shifted here from that of the earlier preface, where the intended audience is "Europeans." Rather, Manuzzi now announces his colors as a patriotic Venetian, or perhaps as both Venetian and Italian, and as a faithful son of the republic from which he has long been separated.

We are in 1705, and such was not always the case. In 1679 or 1680, Manuzzi encountered a fellow Venetian after a long gap. This was the traveling physician Angelo Legrenzi, who writes of meeting a rather different Manuzzi in Aurangabad, when the latter was employed by Shah 'Alam. Here is Legrenzi's description of that encounter:

> [T]he prince entertains several medical men, or rather surgeons, for they practice not only physic but surgery; I do not say in cases of importance — on the contrary, only in more humble operations, such as bloodletting, cupping, blistering, and the like. Among these gentlemen, I thus had the chance to encounter a compatriot by name Nicolò Manucci [Manuzzi], a gentleman with great credit among the grandees, with a stipend that was the most considerable that I have come across in these lands, which is of 300 Rupees a month. I was greatly consoled by having so happy a chance, knowing how rare it was to come across Italians, let alone Venetians. I can hardly state here how much we embraced, how lively the demonstrations of affection were, how long our conversations, and the interrogations, for since he had been absent from the Patria for 30 years, he lived in great curiosity concerning the state of his intimates (even if they were not known to me), of the state of the city of Venice, and of other particularities. Once the ceremonies were over, and the many questions asked, a few days later he began seriously to discuss with me with a view to penetrate my sentiment, by asking me openly whether I desired that he should introduce me into the service of the Prince, all the while assuring me that I would thus come to possess no ordinary fortune, and offered that he himself would intervene by way of recommendations and good offices so far as His Highness was concerned. I thanked him very much for his goodwill in thus favoring me, but with the response that I

> had absolutely no wish to settle outside the Patria, and I had come there only to see those countries and their most notable things, after which my intention was to return [home] to see my blood and intimates once again. Our friend not being satisfied with this reply, asked that I should reflect on the future contingencies surrounding the death of the decrepit King [Aurangzeb], for once the Prince his son would be raised to the throne — for the Crown pertained to him as the eldest — I would then be depriving myself of nothing less than glorious acquisitions; all of these reasons had no effect on me and I replied that I had absolutely no desire to lock up my liberty, above all with Princes who possessed neither reason nor faith [*non possedono ragione ne fede*]. At this statement, our friend became more than a little confused, desiring however that I should instruct him, and remain at his side to shed a little light for him on Medicine, given that in fact he lacked letters as well as a knowledge of the [medical] art; I consoled him however on this point, telling him that I would consent to be entertained for some months, and only leave when the season changed.[53]

Coincidentally, Legrenzi's account was printed in Venice even as Manuzzi's work was on its way to Europe. But its interesting and pointed contrast, between a Legrenzi who was a cultivated and curious traveler but also a devoted patriot, and a semiliterate Manuzzi whose main interest was in accumulating a fortune in India (even if it meant settling there), does not seem to have damaged the latter's reputation in Venice. On the contrary, the reputation of Manuzzi and his work was to soar in the next few years, at least in the exalted Venetian circles that were close to the Senate. This had in part to do with his written text, but it also was linked in good measure to the reception of the book of sixty-six paintings of the "false Gentile gods," and the rituals, customs, and ceremonies of the Gentiles of India.

We can follow the trajectory of the work in early 1705, when it left Pondicherry, and its eventual arrival in Venice. We are aware that Père Eusèbe de Bourges arrived in the port of Lorient on the ship *Saint Louis* in October 1705, and made his way to Paris, and may have made contact with Catrou in order to recover the *Libro Rosso*. In early 1706 he was able to show the contents of his precious package to Lorenzo Tiepolo, Venetian ambassador in that city. Tiepolo quickly wrote to the Senate in February 1706, describing the whole encounter with a "Capuchin religious who came from the East Indies and gave me a letter directed to the Most Excellent Senate from a certain Nicolò Manuci, native of Venice, who after many circuits in the kingdom of the Mogol now lives in Madraspattan."[54] Père Eusèbe had apparently sung the praises of

Manuzzi in an unstinting fashion, describing him as a "man of talent and held in great esteem in those lands in his profession as a doctor." Tiepolo goes on to describe the text and its intention in the following manner:

> This man [Manuzzi] thus still maintaining his veneration for his natural Prince [the doge] has wanted even after so much time [in India] to render him a respectful testimonial by transmitting a long History of that vast Monarchy, together with some drawings of the portraits of those Princes, and others that represent the figures of their false Gods. The History then is pretty voluminous, written in three languages based on the availability of scribes as he states in his letter, that is part Italian, part French, and part Portuguese. It seems that the great length of the same did not permit him the required time to have it all properly rewritten and to bring it to a final state of perfection, it being written in a diverse variety of paper and with several breaks.

He then goes on to note that it would be appropriate for the Senate to write a formal letter to Manuzzi thanking him for the same, and adds that though he has not looked at the history carefully, it appears that the account is faithful; he adds, "and the figures, however they may be, have the merit of representing objects of curiosity [*oggetti di curiosità*]." In the months that followed, Tiepolo continued to correspond episodically with the Senate on the Manuzzi papers, while Père Eusèbe for his part was able to visit Venice briefly, offering the doge a gift from Manuzzi of some bezoar stones with alleged medical properties.[55] Eventually, the ambassador even managed to persuade Catrou to return the *Libro Rosso* to him, but the Jesuit seems to have refused to part with the three other volumes he held. On 25 June 1706, Tiepolo announced to the Senate that he was sending them "all the papers of Manuzzi given to me by the said Capuchin — that is those of the History, the two books of drawings, and fourteen pieces of bezoar stones"; the package arrived in Venice two weeks later.

There seems to have been very little doubt in Venice about the importance of the text, but it was nevertheless deemed necessary to have the whole work examined by a competent authority. It was thus handed over to the authoritative university council, *Riformatori dello Studio di Padova*, in late July, and in late March 1707, a report was presented to the Senate confirming the great significance of the work, but also noting the need to translate the whole into a "single language" [*un sol idioma*]. This task was eventually given to a certain Stefano Neves Cardeiraz, a professor of law in Padua, who with two of his sons began the task in 1708, and only completed it in 1712. A full Italian text now existed of the first four parts, as well as of the captions to the two books of illustrations, but it was still impossible to find a publisher for the whole. From 1706, the *Riformatori* had charged itself with this task, but was unable to come to a satisfactory conclusion with the Printers' Guild (*Stampatori*), especially in view of the costs involved in producing some 130 engravings of quality. These problems had still not been resolved in 1712, when the translation by Cardeiraz and sons was finally ready. Whatever the concrete difficulties in publication, the arrival of the text of the *Storia* in Venice was clearly a matter of some significance for the Manuzzi family itself. By 1706, two of Nicolò Manuzzi's nephews — sons of his brother Andrea — were in considerable difficulty with the law for blasphemy. One of them, also Nicolò by name (and born in 1681) had already been banished from Venice once, and then condemned to five years in the galleys for not adhering to the punishment. In April 1707, Andrea Manuzzi was able to plead successfully that his son should be let off on account of the newly discovered virtues of his brother in India; then again, in March 1708, he pleaded that his other son Antonio be left off for a similar crime, and even be given three hundred ducats to allow him to join his uncle in Madras.

Antonio Manuzzi did make the voyage to India, only to die there shortly after his arrival, aged twenty-four. His uncle wrote back with this news to Venice in February 1711, as follows: "My nephew Antonio Manuchi last year in the month of March, desirous of seeing the world [*di veder il mondo*] embarked for Bengal, from where, setting out in August with the intention of joining the company of other ships, almost all of them [the ships] managed to arrive after a fierce storm at a neighboring port, except the one on which he was, and now that seven months have passed, he has still not appeared, and the general view is that the ships sank and the poor fellow perished."[56] This letter, of February 1711, is the last trace of direct correspondence between Manuzzi and Venice. It was sent by him in the hands of a secular clergyman, Gerolamo Buzzacarino, along with some "cordials and various medicines," as well as the long-announced fifth part of his *Storia*. This volume of ninety folios had arrived in Venice by early 1713, and was rapidly handed over to Cardeiraz, who managed with his sons to finish the translation into Italian (the original being largely in Portuguese) later that year. The problem of publication grew more acute as the work expanded, for each new part rendered the *Storia* less and less coherent. Manifestly unaware of this, Manuzzi wrote in the concluding sections of part V: "With this, I come to the end of the Fifth Part; and if I am allowed the time and have the occasion to speak, I shall continue with a Sixth

Part, to give full satisfaction to the curious Reader." It is unclear whether this was now to be seen as a threat or a promise. Like part IV, this volume too was a curious confection of anecdotes and increasingly virulent diatribes directed at the Jesuits, beginning in January 1705 and moving forward and carrying matters on a mere two years, to the death of Aurangzeb. The very last lines of the text are dedicated to the inscription that appeared on the coins minted by one of the claimants, Prince Muhammad A'zam, with the title A'zam Shah, in March 1707.

Sikka zad dar jahān ba daulat-o-jāh
Pādshāh-i mamālik A'zam Shāh

Coin was struck in the world with fortune and dignity
by the Emperor of Kingdoms, A'zam Shah

Manuzzi had been writing of the imminent death of Aurangzeb for quite some time; and as we have seen, as early as 1680, he had mentioned it to the visiting Legrenzi. But, as it happened, the death of Aurangzeb followed closely on two other deaths, which affected Manuzzi greatly and seem to have sapped his desire to write beyond the fifth part. Of these other deaths, he writes: "Now I shall recount what happened to me on the fifteenth of December 1706. God was served to carry off my wife, with whom I lived together for more than twenty years, which caused me great pain, something that I had until then never felt; and as it is usual that misfortunes never come singly, the same month on the twenty-ninth, Monsieur Martin, governor of Pondicherry which is today called Fort St. Louis, died too, from which death I suffered an equal blow, for he was my old and true friend, and I had received many and great favors, grants, and honors from him."[57] In point of fact, the two deaths must have been connected in Manuzzi's mind by another fact. For it was allegedly on the advice of François Martin that he had contracted his marriage in the first place, in 1686.[58] Here is how he describes this event in an earlier part of his *Storia*, after describing his recent arrival in Madras.

> Being in Madras, all the Portuguese gentlemen who inhabited that said city, knowing of the zeal with which I had served their nation, came to visit me, offering to serve me in all that might occur to me, to whom I graciously gave the necessary thanks. Knowing that Monsieur Francesco Martin had recently arrived from Surat as General of the Royal Company of France in the city of Pulliceri [Pondicherry], I resolved to go and visit him. When I had arrived there, after

> a few days, when he saw that I had decided to return to Europe, he dissuaded me, and gave him as counsel that I should marry in India with a lady, daughter of English parents, but a Roman Catholic, living in Madrastapatan, by name Elisabetta Hardeli, natural and legitimate daughter of Cristovaro Jardeli, an Englishman who had been President of Musilpatem [Masulipatnam], and of Dona Agata Perera, a Portuguese [and] who was the widow of Thomas Kalrk, also an Englishman, and Roman Catholic, who had been a judge and lieutenant of the Governor of Madrastapaton. Under his persuasion, and that of the Reverend Capuchin Fathers, I resolved to remain in India, and returning to Madrasta, I discussed the matter with the Reverend Father Zenone, and the Father Efremo, Capuchins and French by nation, apostolic missionaries, and propagators of Christianity in that said city of Madrastapaton, from whose mouths I had information regarding the qualities of that said lady, and whom I already resolved to marry. And on the day of St. Simon and St. Jude of the year 1686 [28 October], I was married to the said lady, with whom God was served to give me a son, but Heaven did not wish that he should suffer the travails of this ungrateful world.[59]

DEFINING A PECKING ORDER

The year of his marriage can be seen as a defining point in Manuzzi's life. Earlier, as we have seen, he had attempted periodically to leave Mughal India for the Portuguese territories, but these attempts — in Goa, Bassein, Daman, and Bandra — had always ended badly. It was in 1686 that the Venetian turned his back definitively on the Mughals, and decided to live out his life with the Europeans; and, by his own admission, this was after having seriously contemplated returning to Europe. He had spent thirty-odd years in Mughal service; the remaining thirty-four years of his life were to be spent discoursing about the Mughals, and about India more generally, to an audience that he imagined existed both in Europe and among the Europeans in India. Yet, even among the Europeans, it is clear that he had his own sense of a pecking order. Despite the fact that his own wife, Elizabeth Hartley, was in fact half-Portuguese, it is evident that Manuzzi places the Portuguese lowest in his consideration. To him, they are an object lesson to the other Europeans, having once lorded it over the East, and now having sunk to a low state. Thus: "When the Portuguese were masters of India, they were rich and powerful, living in pomp and magnificence. Owing to this fact, the natives of Portugal who came thence to India, never having seen or been accustomed to such grandeur, looked with awe with their fellow countrymen in India. But this is no longer the case nowadays, for in India, they have barely enough for food, and when they marry any girl they obtain on loan almost everything that is wanted for the wedding. The day after the wedding feast, everybody comes and carries off whatever has been loaned. The greater part of the house stands empty, the bride without jewels, the black servants without ornaments."[60] Or again, he remarks acerbically: "I have noticed with this nation [the Portuguese] that if anyone gives them good advice, they are suspicious, and betray their feeling that there was no necessity for it. Sometimes they do the very contrary to what has been suggested, in order not to admit that advice has been received."[61] Large sections of the *Storia*, and in particular the fourth and fifth parts, are devoted to recounting anecdote after anecdote regarding the greed and stupidity of the Portuguese, the fact that the wives routinely cuckold their husbands, and the poor morals of both governors and governed in the Portuguese territories. In contrast, Manuzzi clearly has a far higher opinion of the English, and he declares that the inhabitants of Madras are the best disposed of any city he has encountered.[62] To be sure, he had difficulties with some of the governors of Fort St. George, but with others it is clear that he was on quite close terms. However, it is manifest that his preference is for the French, which must explain his desire (shortly after the death of his wife) to move the principal center of his operations to Pondicherry rather than Madras.

And what of India itself? Here, Manuzzi is categorical. Neither life in Mughal India nor with the Gentiles should be acceptable for any European. If one has to choose between the two, however, it is clear that the Mughals are the lesser of the two evils. Toward the close of part II, he does enter into an extended consideration regarding his own rather paradoxical life story in regard to his relationship with the Mughals. He writes:

> I well know that some who read this History will note how many times I left the lands of the Mogol, and then returned to them, [and] some will persuade themselves that those lands are some sort of Elysian fields [*campos elizios*] and it was on that account I returned to them, but in reality even if with God's favor I had the good luck to find some good fortune there, I never wanted to settle there, because in reality they do not have the things to delight or affect the mind of a person from Europe [*pessoa de Europa*] to want to stay on there, for they are good neither for the body, and even less for the soul: for the body, since it is necessary to constantly live in vigil for there are never words that can be trusted and everything must be judged suspiciously and in the opposite sense to what

> has been said, for they are perfectly accustomed to act as the proverb goes in my land: *good words and sad works mislead the wise and the foolish alike*. So, when they claim to be your greatest friends, it is necessary to watch out doubly. It is not good for the soul, both because of the liberties that there are in them, and because of the lack of Catholic observances, and so when I could withdraw from there, I did so, and never returned there save when I was obliged to by necessity, and I gave many thanks to God that in the end he gave me the means to live freely, and I assure the reader that few Europeans have been able to live with the profits and honors that I attained, and yet have not allowed themselves to be fooled with the hope that by going there [Mughal India], they could find some remedy, for there are few who emerge from there improved, and many are damaged.[63]

The lessons that Manuzzi wishes to point to are hence rather evident. There was nothing to be gained in the long term from employment with the Mughals and like powers, an option that generations of European renegades and mercenaries had attempted since the early sixteenth century. Extended passages of his text and a diversity of anecdotes evoke cases of Portuguese in particular who had attempted to make good with the Mughals, only to come to a bad end. The material regarding Maria de Ataíde, the renegade wife of the great Iranian-born *amīr* 'Ali Mardan Khan, whom he evokes at considerable length, is a rather good case in point.[64]

And yet, if one is to take Manuzzi at his word, there is worse than life with the Mughals. For beyond the pecking order of the Europeans, and far worse than cohabitation with the Moors (or Mughals), is the life that one may lead in a polity and society of the "Gentiles." The pages that Manuzzi devotes to the Gentiles are many, but the most systematic appear in the third part of his text, and in relation to the second collection of illustrations that he sent to Europe (through the mediation of Père Eusèbe de Bourges). The significant sections of the third part bear the general title "Brief Notice concerning what the Gentiles of this India believe and state regarding the essence of God," and the text itself commences with a discussion of Brahma, Vishnu, and Rudra (Shiva). However, the same section then moves on to speak of other matters regarding customs, and government, all of which are marked by the clear — and rather crushing — contempt that Manuzzi felt in regard of these peoples. Concretely, the bulk of Manuzzi's observations seem to concern the Nayaka kingdoms of southern India, and at one point he even mentions quite clearly that his observations derive in particular from the case of the Nayaka principality of Madurai.[65] Thus, his introduction to the "manner of government that they have among themselves" opens as follows: "The government of the Gentiles is the most tyrannical and the most barbarous that one can imagine, because, besides the fact that all the kings are foreigners [*étrangers*], they treat their subjects worse than slaves; all lands belong to the Crown, and there is no subject who has his own lands, or heritage, or possession of any sort that he can leave to his children."[66] There then follow passages of a considerable virulence, where one can see that Manuzzi was influenced to a great extent by the Catholic missionaries, who seem to have been among his greatest intimates in Madras and Pondicherry. The political economy of the "Gentile" kingdoms is eviscerated in some rapid pages, and Manuzzi then turns his contemptuous gaze on the manner in which the Gentiles make war. Here his attention is attracted by the lack of secrecy, the fact that the tactics and strategy of one and the other party are open for all to see, and the role played by money in resolving conflict. He notes: "It is quite normal among the Rajas of this Empire to conclude their wars through money, and the one who is the weakest is frequently the one who gains the greatest advantage, and money alone is what they love, for so far as men are concerned, none of the natives of these lands has any love, either for grandeur or for secrets." Besides, cowardice is the general rule in his view, for "almost all the soldiers in the army have their women and their children with them." Thus encumbered, with their family on the one hand, and their assorted pots and pans on the other, the soldier has nothing lower on his priorities than to fight. The Gentile soldier is quite willing to fight in one army on a certain day, and desert to the other the next day; so, Manuzzi concludes, "it is hardly to be marveled at that when the battle is considered very bloody there are fewer than a hundred dead and wounded, for as soon as the battle begins, one begins to flee from one or the other side, and they are so fearful of the cavalry that forty thousand foot soldiers will not stand up to two thousand horsemen, and as soon as they see them from afar, they begin to run faster than the horses, even if the horsemen carry no firearms."

The view that Manuzzi carries of the Gentiles can be seen most clearly perhaps in the sixty-six "ethnographic portraits" that comprise the complement to the Mughal portraits of the *Libro Rosso*. These works constitute a greater mystery from a variety of viewpoints than the "Mughal" representations. So far as the latter are concerned, we are fairly certain that they were produced by minor artists attached to the Mughal ateliers of the Deccan in the late 1670s or early 1680s. But the drawings of the so-called *Libro Nero* are more complex.[67]

An ascetic or penitent. Biblioteca Nazionale Marciana (Venice), Codice It. VI. 136, fl. 145r.

By permission of the Ministero per i Beni e le Attività Culturali—Biblioteca Nazionale Marciana.

In the first place, they do not correspond clearly to a prototype, unlike those of the *Libro Rosso*. Their composition is also somewhat more complex, since they are at times made up of numbered elements, which carry an explanation at the bottom corresponding to each number. The impression that one has is that these works were produced by more than one hand, and that they date from the Madras period of Manuzzi's life, probably from the 1690s or early 1700s. The fact that their captions are in French suggest that they were initially meant to be sent to France, something that the fiasco with Catrou eventually rendered impossible. Further, there is some evidence to suggest that the artists who painted these portrayals were Indian textile painters of the Madras region, somewhat unaccustomed no doubt to the new format that Manuzzi imposed on them, but creatively adapting the narrative modes of painting to which they were already accustomed.

Manuzzi appears to have worked quite closely with his painters, as we see from the relationship between the visual representation and the textual material that accompanies it. There is little to support his own claim, made by way of excuse to John Pitt in 1699, that he was suffering from "Infirmity and Blindness."[68] A few examples of his involvement in the *Libro Nero* shall suffice here, from among the sixty-six "ethnographic" paintings. The last of the series, for example, shows a Hindu ascetic with his arm raised in the air. This is part of a series showing various sorts of *jogīs* and ascetics, often in ridiculous positions with caricatured expressions. The commentary that accompanies it runs as follows.

> This figure represents a penitent Gentile. The long tresses that hang behind him are made of his own hair. What one sees around his arm and on top of his hand are his nails, which have grown to this prodigious length, and which he has folded and arranged in this manner. What one sees at his feet are also his nails. However indecent and dishonest this getup [*cett equipage*] might appear, I should say that I have added to it in order to cover up that which modesty does not permit to be shown; these unhappy men having no shame at all do not ever hide it; however, if one considers the opinion of the Idolaters with regard to them, one is not at all surprised, since they are greatly venerated and they believe that this getup is a mark of sainthood, and the women out of devotion will even go and kiss that which I cannot name.[69]

One may also consider the following commentary, accompanying one of several scenes involving a *satī*. The painting bears a caption, namely "deplorable events [*évenemens deplorables*]."

> Representation of the tragic end of a woman reported in my History, who having fallen in love with a player of [musical] instruments, was so carried away by her passion that she asked him to put an end to the life of her spouse in the hope of marrying the one who possessed her heart. But on being frustrated in her attempt by the refusal of this man to satisfy her in this matter, even though he had already tasted her lovemaking, she blamed herself greatly for the inhuman parricide [*sic*] that she had just committed on the person who should have been dearest in her life. This woman, distraught, passed quickly from love to rage, and

"Deplorable events," or, a Hindu cremation gone awry. Biblioteca Nazionale Marciana (Venice), Codice It. VI. 136, fl. 66v. *By permission of the Ministero per i Beni e le Attività Culturali—Biblioteca Nazionale Marciana.*

> being obliged by the cruel custom of the land to burn herself with the body of her husband, on arriving at the pyre, dragged her unhappy lover with her.[70]

And finally, we have a representation of the Tirupati temple, with the following brief set of remarks. "I should state to explain the figure opposite this, that in the Third Part of my History, I have written of the pagoda of Tarpeti in the Carnate which this portrait represents. A large number of Indians of both sexes go there out of devotion. It is usual for the Bramenis of this pagoda to choose the most beautiful among the female devotees who go there for their

The Tirupati temple. Biblioteca Nazionale Marciana (Venice), Codice It. VI. 136, fl. 85r.

By permission of the Ministero per i Beni e le Attività Culturali—Biblioteca Nazionale Marciana.

own use, under the pretext that it is the Idol which wishes to honor them with his conversation."[71]

These repeated scenes of trickery, falsity, and bad faith animate a religion and society that to Manuzzi appears even less honorable than that of the Mughals, however distasteful he finds the Mughal polity. The conclusion that one finds elsewhere in the third part is thus easy enough to understand from this perspective: "Having seen the cruelties and the bad treatment with which the Gentiles govern the natives of the land, born their subjects, it is easy enough to imagine what they do to foreigners, and that it is impossible to live among people so barbarous, and enemies of every sort of justice and reason."[72]

CONCLUSION

And yet Manuzzi did not return home, preferring to end his days in India, even if it was in the European enclaves of Pondicherry and Madras. This may represent something of an enigma. However, we do know that he made two attempts late in life to return to Europe. In his last letter to Venice of 1711, he begins by stating that four ships are presently ready to leave Pondicherry for France, and "I had wished to find a passage in one of them, being desirous to spend the rest of my days under the happy clime of Your Most Serene Dominion, and pay tribute to Death in the same native commune where I first drew breath." However, some "motives of a grave consideration" had prevented him from doing so, even though he had received express permission from the French court to embark. Again, in 1715–16, it would seem Manuzzi contemplated leaving for Europe, this time on an English ship from Madras; he once more received permission from the East India Company's Court of Committees, on condition that his "effects be invested in Diamonds and brought hither [to London] on the Company's usual terms." The Council of Fort St. George responded to London in October 1716, stating that "whenever Senhor Nicolas Manuch desires to come to England, [we] will let him; he never was deny'd; his effects will ly in little room." By way of abundant precaution, Manuzzi even appears to have contacted the Venetian ambassador in London, Niccolò Tron, to facilitate his transit through England. However, we gather that he was eventually dissuaded by friends and physicians from the voyage.[73] Neither did lack of resources seem to play a crucial part in his decision to remain in India. We are aware from the testimony of a certain Antonio Gorla, a Carmelite friar who visited Madras in 1699, that it was generally thought at the time that Manuzzi had lost "the greater part of the money he had earned at sea along with an illegitimate son he had." However, the friar visited him in his residence, inspected his rather odd medical practices (involving the making of many "cordials" and the extensive use of bezoar stones), and stated: "At the Mount where he lived, he had purchased two gardens, and had built a house which if it had been any more splendid would have been called a *palazzo*."[74] One of the last traces we have of Manuzzi comes from a suit that he filed against a Muslim resident of Madras, Khoja Baba, in late December 1718, to recover winnings at "backgammon" (perhaps *pachīsī*).[75] Age and infirmity do not seem to have prevented Manuzzi from traveling frequently between Pondicherry and Madras, and very possibly from maintaining two households, a principal one in the Rue Neuve de la Porte de Goudelour in Pondicherry, and the other at "Senhor Manuch's Garden" in Madras. It was very probably on one of his visits to Madras that Manuzzi died, aged about eighty-two, in 1720.

The text of the *Storia* was not published in the eighteenth century; the enterprise was eventually deemed far too expensive by the Venetian Senate, especially in view of the cost of the illustrations. There is every likelihood, however, that Manuzzi managed to transmit a substantial fortune to his brother in Venice, far greater than the sums mentioned in his will of 1712. On his death in 1738, Andrea Manuzzi's son Niccolò (the same who had narrowly escaped a sentence in 1708, on account of his uncle's newfound prestige) left a sum of 136,000 ducats in goods and credit, various precious objects, and a house in the countryside, as against debts of a mere 13,000 ducats.[76] Unlike another celebrated Venetian some four hundred years before him, our Nicolò Manuzzi did not return home but told his tale from afar. But his tale suggests that sometimes it pays to be an alien.

Manuzzi's skills as an artilleryman (or indeed in general as a military specialist) are certainly open to doubt. There are also good reasons to doubt the veracity of some parts of his early travel narrative, as we have seen in the case of his alleged association with Viscount Bellomont. His qualifications as a doctor were also clearly strictly of an informal kind, not based on any recognizable training, as we gather from his compatriot Legrenzi's merciless description of him as one who "lacked letters as well as a knowledge of the [medical] art." It may well be that over time he had learnt informal Indian medical practices from *faqīrs*, *siddhas*, and the like, and his own remarkable longevity in India was certainly an advertisement for whatever sort of medicine it was that he practiced (laced as it was with cordials, and spiced with bezoar stones). However, we may find in this doubtful claim to be a doctor a further source of his tensions with Bernier; while another French doctor, Biron, noted ironically in the early eighteenth century of one of Manuzzi's patent medicines, which he sold in Madras at an *écu* an ounce: "I have no idea what goes into it; this doctor keeps it a great secret."[77]

Of one central moral of his life, there is no doubt: nothing succeeds like success. As an entrepreneur, whether in matters medical, affairs of property, or questions of diplomacy, Manuzzi had a keen nose and put it to good use. But the culture he had was not, for the most part, a written one, and we must treat with the greatest of caution his claims to have unmediated access to written texts of any sort. For instance, it is clear that Manuzzi never had access to any of the major chronicles of the Mughal Empire, or the Deccan sultanates, in Persian; his Persian — unlike that of the Vecchietti brothers or the Jesuit Jerónimo Xavier in the early seventeenth century — was clearly the spoken version that was employed in the military camp and palace courtyard. His "history" of the Mughals thus cannot be tied to any recognizable tradition of written textual transmission. We must hence lay aside the outlandish claims made on his behalf by Catrou, who once stated that Manuzzi had "had access to the chronicles of the Empire of the Mogol," that he had been able to "read and transcribe the true chronicle of the Mogol," and on other occasions had even had materials "translated with all possible accuracy from the Persian of the originals in the Palace."[78] But what sort of orality did Manuzzi live in? Can we locate him in the tradition of the bazaar, and of popular perceptions of the high and mighty, as a sort of historian of the "subaltern" viewpoint? This claim has been made on behalf of more than one European writer on India, and it has even been proposed that the entire European tradition of writing on India from 1500 onward can be divided into a high, erudite, disdainful one, and a more popular and easygoing one.[79] This view, already problematic with respect to Portuguese chroniclers of the sixteenth century, works no better for Manuzzi and his *Storia*. Whatever the reasons for its incapacity to penetrate the European market, and to compete with the narratives of Bernier and Tavernier (and we have seen that these were rather complex), it was certainly not because the *Storia del Mogol* was too kind in its view of India and Indians.

Yet, we should note, the text of the *Storia* was not completely "lost" either. It had for long been supposed that with the exception of the use made of it by Catrou, the original work — with the exception of a few illustrations — had been filed away or ignored until its rediscovery by Irvine in the late nineteenth and early twentieth centuries. This is, however, not entirely true. Between 1723 and 1737, a vast work in eight tomes and nine volumes appeared in Amsterdam purporting to be nothing less than an account of "the religious ceremonies and customs of all the people of the world." Its authors were the engraver Bernard Picart and the publisher Jean-Frédéric Bernard, both linked to the skeptical *milieux* of Freemasons and other adherents of the radical Enlightenment. Their ends were deeply relativist; by placing all religions, ancient and contemporary, side by side, they probably intended to reduce them all to a somewhat similar status.[80] The work was a great success, much translated and greatly admired in particular for its illustrations, which were drawn from various sources. A copy of an English translation even found its way into the personal library of Warren Hastings. The texts and illustrations on India often have predictable sources: the writings of the English minister from Surat in the 1620s Henry Lord, for example, or the extensive and illustrated writings of the Dutch ministers Abraham Rogerius and Philippus Baldaeus (the latter drawing in turn on illustrations by earlier artists).

But one also finds in it — with no attribution — an anonymous text titled "An Historical Dissertation on the Gods of the East-Indians"; it is relatively short, at about thirty-five pages, and ends rather abruptly.[81] This text bears no direct attribution, unlike the previous excerpts in the volume. But its proximate source turns out to be a text by Charles Dellon, born in 1649, a French Huguenot physician who had traveled to Asia and been imprisoned by the Inquisition in Goa. In 1709 (and then again in 1711), there appeared a new edition of his works. In this version we find an addition, namely a section that is titled "Histoire des Dieux qu'adorent les Gentils des Indes."[82] Dellon recounts how he came upon this addition: it had originally been written in Portuguese by a very knowledgeable and very pious Portuguese priest who had spent an extended period of time in India. This priest happened to return to Portugal on the same ship as Dellon, and "on finding himself ill from scurvy, and beyond hope of any cure, placed his extract on the Religion of the Gentiles in his hands." Dellon claimed to have kept this text for a long time without translating it, but that in the end he had done so with the simple purpose of bringing out the "mad beliefs of these Indian idolaters."[83]

Here is how the "Historical Dissertation" begins, simply enough. "The Indian Idolaters, whom we call Gentiles, unanimously agree that there is one God; but there is not one among them, who does not form such Ideas to himself, as are altogether unworthy [of] the Holiness and Majesty of the Supreme Being. These mistaken People have certain Books, in which all they are to believe is contain'd, which are of as great Authority among them as the holy Scriptures with us."[84] Now it turns out that this passage, and the pages that follow it, are closely related to a section of Manuzzi's text that we have referred to briefly above, titled "Breve notizia di quel che credono e discorrono gli Gentili di quest'India circa l'essenza di Dio."[85] This was a part that had found its way to Venice, but a French copy of which was also in the possession of the Jesuit college in Paris.[86] Did Dellon plagiarize Manuzzi then, or was it the other way around? In fact, it is now increasingly clear that Manuzzi and Dellon both had the same source, namely an earlier text written by a third party or parties, and which can be found in several manuscript recensions as "Relation des erreurs qui se trouvent dans la religion des gentils malabars de coste de Coromandel dans l'Inde."[87] We cannot but savor this last irony then, for what this implies is that the acerbic views on Indian religion to which Manuzzi was happy to put his name came eventually to circulate, albeit anonymously, in published form in a text not of the Catholics, but of a skeptical project that cast doubt — among many other things — on Catholicism itself.

5 By Way of Conclusion

I besetch you good Madam speak, & lett mee know how I am, for I know whatt I am: which I will never chaundg from, thoughe I indur mor with the greatest patience ever.
—Anthony Sherley to the Countess of Cumberland (1602)[1]

My conclusion will be brief and somewhat schematic. In the preceding chapters, the method followed has essentially been one of the case study, bridging as it were the gap between microhistory and world history.[2] We have looked at three instances, running from the 1530s through to the 1720s, and in a large space that has taken us from western India to the western Mediterranean. We have examined some quite complex itineraries and processes of circulation, often—but not exclusively—framed within the world that was made by the Iberian empires of the early modern period. These empires came initially to be constructed in a Mediterranean and Atlantic context over the fifteenth century, and then mushroomed in a major way in the half century between about 1490 and 1540. By the last quarter of the sixteenth century, the Union of the Crowns of Spain and Portugal meant that the Habsburgs ruled over domains with worldwide coverage, even if the extent of their territorial control was quite limited in both Africa and Asia. Writing in the early 1620s, Anthony Sherley could address the Count-Duke of Olivares as the "sole master who guides the wheels of this great clock" of the world; and even if he was flattering him, there was a real sense here that the domain of circulation (and thus of power) was now a global one.[3]

Yet, we cannot assume that such an expansion in terms of horizons meant that those who inhabited this world made a smooth and rapid transformation from being merely rooted inhabitants of Bijapur, Sussex, or Venice, to being cosmopolitans, and thus citizens of the world. In a sense, therefore, this work has been about friction and discomfort, at both the existential and the conceptual levels. It has turned out that the three principal actors whom we have looked at here—'Ali bin Yusuf 'Adil Khan, Anthony Sherley, and Nicolò

Manuzzi—but also a whole host of other actors who dealt with them, did not assume with any level of complacency that the world was somehow their oyster. Further, it can be shown that they would have been rather foolish to assume an attitude of complacency in the face of circumstances that were in reality difficult if not altogether intractable. The question then arises of what the nature of the difficulty or intractability was.

A little more than a quarter century ago, the question of intercultural "encounters" in the Iberian empires of the early modern period was at the heart of a series of important discussions. The work of Tzvetan Todorov on "the question of the Other" in the Spanish conquest of America sparked off an extended debate on how such matters were to be addressed.[4] Todorov's preferences were to approach the question of encounters through semiotics and structural comparison, and he effectively argued that the Iberians and the Mesoamericans had entirely different and largely incompatible systems of communication at the time that Hernán Cortés and his men landed on the American mainland in 1519. If this approach opened up some valuable insights, it also left a number of puzzles to be answered. How, after all, did common Spanish soldiers function in the markets of Tenochtitlán in order to carry out day-to-day transactions while the "conquest" was being carried out? What was the nature, as well as the deeper meaning, of translation in the whole process, mediated as it was by one or perhaps more than one intervening social layer? Could one assume that the fact that communication was not merely possible but also regular after the conquest meant that one cultural system had entirely collapsed, and been folded into the other?

The great quality of Todorov's intervention lay not merely in its theoretical sophistication but also in its astute choice of example: Cortés in Mexico was after all the most dramatic of all possible early modern intercultural encounters. No matter what the Vikings had achieved some centuries before in Newfoundland, it was clear that the core populations of Europe and America had had no previous contact for many centuries preceding the Spanish landing in Yucatán. It was therefore not self-evident that the Todorov "model," even if it held true for America, could work in the Eurasian space where ideas and conceptions had regularly circulated over the centuries. Yet, emboldened perhaps by the success of Todorov's radical structural opposition, a model similar to his was proposed in the Indian context by Bernard Cohn in 1985. Cohn argued, using the instance of Sir Thomas Roe's embassy (on behalf of the English East India Company) to the court of the Mughal emperor Jahangir in the 1610s, that two entirely different cultural systems found themselves face-to-face at the moment of the embassy: while "Europeans of the seventeenth century lived in a world of signs and correspondences," they were confronted on the other side by "Hindus and Muslims [who] operated with an unbounded substantive theory of objects and persons."[5] Indians, whether Hindu or Muslim, were thus apparently more-or-less unfamiliar with the market and notions of price (including those that might operate in a context of political corruption), while Europeans like Roe apparently were wholly driven by such ideas.

It may seem strange that constructs such as these, based as they are on essentialized categories of nomenclature and identity, were thought to be convincing a mere quarter century ago. On this view, cultures are contained, watertight, and largely impermeable until and unless they are subject to the sorts of direct and epistemological violence that colonialism usually entails. Then, under conditions of subordination, cultural change may reluctantly begin, but it is a degrading and impoverishing change of a sort that Claude Lévi-Strauss famously decried in his *Tristes Tropiques*. At the time of these formulations, many would have accepted Geertz's view that culture is "an historically transmitted pattern of meanings embodied in symbols, a system of inherited conceptions expressed in symbolic forms by means of which men communicate, perpetuate, and develop their knowledge about and their attitudes toward life."[6] But Geertz significantly says nothing about the impermeability or self-sustaining nature of cultures, contenting himself to make claims regarding inheritance, on the one hand, and systematic character, on the other. This therefore leaves quite open issues of cross-cultural mediation as well as processes of cultural transformation.

We might say that the Todorov-Cohn position is heavily invested in one way or another in the incommensurability between cultures.[7] To be sure, it could be argued, one might have cultures that are more or less proximate, and thus or more or less commensurable. At the other extreme are those in more recent times who see cultures as entirely malleable and possessed of no systemic character, and individuals as wholly mobile. There are apparently no natives and no strangers, and never have been. The position is pushed to its most extreme point by a recent historian of South Asia who demands: "Where does one get a domiciliary certificate for an eighteenth-century culture"?[8] And yet, when one uses any of a number of adjectives such as "Genoese," or "Iranian," to describe eighteenth-century actors, something that historians constantly do, a statement is indeed being made about belonging not merely to a place but to a culture. One can therefore still return usefully to Georg Simmel's brief but important analysis on the "stranger" (titled "Exkurs über den Fremden") from a century ago, despite one's discomfort with the transhistorical and transcultural nature of his claims. The stranger, Simmel notes, "is fixed within a spatial group, or within a group whose boundaries are similar to spatial boundaries. But his position in this group is determined, essentially, by the fact that he has not belonged to it from the beginning [*dass er nicht von vornherein in ihn gehört*], that he imports qualities into it, which do not and cannot stem from the group itself." The most obvious such stranger is of course the trader, but one can easily expand the category to include other sorts of go-betweens, or *passeurs*.[9] Simmel concludes his brief reflection by noting that "in spite of being inorganically appended to it, the stranger is yet an organic member of the group. . . . Only we do not know how to designate the peculiar unity of this position other than by saying that it is composed of certain measures of nearness and distance."[10]

Now the term *Fremd* can of course equally be translated as "alien," and to that extent Simmel's essay surely speaks directly to the contents of this book. Our three instances are clearly illustrative of different aspects of the problem of the "alien" in the context of the early modern world. In the case of 'Ali bin Yusuf, the prince from Bijapur, we witness a multiple displacement: originating in a Turkoman family from Iran, this Persophone aristocrat grew up in the Deccan, then fled to Gujarat, and eventually spent about half of his life with the Portuguese in Goa, but remained a Muslim in the midst of the Counter-Reformation. This aspect of his cultural difference was in fact deliberately maintained by the Portuguese, as part of a political strategy to ensure that he could return to Bijapur as sultan when the occasion presented itself, but it also reflects his consistent image as a "great observer of Muhammad [*grande observador de Maphoma*]." We may recall, too, the manner in which his son Yusuf Khan presented himself to Philip II in the early 1580s: "I was born here [Goa] and was brought up here with nothing lacking for me to be a native except that I was of another law [*sem me faltar nada pera natural mais que ser doutra ley*]." Later generations of the family would assimilate entirely, taking "Meale" as a family name and being entirely absorbed into the petty Iberian overseas aristocracy. Does the case of 'Ali bin Yusuf correspond then to one where "personal identity has to be continually made, and is continually revised and remade, throughout an individual career in contingent social and cultural settings"?[11] This view, of the "self as a protean cultural artifact," does not to my mind render much justice to this situation, or to the heavy constraints within which choices were made (and which the weak concept of "settings" hardly clarifies).[12]

With Anthony Sherley, we seem to move to another aspect of Simmel's presentation of the "stranger." For Sherley's espousal and development of realpolitik on a world scale corresponds precisely to "the objectivity of the stranger," which is not at all an attitude of nonparticipation but rather an attitude "which allows the stranger to experience and treat even his close relationships as though from a bird's-eye view [*aus der Vogelperspektive*]." To be sure, this was very much a conceit and even a form of artifice on the part of Sherley. It also allowed him to positively valorize himself, and to claim that he alone could carry out a certain number of tasks. At the same time, it made him the object of continuous suspicion, as an "inconstant" man of infinite projects, but also as someone whose very religion was open to question.[13] We have noted Sherley's ostensible conversion to Catholicism after his return from Iran, but many of his contemporaries seem to have seen this as a form of dissimulation, or at least an act of convenience rather than conviction. This may in part have accounted, along with a number of other factors, for his reluctance to return to England after 1600 (and the fact that he never did so until the end of his life).

If Sherley can be added to the gallery of those who made up what has been termed the "Age of Dissimulation," the trajectory of Nicolò Manuzzi is quite distinct from it.[14] Contrary to what has sometimes been claimed, Manuzzi may have lied or prevaricated regularly about events, and the extent of his wealth, the depth of his medical knowledge, or even the state of his eyesight, but there is little evidence that he donned masks with regard to his identity as a Catholic and a Venetian. While his compatriot and acquaintance Legrenzi may have criticized him for his excessive proximity to the Mughals, "princes who possessed neither reason nor faith [*non possedono ragione ne fede*]," he did not imply that Manuzzi had converted to Islam as so many other Europeans in the Mughal domains at the time did. To be sure, Manuzzi was a far more playful character than many, but he clearly saw little interest in giving up either his religion (to which he was, by all evidence, very devoted) or the positive benefits he derived from being a "Frank," whether as artilleryman or medicine man. On the contrary, he eventually seems in an interesting way to have translated this received identity as Frank (*firangī*, in Persian) to his own notion that while he was Venetian and Italian, his primary affinities in India were—in that order—with the French and the English, and that he was therefore a "European." 'Ali bin Yusuf died in Goa, very probably in a state of acute disgruntlement with the Portuguese administration and with the tolling bells of his Jesuit neighbors, and never managed to return to Bijapur. Anthony

Sherley died in Granada, none too prosperous perhaps, but still able even in the last decade of his life to have the ear of kings and powerful ministers. Nicolò Manuzzi too died as an alien in an Indian exile, but it was one that he chose, for we have seen that he could certainly have returned to Europe after 1706. Perhaps his health and advancing age made him nervous about such a long voyage. Or, then again, it may be that he had crossed a threshold, and would have been no less of an alien in Venice had he returned there — like a Rip van Winkle *avant la lettre* — after an absence of a half-century and more. It is not space alone, but time too that can make one a stranger.

Notes

1. INTRODUCTION

1. Annamayya, *God on the Hill: Temple Poems from Tirupati*, trans. Velcheru Narayana Rao and David Shulman (New York, 2005), p. 5.
2. Jean Aubin, *Le Latin et l'Astrolabe, III: Études inédites sur le règne de D. Manuel, 1495–1521* (Paris, 2006), p. 211.
3. Yahya himself signed his letters in Arabic as Abu Zakariya Yahya bin Muhammad, with Ta'fuft being a place-name; cf. Bernard Rosenberger, "Yaḥyā U Tā'fuft, 1506–1518: Des ambitions déçues," *Hespéris-Tamuda* 31 (1993): 21–59, reference on p. 21.
4. In this context, see for instance Miles Ogborn, *Global Lives: Britain and the World, 1550–1800* (Cambridge, 2008).
5. See the wide-ranging, but rather inconclusive, survey by Sabina Loriga, "La biographie comme problème," in Jacques Revel, ed., *Jeux d'échelles: La microanalyse à l'expérience* (Paris, 1996), pp. 209–31.
6. Pierre Bourdieu, "L'illusion biographique," *Actes de la Recherche en Sciences sociales* 62–63 (1986): 69–72. Significantly, in this brief essay, Bourdieu cites the theorist and practitioner of the *nouveau roman* Alain Robbe-Grillet. His main concern appears to be to restitute the fragmentary and nonteleological content in the account of a life.
7. Jacques Le Goff, *Saint Louis* (Paris, 1996). Also see the review of the book by William Chester Jordan in *Speculum* 72, no. 2 (1997): 518–20, which concludes by reminding us that Le Goff's question "is not a call to the extreme and nihilistic critiques of some armchair postmodernists; it is rather an earnest exhortation to new and profounder engagement with the sources of the past."
8. Roland Barthes, "Le discours de l'histoire," in Barthes, *Œuvres complètes, Tome II, 1966–1973*, ed. Éric Marty (Paris, 1994), pp. 417–27.
9. Support given to variants of the concept of the "modal biography" seems to derive largely from this position. For examples of biographical studies of such a type, see Paul S. Seaver, *Wallington's World: A Puritan Artisan in Seventeenth-Century London* (Stanford, 1985); Jacques-Louis Ménétra, *Journal of My Life*, introduction and commentary by Daniel Roche, trans. Arthur Goldhammer (New York, 1986); Alain Corbin, *The Life of an Unknown: The Rediscovered World of a Clog Maker in 19th-Century France*, trans. Arthur Goldhammer (New York, 2001). For a South Asian example, see Rupert Snell, "Confessions of a 17th-

Century Jain Merchant: The *Ardhakathānak* of Banārasīdās," *South Asia Research* 25, no. 1 (2005): 79–104.

10. Edoardo Grendi, "Microanalisi e storia sociale," *Quaderni storici* 35 (1977): 506–20; for a useful reflection on this author and his work, see Osvaldo Raggio and Angelo Torre, "Prefazione," in Edoardo Grendi, *In altri termini: Etnografia e storia di una società di antico regime* (Milan, 2004), pp. 5–34. It is of course an elementary fact that one cannot reconstruct a distribution from a single observation. For an interesting attempt to reconcile microhistory and a statistical approach, see Raul Merzario, *Il paese stretto: Strategie matrimoniali nella diocesi di Como, secoli XVI–XVIII* (Turin, 1981), which has in turn been critiqued for abandoning the larger context by Cristiana Torti, "Un paese troppo stretto? A proposito di un libro di Raul Merzario," *Società e storia* 17 (1982): 657–82. An attempt to reconcile various quite disparate positions may be found in Giovanni Levi, "Les usages de la biographie," *Annales ESC* 44, no. 6 (1989): 1325–36, which already differs from the position taken by the same author in his study of the exorcist Giovan Battista Chiesa; see Levi, *Inheriting Power: The Story of an Exorcist,* trans. Lydia G. Cochrane (Chicago, 1988).
11. Roberta Garner, "Jacob Burckhardt as a Theorist of Modernity: Reading *The Civilization of the Renaissance in Italy,*" *Sociological Theory* 8, no. 1 (1990): 48–57. For the original text, see Jacob Burckhardt, *Die Kultur der Renaissance in Italien,* ed. Horst Günther (Frankfurt, 1989). For Cellini's text, see Orazio Bacci, ed., *La vita di Benvenuto Cellini* (Florence, 1961).
12. Inevitably, Burckhardt's view has not been retained by modern scholarship; cf. Victoria C. Gardner, "*Homines non nascuntur, sed figuntur*: Benvenuto Cellini's *Vita* and the Self-presentation of the Renaissance Artist," *Sixteenth Century Journal* 28, no. 2 (1997): 447–65. Also see the implicit counterargument (and attempt to "rescue" Burckhardt, and in passing throw a lifeline to the Renaissance), in Randolph Starn, "A Postmodern Renaissance?" *Renaissance Quarterly* 60, no. 1 (2007): 1–24.
13. Stephen J. Greenblatt, *Renaissance Self-fashioning: From More to Shakespeare* (Chicago, 1980), pp. 2–9. For a critical but appreciative reading, see John Martin, "Inventing Sincerity, Refashioning Prudence: The Discovery of the Individual in Renaissance Europe," *The American Historical Review* 102, no. 5 (1997): 1309–42.
14. Greenblatt, *Renaissance Self-fashioning,* p. 9.
15. Vincent J. Cornell, "Socioeconomic Dimensions of Reconquista and Jihad in Morocco: Portuguese Dukkala and the Sadid Sus, 1450–1557," *International Journal of Middle East Studies* 22, no. 4 (1990): 379–418, discussion on 386–87. Cornell's characterization depends heavily on the earlier work by Ahmad Bushurrab (Boucharb), *Dukkālah wa'l-isti'mār al-Burtughālī ilā sanat ikhlā'Asafī wa-Azammūr (-qabla 28 Ghusht 1481 — Uktūbir 1541)* (Casablanca, 1984). For remarks on this work, see Rosenberger, "Yaḥyā U Tā'fuft, 1506–1518," p. 52.

16. Matthew T. Racine, "Service and Honor in Sixteenth-Century Portuguese North Africa: Yahya-u-Ta'fuft and Portuguese Noble Culture," *Sixteenth Century Journal* 32, no. 1 (2001): 67–90.
17. Racine, "Service and Honor," pp. 88–89. Here, Racine interestingly links his discussion with that in Mervyn James, *English Politics and the Concept of Honour, 1485–1642* (Oxford, 1978).
18. On Ataíde, see André Pinto Teixeira, "Nuno Fernandes de Ataíde, o nunca está quedo, capitão de Safim," in João Paulo Oliveira e Costa, ed., *A Nobreza e a Expansão: Estudos biográficos* (Cascais, 2000), pp. 159–205.
19. For these and other details, see Maria Augusta Lima Cruz, "Mouro para os Cristãos e Cristão para os Mouros — O caso Bentafufa," *Anais de História de Além-Mar* 3 (2002): 39–63.
20. Aubin, *Le Latin et l'Astrolabe, III*, pp. 194–96.
21. Aubin, *Le Latin et l'Astrolabe, III*, p. 210.
22. It has also been suggested that his death in 1518 was a key moment permitting the conquest of Marrakesh by the Sa'di dynasty; Mercedes García-Arenal, "*Mahdī, Murābiṭ, Sharīf*: L'avènement de la dynastie sa'dienne," *Studia Islamica* 71 (1990): 77–114, especially p. 111: "En 1518, mourut Yaḥyā ibn Ta'fuft, et avec lui disparut le principal rival des Sa'diens."
23. Daniel J. Vitkus, "Turning Turk in Othello: The Conversion and Damnation of the Moor," *Shakespeare Quarterly* 48, no. 2 (1997): 145–76.
24. Abraham Rute has often been confused with Abraham Ben Zamerro; this confusion has been definitively resolved by José Alberto Rodrigues da Silva Tavim, *Os Judeus e a expansão portuguesa em Marrocos durante o século XVI* (Braga, 1997), pp. 195–203.
25. Racine, "Service and Honor," pp. 89–90. Compare Rosenberger, "Yaḥyā U Tā'fuft, 1506–1518," p. 53: "Au Portugal, les mœurs de l'aristocratie, au sein de laquelle Yaḥyā a vécu, restaient fortement marqués par la féodalité. Si l'on met à part les différences religieuses, la distance entre cette société et celle d'où il provenait n'était pas aussi grande que le fosse qui séparait cette dernière du monde occidental au XIXe ou au XXe siècle."
26. Instituto dos Arquivos Nacionais/Torre do Tombo, Lisbon (henceforth IAN/TT), Corpo Cronológico, I-108–94, letter from Dom Antão de Noronha to Queen Dona Catarina, Goa, 22 December 1567, in Josef Wicki, "Dokumente und Briefe aus der Zeit des indischen Vizekönigs D. Antão de Noronha (1563–1568)," *Aufsätze zur portugiesischen Kulturgeschichte* 1 (1960): 280.
27. Bartolomé Bennassar and Lucile Bennassar, *Les chrétiens d'Allah: L'histoire extraordinaire des renégats, XVIe et XVIIe siècles* (Paris, 1989); from a different perspective, see Ellen G. Friedman, *Spanish Captives in North Africa in the Early Modern Age* (Madison, 1983).
28. See the useful overview in Mercedes García-Arenal, "Les conversions

d'Européens à l'islam dans l'histoire: Esquisse générale," *Social Compass* 46, no. 3, 1999): 273–81. For a pioneering study on Portuguese Asia, see Maria Augusta Lima Cruz, "Exiles and Renegades in Early Sixteenth-Century Portuguese India," *The Indian Economic and Social History Review* 23, no. 3 (1986): 249–62. Also see the wide-ranging but rather unsystematic view in G. V. Scammell, "European Exiles, Renegades and Outlaws and the Maritime Economy of Asia c. 1500–1750," *Modern Asian Studies* 26, no. 4 (1992): 641–61; and, for an analysis of more recent times, Linda Colley, "Going Native, Telling Tales: Captivity, Collaborations and Empire," *Past and Present* 168 (2000): 170–93.

29. Jean Cantineau, "Lettre du Moufti d'Oran aux musulmans d'Andalousie," *Journal Asiatique* 210 (1927): 1–17; L. P. Harvey, "Crypto-Islam in Sixteenth-Century Spain," in *Actas del Primer Congreso de Estudios Arabes e Islamicos* (Madrid, 1964), pp. 163–81. The use of the term *taqiyya* is often attributed to this text, but without a clear source.

30. Leila Sabbagh, "La religion des moriscos entre deux fatwas," in *Les morisques et leur temps* (Paris, 1983), pp. 45–56; more recently, Devin Stewart, "The Identity of 'The *Muftī* of Oran,' Abū l-'Abbās Aḥmad b. Abī Jum'ah al-Maghrāwī al-Wahrānī (d. 917/1511)," *Al-Qanṭara* 27, no. 2 (2006): 265–311.

31. Kathryn A. Miller, "Muslim Minorities and the Obligation to Emigrate to Islamic Territory: Two *fatwās* from Fifteenth-Century Granada," *Islamic Law and Society* 7, no. 2 (2000): 256–88. The essay reviews earlier conclusions in an important essay by Khaled Abou El Fadl, "Islamic Law and Muslim Minorities: The Juristic Discourse on Muslim Minorities from the Second/Eighth to the Eleventh/Seventeenth Centuries," *Islamic Law and Society* 1, no. 2 (1994): 141–87.

32. Pieter Sjoerd van Koningsveld and Gerard A. Wiegers, "The Islamic Statute of the Mudejars in the Light of a New Source," *Al-Qanṭara* 17, no. 1 (1996): 19–59; also Van Koningsveld and Wiegers, "Islam in Spain during the Early Sixteenth Century: The Views of the Four Chief Judges in Cairo (Introduction, Translation, and Arabic Text)," in Otto Zwartjes, Geert Jan van Gelder, and Ed de Moor, eds., *Poetry, Politics and Polemics: Cultural Transfer between the Iberian Peninsula and North Africa* (Amsterdam, 1996), pp. 133–52.

33. The wide-ranging but problematic work by Perez Zagorin, *Ways of Lying: Dissimulation, Persecution, and Conformity in Early Modern Europe* (Cambridge, Mass., 1990), addresses a number of diverse instances. On theological perspectives among Shi'is, see Etan Kohlberg, "Some Imāmī-shī'ī Views on *Taqiyya*," *Journal of the American Oriental Society* 95, no. 3 (1975): 395–402.

34. See the early work by Carlo Ginzburg, *Il nicodemismo: Simulazione e dissimulazione religiosa nell'Europa del '500* (Turin, 1970).

35. David Turnbull, *Masons, Tricksters and Cartographers: Comparative Studies in the Sociology of Scientific and Indigenous Knowledge* (Amsterdam, 2000); more recently, Natalie Zemon Davis, *Trickster Travels: A Sixteenth-Century Muslim*

between Worlds (New York, 2006), pp. 188–90, passim. Here, Davis studies the trajectory of Hasan al-Wazzan or Leo Africanus, initially suggests that he might have justified his dissimulation through the idea of taqiyya, but concludes on a speculative tone that "this crafty and curious bird had more in play than taqiyya alone."

36. James Clifford, *The Predicament of Culture: Twentieth-Century Ethnography, Literature, and Art* (Cambridge, Mass., 1988), p. 17.
37. John H. Humins, "Squanto and Massasoit: A Struggle for Power," *The New England Quarterly* 60, no. 1 (1987): 54–70; Neal Salisbury, "Squanto: Last of the Patuxets," in David Sweet and Gary B. Nash, eds., *Struggle and Survival in Colonial America* (Berkeley, 1981), pp. 228–44.
38. Arnold Krupat, "Ethnographic Conjuncturalism: The Work of James Clifford," in Krupat, *Ethnocriticism: Ethnography, History, Literature* (Berkeley, 1992), p. 113.
39. Alan Holder, "'What Marvelous Plot . . . Was Afoot?': History in Barth's *The Sot-Weed Factor*," *American Quarterly* 20, no. 3 (1968): 596–604.
40. Philippe Jacquin, *Les Indiens blancs: Français et Indiens en Amérique de Nord, XVIe–XVIIIe siècle* (Montreal, 1996).
41. Manfred Puetz, "John Barth's *The Sot-Weed Factor*: The Pitfalls of Mythopoesis," *Twentieth Century Literature* 22, no. 4 (1976): 454–66, quotation on 459.
42. For a classic case of sixteenth-century imposture, see Miriam Eliav-Feldon, "Invented Identities: Credulity in the Age of Prophecy and Exploration," *Journal of Early Modern History* 3, no. 3 (1999): 203–32. For a seventeenth-century Mughal-Safavid instance, see Jorge Flores and Sanjay Subrahmanyam, "The Shadow Sultan: Succession and Imposture in the Mughal Empire, 1628–1640," *Journal of the Economic and Social History of the Orient* 47, no. 1 (2004): 80–121.
43. There is a considerable literature on Nikitin. See, most recently, Mary Jane Maxwell, "Afanasii Nikitin: An Orthodox Russian's Spiritual Voyage in the *Dar al-Islam*, 1468–1475," *Journal of World History* 17, no. 3 (2006): 243–66.
44. An early and important work is that of Margaret T. Hodgen, *Early Anthropology in the Sixteenth and Seventeenth Centuries* (Philadelphia, 1964); also see the later, but still classic, work of Anthony Pagden, *The Fall of Natural Man: The American Indian and the Origins of Comparative Ethnology* (Cambridge, 1982).
45. See Robert Bartlett, *Gerald of Wales, 1146–1223* (Oxford, 1982).
46. André Miquel, *La Géographie humaine du monde musulman jusqu'au milieu du XIe siècle*, 4 vols. (Paris, 1967–88), especially vol. II, *La représentation de la terre et de l'étranger*; Felicia J. Hecker, "A Fifteenth-Century Chinese Diplomat in Herat," *Journal of the Royal Asiatic Society*, ser. 3, 3, no. 1 (1993): 86–98; and, for a very wide-ranging collection on these themes, see Stuart Schwartz, ed., *Implicit Understandings: Observing, Reporting, and Reflecting on the Encounters between Europeans and Other Peoples in the Early Modern Era* (New York, 1994).

47. Bernard Cohn, "The Census, Social Structure and Objectification in South Asia," in Cohn, *An Anthropologist among the Historians and Other Essays* (Delhi, 1987), pp. 224–54; Nicholas B. Dirks, "Castes of Mind," *Representations* 37 (1992): 56–78.
48. Eric Hobsbawm and Terence Ranger, eds., *The Invention of Tradition* (Cambridge, 1983).
49. Abner Cohen, "Cultural Strategies in the Organization of Trading Diaspora," in Claude Meillassoux, ed., *The Development of Indigenous Trade and Markets in West Africa* (London, 1971), pp. 266–81; Philip Curtin, *Cross-cultural Trade in World History* (Cambridge, 1984).
50. See Ina Baghdiantz McCabe, Gelina Harlaftis, and Ioanna Pepelasis Minoglou, eds., *Diaspora Entrepreneurial Networks: Four Centuries of History* (Oxford, 2005).
51. For the Indian case, see the recent survey of literature by Bhaswati Bhattacharya, "Armenian-European Relationship in India, 1500–1800: No Armenian Foundation for European Empire?" *Journal of the Economic and Social History of the Orient* 48, no. 2 (2005): 277–322.
52. Nicolas de Nicolay, *Dans l'empire de Soliman le Magnifique*, ed. Marie-Christine Gomez-Géraud and Stéphane Yérasimos (Paris, 1989).
53. George Roques, *La manière de négocier aux Indes, 1676–1691: La compagnie des Indes et l'art du commerce,* ed. Valérie Bérinstain (Paris, 1996), pp. 147–49.
54. Edmund M. Herzig, "The Deportation of the Armenians in 1604–1605 and Europe's Myth of Shah Abbas I," in Charles Melville, ed., *Persian and Islamic Studies in Honor of P. W. Avery* (Cambridge, 1990), pp. 59–71.
55. Glenn Joseph Ames, "Colbert's Indian Ocean Strategy of 1664–1674: A Reappraisal," *French Historical Studies* 16, no. 3 (1990): 536–59.
56. Gabriel Rantoandro, "Un marchand arménien au service de la Compagnie française des Indes: Marcara Avanchinz," *Archipel* 17 (1979): 99–114; Ina Baghdiantz McCabe, *The Shah's Silk for Europe's Silver: The Eurasian Trade of the Julfa Merchants in Safavid Iran and India (1530–1750)* (Atlanta, 1999), pp. 295–325.
57. C. R. Boxer, ed., *A True Description of the Mighty Kingdoms of Japan & Siam, by François Caron & Joost Schouten; Reprinted from the English Edition of 1663* (London, 1935); the original Dutch text was published in The Hague in 1662.
58. McCabe, *The Shah's Silk,* pp. 317–18. In anonymous pamphlets circulated in Paris at the time of the trial, Marcara was also described as the "son of a butcher, a horse-groom, a rag-and-bone picker."
59. Sebouh Aslanian, "Social Capital, 'Trust' and the Role of Networks in Julfan Trade: Informal and Semi-formal Institutions at Work," *Journal of Global History* 1 (2006): 383–402.
60. García-Arenal, "Les conversions d'Européens," p. 277.

61. Wheeler M. Thackston, ed. and trans., *The Baburnama: Memoirs of Babur, Prince and Emperor* (New York, 2002), p. 3.

2. A MUSLIM PRINCE IN COUNTER-REFORMATION GOA

1. Fr. Fernão de Álvares at Daman to António de Quadros at Goa, 19 February 1561, in Josef Wicki, ed., *Documenta Indica, V (1561–1563)* (Rome, 1958), doc. 18, p. 107.
2. Biblioteca Nacional de Madrid, Ms. 3217, "Livro das cidades, e fortalezas, que a Coroa de Portugal tem nas partes da Índia, e das capitanias, e mais cargos que nellas há, e da importância delles," facsimile edition by Francisco Paulo Mendes da Luz, *Studia* 6, 1960, fls. 5r–5v.
3. One of the best discussions of the topography of the city remains Boies Penrose, *Goa — Rainha do Oriente* (Goa — Queen of the East) (Lisbon, 1960), pp. 50–75, with the maps of Linschoten and Erédia.
4. See José Nicolau da Fonseca, *An Historical and Archaeological Sketch of the City of Goa* (preceded by a short statistical account of the territory of Goa) (Bombay, 1878), map facing p. 111.
5. Catarina Madeira Santos, *"Goa é a chave de toda a Índia": Perfil politico da capital do Estado da Índia (1505–1570)* (Lisbon, 1999), pp. 211–78.
6. For the fiscal structure of the Bijapur Sultanate, see Hiroshi Fukazawa, "The Local Administration of the Adilshahi Sultanate (1489–1686)," in Fukazawa, *The Medieval Deccan: Peasants, Social Systems and States (Sixteenth to Eighteenth Centuries)* (Delhi, 1991), pp. 1–48. Less helpful is the older study by Iftikhar Ahmed Ghauri, "Central Structure of the Kingdom of Bijapur," *Islamic Culture* 44, no. 1 (1970): 19–33, which tends to read backward from the seventeenth century.
7. Georg Schurhammer, *Francis Xavier: His Life, His Times*, trans. M. Joseph Costelloe, 4 vols. (Rome, 1973–82), especially vol. II, *India, 1541–1544*.
8. Teotónio R. de Souza, *Goa Medieval: A Cidade e o Interior no Século XVII* (Lisbon, 1994), pp. 111–12. The wider discussion of Goa's population in M. N. Pearson, "Goa during the First Century of Portuguese Rule," *Itinerario* 8, no. 1 (1984): 36–57, is helpful but rather opaque at times. He suggests an urban population of about 60,000 in the 1580s, and also proposes that the rural population comprised a far higher proportion of Hindus than Christians, even as late as the 1630s.
9. "Relazione dell'Impero Ottomano del clarissimo Daniele Barbarigo tornato bailo da Costantinopoli nel 1564," in Eugenio Albèri, ed., *Relazioni degli Ambnasciatori veneti al Senato*, serie III, vol. III (Florence, 1844), p. 9.
10. See Gülru Necipoğlu, *The Age of Sinan: Architectural Culture in the Ottoman Empire* (Princeton, N.J., 2005).
11. Indeed, as late as 1753, the number of Muslims in Goa was still 298, or 0.2% of the

population: 23 in Ilhas, 62 in Bardez, and 213 in Salsete. In 1781, the number in Bardez was 159, and in 1793 it had come down to 56: Maria de Jesus dos Mártires Lopes, *Goa Setecentista: Tradição e Modernidade (1750–1800)* (Lisbon, 1996), pp. 88–90. For a panoramic though rather suspect synthesis, see Alberto C. Germano da Silva Correia, *Les Musulmans de l'Inde Portugaise: Histoire, Démographie, Anthropométrie, Morphologie médicale, Anthropo-sérologie, Ethnographie* (Bastorá, 1937).

12. Fr. Luís Fróis at Goa to the Society of Jesus in Coimbra, 30 November 1557, in Josef Wicki, ed., *Documenta Indica, III (1553–1557)* (Rome, 1954), doc. 111, p. 728. Fróis (1532–97) is best known for his massive *História de Japam*, ed. José Wicki, 5 vols. (Lisbon, 1976–84).
13. Fr. Luís Fróis at Goa to Father Francisco Rodrigues in Lisbon, 12 December 1557, in Wicki, ed., *Documenta Indica, III (1553–1557)*, doc. 113, pp. 732–43. The Portuguese word *moçafo*, derived from the Arabic *muṣḥaf*, means the collected writings integrated into the Qur'an, brought together into a fixed order in the form of a volume. The phrase is thus somewhat redundant.
14. Jorge Manuel dos Santos Alves, *Um porto entre dois impérios: Estudos sobre Macau e as relações luso-chinesas* (Macao, 1999), pp. 68–82; Georg Schurhammer, "Doppelgänger in Portugiesisch-Asien," in Schurhammer, *Gesammelte Studien*, ed. László Szilas, 4 vols. in 5 parts (Lisbon, 1962–65), *Orientalia*, pp. 139–42.
15. Maria Toscana de Brito (or Toscano de Brito) belonged to an important family in Portuguese Asia; in the letter by Fróis, he mentions "three or four brothers of Maria Toscana," among whom we know in particular of Gil de Góis and Jorge Toscano de Lacerda.
16. Sebastião Gonçalves, *Primeira Parte da História dos Religiosos da Companhia de Jesus e do que fizeram com a divina graça na conversão dos infieis a nossa sancta fee cathólica nos reynos e províncias da Índia Oriental*, ed. Josef Wicki, 3 vols. (Coimbra, 1957–62), vol. II, pp. 331–34; also see Alessandro Valignano, *Historia del principio y progresso de la Compañía de Jesús en las Indias Orientales (1542–64)*, ed. Josef Wicki (Rome, 1944), pp. 349–52.
17. Some of these themes and materials have already been dealt with in an earlier essay, namely Sanjay Subrahmanyam, "Notas sobre um rei congelado: O caso de Ali bin Yusuf Adil Khan, chamado Mealecão," in Rui Manuel Loureiro e Serge Gruzinski, eds., *Passar as fronteiras: II Colóquio Internacional sobre Mediadores Culturais, séculos XV a XVIII* (Lagos, 1999), pp. 265–290.
18. On this subject, see P.S.S. Pissurlencar, *Agentes da diplomacia portuguesa na Índia* (Bastorá-Goa, 1952); also, Peter J. Bury, "The Indian Contribution to Portuguese Rule in the East, 1500–1580" (Ph.D. diss., Cambridge University, 1975). There are also several studies by the English historian Geoffrey Scammell, of somewhat limited value; see, for example, G. V. Scammell, "Indigenous Assistance in the Establishment of Portuguese Power in the Indian Ocean," in John Correia-

Afonso, ed., *Indo-Portuguese History: Sources and Problems* (Bombay, 1981), pp. 163–73.

19. Diogo do Couto, *Da Ásia, Década IV* (Lisbon, 1778), book 10, pp. 426–29, passim; Gaspar Correia, *Lendas da Índia,* ed. M. Lopes de Almeida, 4 vols. (Oporto, 1975), vol. III, pp. 639–44, 869; vol. IV, pp. 25–26, 314–17, 331–34, passim.
20. B S. Shastry, "Identification of 'Mealecão,' the Rebel Prince of Bijapur," *Indica* 20, no. 1 (1983)): 17–24.
21. Some Indian historians who did not consult the Portuguese printed sources directly (and even less the archives) have helped to confound the confusion; see, for instance, P. M. Joshi, "Relations between the Adilshahi Kingdom of Bijapur and the Portuguese at Goa during the Sixteenth Century," in S. M. Katre and P. K. Gode, eds., *A Volume of Indian and Iranian Studies: Presented to Sir E. Denison Ross* (Bombay, 1939), pp. 161–70, or even M. A. Nayeem, *External Relations of the Bijapur Kingdom (1489–1686 AD): A Study in Diplomatic History* (Hyderabad, 1974), pp. 218–24.
22. The correct version is "Sāwawī" or "Sāwajī," of which "Sawā'ī" appears to be an Indianization. I am grateful to John Gurney for pointing this out. Sawaji was the form used by the celebrated poet Salman Sawaji (d. 1376).
23. D. Fernando de Castro, *Crónica do Vice-Rei D. João de Castro,* ed. Luís de Albuquerque and Teresa Travassos Cortez da Cunha Matos (Tomar, 1995), pp. 49–50. Oddly, the author of this text identifies Meale as the "brother-in-law" (*cunhado*) of Ibrahim 'Adil Shah.
24. For the relevant passage from Firishta, see Muhammad Qasim Hindushah Astarabadi 'Firishta,' *Tārīkh-i Firishta: Muslim 'ahd kī 'aẓīm tarīkhī dāstān kā mustanad aur mu'arkata ālārā muraqqa'*, Urdu trans. by Khwaja 'Abdul Ha'i, 2 vols. (Lahore, 1962). For a discussion of the credibility of this version (or lack thereof) in the eyes of other contemporary writers, see T. N. Devare, *A Short History of Persian Literature at the Bahmani, the Adilshahi and the Qutbshahi Courts* (Pune, 1961), pp. 67–68. According to Rafi'-ud-Din, Sultan Mahmud Beg was killed during the rule of the Aqqoyunulu dynasty in Iran; his son Yusuf then moved from Sawah to Isfahan, then to Shiraz, and eventually to the Deccan; he claimed to have heard this version in about 1560 at the 'Adil Shahi necropolis in Gogi from a ninety-year-old man called Shams-ud-Din Khizri. For this neglected chronicler, also see Devare, *A Short History*, pp. 312–18, which gives his lifetime as 947–1020 H/1540–1612 CE, and which also summarizes his career usefully; and Iqtidar Alam Khan, "The Tazkirat ul-Muluk by Rafi'uddin Ibrahim Shirazi: As a Source on the History of Akbar's Reign," *Studies in History*, n.s., 2, no. 1 (1980): 41–55.
25. On the history of Bijapur, see the important study by Richard M. Eaton, *Sufis of Bijapur, 1300–1700: Social Roles of Sufis in Medieval India* (Princeton, N.J., 1978); and for a general account of the political history of the Sultanate, H. K. Sherwani

and P. M. Joshi, eds., *History of Medieval Deccan, 1295–1724*, 2 vols. (Hyderabad, 1973–74).

26. For inscriptions of Isma'il under the title 'Adil Khan, see the series *Epigraphia Indo-Moslemica*, 19 vols. (Calcutta, 1909–50), *Epigraphia Indo-Moslemica, 1931–32*, p. 19, inscription from a mosque in Sagar or Nusratabad (Gulbarga), 931 H/1524–25 CE; and *Epigraphia Indo-Moslemica, 1931–32*, p. 22, inscription from a shrine in Sagar. For Ibrahim 'Adil Shah, see *Epigraphia Indo-Moslemica, 1929–30*, p. 2, inscription from Yadgir (Gulbarga), 953 H/August 1546; *Epigraphia Indo-Moslemica, 1931–32*, p. 2, inscription from Shahpur (Gulbarga), 962 H/July 1555; *Epigraphia Indo-Moslemica, 1929–30*, p. 3, inscription from Yadgir, 963 H/October 1556. For a partial overview of the inscriptional corpus, see V. S. Bendrey, *A Study of Muslim Inscriptions, with Special Reference to the Inscriptions Published in the 'Epigraphia Indo-Moslemica' 1907–1938, together with Summaries of Inscriptions Chronologically Arranged* (Bombay, 1944).
27. Diogo do Couto, *Década Quinta da Ásia*, ed. Marcus de Jong (Coimbra, 1937), pp. 585–87.
28. The problem of the "treasure" was treated by Georg Schurhammer, "O tesoiro de Asad Khan: Relação do intérprete António Fernandes (1545)," in Schurhammer, *Gesammelte Studien*, ed. László Szilas, 4 vols. in 5 parts (Lisbon, 1962–65), vol. IV, *Varia*, pp. 31–45.
29. Instituto dos Arquivos Nacionais/Torre do Tombo, Lisbon (hereafter IAN/TT), Corpo Cronológico (CC), I-76–118, letter from Goa to the king Dom João III, 25 October 1545, passage cited in Schurhammer, "O tesoiro de Asad Khan," pp. 44–45.
30. IAN/TT, CC, I-74–32, "Carta de D. Garcia de Castro a El Rey sobre a Armada do Governador e do que lhe soscedera," Goa, 3 December 1543, published by Luís de Albuquerque and José Pereira da Costa, "Cartas de 'serviços' da Índia (1500–1550)," *Mare Liberum* 1 (1990)): 309–96, particularly 344–46.
31. Vítor Luís Gaspar Rodrigues, "Sebastião Lopes Lobato: From Soldier to *Ouvidor-Geral* of India," in Kenneth McPherson and Sanjay Subrahmanyam, eds., *From Biography to History: Essays in the History of Portuguese Asia (1500–1800)* (New Delhi, 2005), pp. 253–69.
32. IAN/TT, CC, I-74–46, "Carta de D. Garcia de Castro a El Rey sobre a vinda do Mouro àquella cidade e do que sosedera," Goa, 29 December 1543.
33. It is hence all the more astonishing to read a letter from Dom João III to Dom João de Castro, ordering him in March 1547 to open secret negotiations to sell Bardes and Salcete (*as terras firmes de Goa*) to either the 'Adil Shah or the Nizam Shah; these aberrant orders were never implemented. See Armando Cortesão and Luís de Albuquerque, eds., *Obras Completas de D. João de Castro*, vol. III (Coimbra, 1976), pp. 373–74.

34. See Luís de Albuquerque and Inácio Guerreiro, "Khoja Shams-ud-din, comerciante de Cananor na primeira metade do século XVI," in Albuquerque and Guerreiro, eds., *Actas do II Seminário Internacional de História Indo-Portuguesa* (Lisbon, 1985), pp. 231–39. This useful account unfortunately stops in about 1548. The brief essay by K. S. Mathew, "Khwaja Shams-ud-din Giloni [*sic*]: A Sixteenth Century Entrepreneur in Portuguese India," in Roderich Ptak and Dietmar Rothermund, eds., *Emporia, Commodities and Entrepreneurs in Asian Maritime Trade, c. 1400–1750* (Stuttgart, 1991), pp. 363–71, adds little to it.
35. IAN/TT, CC, I-77-6, "Carta de Pedro de Faria a El Rey em que lhe diz que aquellas partes são de muita emportancia . . ." etc, Goa, 11 November 1545. Also see IAN/TT, CC, I-76-102, letter from Pêro de Faria to the king Dom João III, Goa, 8 October 1545, in Albuquerque and Costa, "Cartas de 'Serviços' da Índia," pp. 352–55.
36. IAN/TT, CC, I-77-59, "Carta de Antonio Cardozo para El Rey em que lhe dava comta que o Idalcão estava para armar guerra com Goa por respeito de hum mouro que lla estava cativos, pello qual davão cincoenta mil pardaos. . . ."
37. IAN/TT, CC, I-77-52, "Carta de Pero Fernandes a El Rey dando lhe conta do grande perigo em que Martim Affonço de Souza deixava aquella terra . . . ," Goa, 20 December 1545.
38. D. Fernando de Castro, *Crónica do Vice-Rei D. João de Castro*, pp. 52–60.
39. Cortesão and Albuquerque, eds., *Obras Completas de D. João de Castro*, vol. III, pp. 70–71.
40. Cortesão and Albuquerque, eds., *Obras Completas de D. João de Castro*, vol. III, pp. 99–100.
41. Cortesão and Albuquerque, eds., *Obras Completas de D. João de Castro*, vol. III, pp. 129–30 (for the treaty) and pp. 282–83 (for an account by Castro to Dom João III written from Diu on 16 December 1546).
42. Rui Gonçalves de Caminha to Dom João de Castro, Goa, 9 February 1547, in Cortesão and Albuquerque, eds., *Obras Completas de D. João de Castro*, vol. III, p. 372.
43. IAN/TT, CC, II-241-24, "Carta de Crisna em que da conta a El Rey do serviço que lhe tem feito . . . ," Bijapur, 6 December 1546, in Pissurlencar, *Agentes da diplomacia portuguesa*, pp. 19–21. On Krishna's earlier difficulties as *tanadar-mór*, also see the letter from Dom João de Mascarenhas at Diu to Dom João de Castro, dated 23 March 1546, in Cortesão and Albuquerque, eds., *Obras Completas de D. João de Castro*, vol. III, pp. 144–45.
44. In a letter from Rui Gonçalves de Caminha to Dom João de Castro dated 11 March 1547, he mentions that on that day he "had received a letter from Crinaa [*sic*]," who was apparently still in Bijapur; Cortesão and Albuquerque, eds.,

Obras Completas de D. João de Castro, vol. III, p. 372. This follows an earlier letter he had received on 8 February (*Obras*, vol. III, p. 364).

45. Leonardo Nunes, *Crónica de Dom João de Castro,* ed. J.D.M. Ford (Cambridge, [Mass.], 1936), p. 170.
46. Letter from Tristão de Paiva to Dom João de Castro, Vijayanagara [Bisnaga], 16 February 1548, in Elaine Sanceau, ed., *Colecção de São Lourenço*, vol. III (Lisbon, 1983), pp. 436–38; also reproduced in Cortesão and Albuquerque, eds., *Obras Completas de D. João de Castro*, vol. III, pp. 518–19.
47. IAN/TT, CC, I-81–119, "Terlado da carta d'Abraem Idallcão a el Rey noso senhor" (summary title from the period), 20 December 1548. For the larger context, see Maria Augusta Lima Cruz, "Notes on Portuguese Relations with Vijayanagar, 1500–1565," in Sanjay Subrahmanyam, ed., *Sinners and Saints: The Successors of Vasco da Gama* (Delhi, 1998), pp. 13–39.
48. On this subject, see Sanjay Subrahmanyam, "The Trading World of the Western Indian Ocean, 1546–1565: A Political Interpretation," in Artur Teodoro de Matos and Luís Filipe F. Reis Thomaz, eds., *A Carreira da Índia e as Rotas dos Estreitos: Actas do VIII Seminário Internacional de História Indo-Portuguesa* (Angra do Heroísmo, 1998), pp. 207–27.
49. IAN/TT, CC, I-81–100, "Carta de Mealecão pedindo a El Rey o deixe hir e vir por onde lhe parecer," Goa, 6 December 1548.
50. Biblioteca Municipal de Elvas, 5/381, "Livro que trata das cousas da Índia e do Japão," (1548), published by Adelino de Almeida Calado in the *Boletim da Biblioteca da Universidade de Coimbra* 24 (1960): 1–138. A major informant for this text was Rui Gonçalves de Caminha: see for example "Emformação do que remde Guoa, dada per Rui Guomçalvez de Caminha, veador da fazenda," pp. 125–28.
51. See, for instance, the letter written by Khwaja Shams-ud-Din to D. João de Castro, Cananor [Kannur], 17 August 1546, in Sanceau, ed., *Colecção de São Lourenço*, vol. III, pp. 354–55: "La mamdo Myalle com duas fustas muito bem esquypadas pera servyrem Vosa Senhoria nesa vyagem em que embora vay e depoys dela aquabada no que elle mamdar."
52. IAN/TT, CC, I-83–36, "Carta de Amealecão a El Rey em que lhe agradece o cuidado que tem delle em lhe escrever e lhe pede huma provizão etc," Goa, 4 November 1549.
53. IAN/TT, CC, I-38–64, "Carta de Mialicão a El Rey em que lhe mandava agradecer huma tença que lhe tinha dado etc," Goa, 30 November 1551.
54. Diogo do Couto, *Década Quinta*, ed. de Jong, p. 585.
55. On Husain Nizam Shah's reign, a valuable text (with very unusual illustrations) is the *maṣnawī* text of Aftabi, *Ta'rīf-i Husain Shāh Bādshāh Dakhan,* ed. and trans. G. T. Kulkarni and M. S. Mate (Pune, 1987). The text passes from an erotic register, describing the Sultan's courtship of Humayun Shah, to a warlike one,

with a description of the celebrated battle against Vijayanagara in early 1565. Also see the interesting, somewhat earlier, *maṣnawī* text in Dakhni by Hasan Shauqi titled "Fath-Nāma-yi Nizām Shāh," in *Dīwān-i Hasan Shauqī,* ed. Jamil Jalibi (Karachi, 1971), pp. 71–118.

56. Diogo do Couto, *Da Ásia, Década VII,* book 1, p. 89.
57. IAN/TT, CC, I-95–50, "Trelados dos comtratos de Meale Ydalcão que forão feitos em Guoa com o visso rey Dom Pedro Mascarenhas aos xxiiij dias do mes dabril de 1555." The text was signed however on 30 April. The document also contains other letters from May and August 1555 that are cited below.
58. Diogo do Couto, *Da Ásia, Década VII,* book 1, pp. 93–103.
59. IAN/TT, CC, I-97–38, "Carta de Rodrigo Anes Lucas em que da algumas noticias dos estados da India," Goa, 22 December 1555.
60. Diogo do Couto, *Da Ásia, Década VII,* book 2, pp. 160–67.
61. IAN/TT, CC, I-100–28, "Carta de Francisco Pereira de Miranda a El Rey no que lhe da conta que a fortaleza de Chaul esta muito aruinada e que he precizo acudirlhe etc," Chaul, 18 December 1556.
62. IAN/TT, CC, I-100–72, "Carta de Duarte Roiz de Bulhão para El Rey," Cochin, 10 January 1557.
63. No mention may be found of him in viceregal or other letters of the 1560s; see, for example, José Wicki, "Duas cartas oficiais de Vice-reis da Índia, escritas em 1561 e 1564," *Studia* 3 (1959): 36–89, with letters from Dom Francisco Coutinho, Conde do Redondo to D. Sebastião, Goa, 20 December 1561, IAN/TT, CC, I-105–79, and Dom Antão de Noronha to Dom Sebastião, Goa, 30 December 1564, IAN/TT, CC, I-107–38. Also see the letter from Lopo Vaz de Sequeira to Dom Sebastião, Bardez, 30 November 1566, IAN/TT, CC, I-108–12, as indeed in the wide-ranging letter from Dom Antão de Noronha to Dom Sebastião, Goa, 17 December 1566, IAN/TT, CC, I-108–15, in António da Silva Rego, ed., *Documentação para a história das missões do padroado português do Oriente: Índia,* vol. X (Lisbon, 1953), pp. 150–67, or in the missive from Dom Antão de Noronha to the Queen, Goa, 22 December 1566, IAN/TT, CC, I-108–19. These three letters may also be found in Josef Wicki, "Dokumente und Briefe aus der Zeit des indischen Vizekönigs D. Antão de Noronha (1563–1568)," *Aufsätze zur portugiesischen Kulturgeschichte* 1 (1960): 225–315. Nor does he appear in reports from 1568 to 1569, when he was presumably recently dead; see José Wicki, "Duas relações sobre a situação da Índia portuguesa nos anos 1568 e 1569," *Studia* 8 (1961): 133–220.
64. Also see Sanjay Subrahmanyam, "Palavras do Idalcão: Um encontro curioso em Bijapur no ano de 1561," *Cadernos do Noroeste* 15, nos. 1–2 (2001): 513–24.
65. Diogo do Couto, *Da Asia, Década IV* (Lisboa, 1778), book 10, p. 423. Also see Maria Augusta Lima Cruz, "A 'Crónica da Índia' de Diogo do Couto," *Mare Liberum* 9 (1995): 383–91.
66. Correia, *Lendas da Índia,* vol. III, p. 869. On Correia's characteristics as a

chronicler, see Maurice Kriegel and Sanjay Subrahmanyam, "The Unity of Opposites: Abraham Zacut, Vasco da Gama and the Chronicler Gaspar Correia," in Anthony Disney and Emily Booth, eds., *Vasco da Gama and the Linking of Europe and Asia* (Delhi, 2000), pp. 48–71.

67. P. Balthasar da Costa S.I. in Goa to the Society of Jesus in Portugal, Europe etc, 4 December 1562, in Josef Wicki, ed., *Documenta Indica (1561–1563)*, vol. V (Rome, 1958), doc. 88, pp. 605–7.
68. Bibliothèque Nationale de France, Paris, Fonds Portugais, Mss. 23, fls. 399r–99v.
69. Couto, *Da Asia, Década Décima* (Lisbon, 1778), book 4, pp. 454–57.
70. See Paulo Jorge Sousa Pinto, "Purse and Sword: D. Henrique Bendahara and Portuguese Melaka in the Late 16th Century," in Subrahmanyam, ed., *Sinners and Saints*, p. 89.
71. IAN/TT, Documentos Remetidos da Índia, book 24, fl. 87v.
72. IAN/TT, Documentos Remetidos da Índia, book 23, fl. 374.
73. Muhammad Qasim Ferishta, *History of the Rise of Mahomedan Power in India*, trans. John Briggs, 4 vols. (reprint, Delhi, 1989), vol. III, p. 19.
74. See Sanjay Subrahmanyam, "Quisling or Cross-cultural Broker? Notes on the Life and Worlds of Dom Martinho de Alemão, Prince of Arakan," in McPherson and Subrahmanyam, eds., *From Biography to History*, pp. 221–51; also, M. Ana Marques Guedes, "D. Martim, um príncipe arracanês ao serviço do Estado da Índia e das pretensões portuguesas de submissão da Birmânia," *Mare Liberum* 6 (1993): 67–82.
75. Nicolas Vatin, *Sultan Djem: Un prince ottoman dans l'Europe du XVe siècle d'après deux sources contemporaines: "Vaki'at Sultan Cem," Œuvres de Guillaume Caoursin* (Ankara, 1997); and for a popular account Didier Delhoume, *Le turc et le chevalier: Djem Sultan, un prince ottoman entre Rhodes et Bourganeuf au XVe siècle* (Limoges, 2004). For an understanding of the events of the period, the older account by Sydney Nettleton Fisher, "Civil Strife in the Ottoman Empire, 1481–1503," *Journal of Modern History* 13, no. 4 (1941): 449–66, remains useful. For a retrospective account of Cem, also see Barbara Flemming, "A Sixteenth-Century Apology for Islam: The *Gurbetnâme-i Sultân Cem*," *Byzantinische Forschungen* 16 (1990): 105–21.
76. Kate Fleet, review of Nicolas Vatin, *Sultan Djem*, in *Bulletin of the School of Oriental and African Studies, University of London* 64, no. 2 (2001): 290–91.
77. An excellent example of this bewilderment can be found in the following intriguing text, written in the late sixteenth century and subsequently reworked: Anonymous, *Primor e Honra da Vida Soldadesca no Estado da Índia* (1630), ed. Laura Monteiro Pereira, revised Maria Augusta Lima Cruz and Maria do Rosário Laureano Santos (Ericeira, 2003).

3. THE PERILS OF REALPOLITIK

1. Muzaffar Alam and Sanjay Subrahmanyam, "Envisioning Power: The Political Thought of a Late Eighteenth-Century Mughal Prince," *Indian Economic and Social History Review* 43, no. 2 (2006): 131–61.
2. Münevver Okur, *Cem Sultan: Hayatı ve şiir dünyası* (Ankara, 1992). For translations, see Kemal Silay, ed., *Anthology of Turkish Poetry* (Bloomington, 1996).
3. In a comparative vein, also see Randolph Starn, *Contrary Commonwealth: The Theme of Exile in Medieval and Renaissance Italy* (Berkeley, 1982).
4. Lisa Hopkins, "Acting the Self: John Ford's *Perkin Warbeck* and the Politics of Imposture," *Cahiers Elisabéthains: Late Medieval and Renaissance Studies* 48 (1995): 31–36; Dale B. J. Randall, *'Theatres of Greatness': A Revisionary View of Ford's 'Perkin Warbeck'* (Victoria, B.C., 1986). Ford's play drew in some measure on Thomas Gainsford, *The true and wonderfull history of Perkin Warbeck, proclaiming himselfe Richard the fourth* (London, 1618).
5. Glen Carman, "The Means and Ends of Empire in Hernán Cortés's 'Cartas de relación,'" *Modern Language Studies* 27, nos. 3–4 (1997): 113–37.
6. J. H. Elliott, "The mental world of Hernán Cortés," in Elliott, *Spain and Its World, 1500–1700: Selected Essays* (New Haven, 1989), pp. 38–39.
7. See the excellent analysis by T. F. Earle, "History, Rhetoric, and Intertextuality," in T. F. Earle and John Villiers, *Albuquerque, Caesar of the East* (Warminster, 1990), pp. 25–49. This may be usefully contrasted to the rather ill-informed reflection in Francisco Bethencourt, "The Political Correspondence of Albuquerque and Cortés," in F. Bethencourt and Florike Egmond, eds., *Cultural Exchange in Early Modern Europe*, vol. III: *Correspondence and Cultural Exchange in Europe, 1400–1700* (Cambridge, 2007), pp. 219–73.
8. Armando Cortesão and Luís de Albuquerque, eds., *Obras Completas de D. João de Castro*, vol. III (Coimbra, 1976), pp. 99, 283–84.
9. Anthony Disney, "The *Estado da Índia* and the Young Nobleman Soldier: The Case of Dom Fernando de Noronha," in Kenneth McPherson and Sanjay Subrahmanyam, eds., *From Biography to History: Essays in the History of Portuguese Asia (1500–1800)* (New Delhi, 2005), p. 207.
10. James D. Tracy, *Erasmus of the Low Countries* (Berkeley, 1996), p. 195.
11. For a discussion of this and related texts, see Sanjay Subrahmanyam, "On World Historians in the Sixteenth Century," *Representations* 91 (2005): 26–57; also Serge Gruzinski, *Quelle heure est-il là-bas? Amérique et islam à l'orée des temps modernes* (Paris, 2008).
12. He was also the editor of Scott F. Surtees, *Emigrants' Letters from Settlers in Canada and South Australia Collected in the Parish of Banham Norfolk* (Norwich, 1852), and various other works. Sherley does make a brief appearance in Walter

Cohen, "The Merchant of Venice and the Possibilities of Historical Criticism," *ELH* 49, no. 4 (1982): 765–89, but only to demonstrate the moral distinction made by him between merchants and usurers.

13. Incidentally, the same year, 1888, also saw the publication of the massive work of Ignatius Donnelly, *The Great Cryptogram: Francis Bacon's Cipher in the So-Called Shakespeare Plays* (Chicago, 1888).
14. For a recent survey of debates on the "real" authorship of Shakespeare's plays, see James Shapiro, *Contested Will: Who Wrote Shakespeare?* (New York, 2010).
15. *A True Report of Sir Anthony Shierlies Journey Overland to Venice, from thence by sea to Antioch, Aleppo, and Babilon, and soe to Casbine in Persia* (London, 1600). This pamphlet was suppressed and its printer fined in October 1600, but the suppression order was apparently not followed.
16. Kathryn Babayan, "The Safavid Synthesis: From Qizilbash Islam to Imamite Shi'ism," *Iranian Studies* 27, nos. 1–4 (1994): 135–61. On the Sufis of Lahejan, see Jean Aubin, "Revolution chiite et conservatisme: Les soufis de Lahejan, 1500–1514," *Moyen Orient et Océan Indien* 1 (1984): 1–40.
17. *The Suma Oriental of Tomé Pires and the Book of Francisco Rodrigues*, ed. and trans. Armando Cortesão, 2 vols. (London, 1944), vol. I, pp. 26–29.
18. J. J. Scarisbrick, "The First Englishman round the Cape of Good Hope?" *Historical Research* 34 (1961): 165–77; Jean Aubin, "La mission de Robert Bransetur: Frontière du Danube et route de Basra," in Aubin, *Le Latin et l'Astrolabe: Recherches sur le Portugal de la Renaissance, son expansion en Asie et les relations internationales,* 2 vols. (Paris, 1996–2000), vol. I, pp. 385–405.
19. Letter from Wyatt to Henry VIII, 7 January 1540, in James Gairdner and R. H. Brodie, eds., *Letters and Papers, Foreign and Domestic, of the Reign of Henry VIII*, vol. XV (London, 1896), p. 15.
20. Text in Aubin, "La mission de Robert Bransetur," p. 405.
21. Aubin, "Per viam portugalensem: Autour d'un projet diplomatique de Maximilien II," in Aubin, *Le Latin et l'Astrolabe*, vol. I, pp. 407–46. Also see the earlier study by Barbara von Palombini, *Bündniswerben abenländischer Mächte um Persien, 1453–1600* (Wiesbaden, 1968).
22. Michele Membré, *Mission to the Lord Sophy of Persia (1539–1542),* trans. and ed. A. H. Morton (London, 1993).
23. E. Delmar Morgan and C. H. Coote, eds., *Early Voyages and Travels to Russia and Persia by Anthony Jenkinson and Other Englishmen* (London, 1886), pp. 112–14.
24. Morgan and Coote, eds., *Early Voyages and Travels to Russia and Persia by Anthony Jenkinson,* pp. 145–47.
25. Roberto Almagià, "Giovan Battista and Gerolamo Vecchietti, viaggiatori in Oriente," *Atti della Accademia Nazionale dei Lincei: Rendiconti di Scienze morali, storiche e filologiche,* 8th ser., 11 (1956): 313–50.
26. Now decidedly dated in many respects is Ronald W. Ferrier, "The European

Diplomacy of Shāh 'Abbās I and the First Persian Embassy to England," *Iran* 11 (1973): 75–92. The important if controversial work by Niels Steensgaard, *The Asian Trade Revolution of the Seventeenth Century: The East India Companies and the Decline of the Caravan Trade* (Chicago, 1974), still retains much interest on the question. For more recent interventions, see Rudolph P. Matthee, *The Politics of Trade in Safavid Iran: Silk for Silver, 1600–1730* (Cambridge, 1999), and Ina Baghdiantz McCabe, *The Shah's Silk for Europe's Silver: The Eurasian Trade of the Julfa Armenians in Safavid Iran and India (1530–1750)* (Atlanta, 1999), as well as 'Abd al-Husain Nawa'i, *Rawābit-i siyāsī-yi Īrān wa Urūpā dar 'asr-i Safawī* (Tehran, 1372 H/1993 CE). Nawa'i's work is heavily indebted however to Nasr Allah Falsafi, *Tārīkh-i Rawābit-i Īrān wa Urūpā dar daura-i Safawī* (Tehran, 1316 H/1938 CE).

27. Vladimir Minorsky, "Review of L. L. Bellan, *Shāh 'Abbās I, sa vie, son histoire* (Paris, 1932)," *Bulletin of the School of Oriental Studies* 7, no. 2 (1934): 455–57.
28. Andrew J. Newman, *Safavid Iran: Rebirth of a Persian Empire* (London, 2006), pp. 71–72.
29. Muzaffar Alam and Sanjay Subrahmanyam, "A Place in the Sun: Travels with Faizî in the Deccan, 1591–93," in François Grimal, ed., *Les sources et le temps/ Sources and Time: A Colloquium* (Pondicherry, 2001), pp. 265–307.
30. See Anthony Nixon, *The Three English Brothers* (London, 1607), including "Sir Anthony Sherley his Embassage to the Christian Princes," or "Sir Anthony Sherley, his Adventures, and Voyage into Persia." On Nixon himself, see Lambert Ennis, "Anthony Nixon: Jacobean Plagiarist and Hack," *The Huntington Library Quarterly* 3, no. 4 (1940): 377–401.
31. "Sir Anthony Sherley, his Adventures, and Voyage into Persia," pp. G1r–G1v.
32. See Juan E. Tazón, *The Life and Times of Thomas Stukeley (c. 1525–78)* (Aldershot, 2003).
33. *The Stukeley Plays: The Battle of Alcazar by George Peele; The famous history of the life and death of Captain Thomas Stukeley*, ed. Charles Edelman (Manchester, 2005).
34. "Sir Anthony Sherley, his Adventures, and Voyage into Persia," pp. G1v–G2r.
35. Modern accounts include E. Denison Ross, *Sir Anthony Sherley and His Persian Adventure* (London, 1933); Boies Penrose, *The Sherleian Odyssey, Being of the Travels and Adventures of Three Famous Brothers during the Reigns of Elizabeth, James I, and Charles I* (Taunton, 1938); Samuel C. Chew, *The Crescent and the Rose: Islam and England during the Renaissance* (Oxford, 1937), pp. 239–97; and D. W. Davies, *Elizabethans Errant: The Strange Fortunes of Sir Thomas Sherley and His Three Sons, as Well in the Dutch Wars, as in Muscovy, Morocco, Persia, Spain, and the Indies* (Ithaca, N.Y., 1967). The most recent reconsideration is Vasco Resende, "'Un homme d'inventions et inconstant': Les fidélités politiques d'Anthony Sherley, entre l'ambassade safavide et la diplomatie européenne," in Dejanirah

Couto and Rui Manuel Loureiro, eds., *Revisiting Hormuz: Portuguese Interactions in the Persian Gulf in the Early Modern Period* (Wiesbaden, 2008), pp. 235–60.

36. Anthony Sherley, *His Relation of his Travels into Persia* (London, 1613), pp. 1–2.
37. Cited in Paul E. J. Hammer, *The Polarization of Elizabethan Politics: The Political Career of Robert Devereux, 2nd Earl of Essex, 1585–1597* (Cambridge, 1999), p. 218.
38. R. A. Roberts et al., *Calendar of the Manuscripts of the Most Hon. The Marquis of Salisbury, K.G., etc, preserved at Hatfield House, Hertfordshire,* vol. VIII (London, 1899), pp. 116–17.
39. George Gilpin to the Earl of Essex, The Hague, 30 April 1598, in Roberts et al., *Calendar of the Manuscripts of the Marquis of Salisbury,* vol. VIII, p. 151.
40. Hammer, *The Polarization of Elizabethan Politics,* pp. 258–59.
41. For Davis's participation in this expedition, see Clements R. Markham, *A Life of John Davis, the Navigator, 1550–1605, Discoverer of Davis Straits* (New York, 1889), pp. 179–94.
42. See W. S. Unger, ed., *De Oudste Reizen van de Zeeuwen naar Oost-Indië, 1598–1604* (The Hague, 1948).
43. Angelo Michele Piemontese, "I due ambasciatori di Persia ricevuti da Papa Paolo V al Quirinale," *Miscellanea Bibliothecae Apostolicae Vaticanae* 12 (2005): 357–425, especially 360–62.
44. Letter from Thomas Chaloner to Anthony Bacon, Lyons, 2 June 1598, in Roberts et al., *Calendar of the Manuscripts of the Marquis of Salisbury,* vol. VIII, pp. 188–89.
45. For Venetians' relations with and knowledge of Iran at this time, see Guglielmo Berchet, *La Repubblica di Venezia e la Persia* (Turin, 1865); also G. Berchet, "La Repubblica di Venezia e la Persia: Nuovi documenti e regesti," *Raccolta veneta* 1, no. 2 (1866): 5–62.
46. Davies, *Elizabethans Errant,* p. 93.
47. Sherley, *Relation of his Travels into Persia,* p. 64.
48. Many of these accounts appear in Ross, *Sir Anthony Sherley and His Persian Adventure*: William Parry's "New and Large Discourse," pp. 98–136; Abel Pinçon's "Relation," pp. 137–74; Mainwaring's "True Discourse," pp. 175–226.
49. Ross, *Sir Anthony Sherley and His Persian Adventure,* p. 206.
50. Ross, *Sir Anthony Sherley and His Persian Adventure,* pp. 118–19.
51. Sherley, *Relation of his Travels into Persia,* p. 66.
52. Chew, *The Crescent and the Rose,* p. 258, suggests that it is a "valid surmise" that these works included Paul Ive's *Practice of Fortification* (1589). For this text, see Charles Stephenson, *'Servant to the King for His Fortifications': Paul Ive and the Practise of Fortification* (Doncaster, 2008). Whatever the texts, they must have been illustrated to attract the attention of Shah 'Abbas.
53. Davies, *Elizabethans Errant,* p. 109.
54. Sherley, *Relation of his Travels into Persia,* pp. 81–82.

55. On these royal slaves in general (and Allah Virdi Khan in particular), see Sussan Babaie, Kathryn Babayan, Ina Baghdiantz-McCabe, and Massumeh Farhad, *Slaves of the Shah: New Elites of Safavid Iran* (London, 2004).
56. Sherley, *Relation of his Travels into Persia*, p. 126.
57. Ross, *Sir Anthony Sherley and His Persian Adventure*, pp. 237–43.
58. Joaquim Veríssimo Serrão, *O reinado de D. António Prior do Crato* (Coimbra, 1956); Sanjay Subrahmanyam "A Matter of Alignment: Mughal Gujarat and the Iberian World in the Transition of 1580–81," *Mare Liberum* 9 (1995): 461–79.
59. Berchet, *La Repubblica di Venezia e la Persia*, pp. 43–44, 192–95. This refers to the arrival in Venice in June 1600 of the Safavid merchant-envoy 'Iffat Beg. A copy of Shah 'Abbas's Persian letter carried by him may be found in Archivio di Stato di Venezia, Documenti Persia, busta unica, doc. 3.
60. Ross, *Sir Anthony Sherley and His Persian Adventure*, pp. 25–26. For the Italian original of Sherley's letter from Gilan, dated 24 May 1599, see Berchet, "La Repubblica di Venezia e la Persia: Nuovi documenti e regesti," pp. 8–9.
61. Sherley kept track of his master's fluctuating fortunes even while in Russia. See his letter to Essex from Archangelsk, dated 20 June 1600, in R. A. Roberts et al., *Calendar of the Manuscripts of the Most Hon. The Marquis of Salisbury, K.G., etc, preserved at Hatfield House, Hertfordshire*, vol. X (London, 1904), p. 190.
62. Anna Maria Crinò, "Lettere autografe inedite di Sir Henry Wotton nell'Archivio di stato di Firenze," in Crinò, *Fatti e figure del seicento anglo-toscano: Documenti inediti sui rapporti letterari, diplomatici, culturali fra Toscana e Inghilterra* (Florence, 1957), pp. 12–13.
63. Carlos Alonso, OSA, "Embajadores de Persia en las Cortes de Praga, Roma y Valladolid (1600–1601)," *Anthologica Annua* 36 (1989): 11–271, on 209.
64. Alonso, "Embajadores de Persia en las Cortes de Praga, Roma y Valladolid (1600–1601)," p. 179.
65. Alonso, "Embajadores de Persia en las Cortes de Praga, Roma y Valladolid (1600–1601)," p. 222.
66. Penrose, *The Sherleian Odyssey*, pp. 256–57.
67. For Sherley in Morocco, see Franz Babinger, "Sir Anthony Sherley's marokkanische Sendung (1605/06)," in Babinger, *Sherleiana* (Berlin, 1932), pp. 31–51.
68. See Anne Dubet, "El arbitrismo como práctica política: El caso de Luis Valle de la Cerda (¿1552?–1606)," *Cuadernos de Historia Moderna* 24 (2000): 107–33. The suggestion to place Sherley's work squarely in the tradition of the Spanish *arbitristas* of the period was first made, I believe, in John H. Elliott, "Self-Perception and Decline in Early Seventeenth-Century Spain," *Past and Present* 74 (1977): 41–61.
69. The bulk of these projects and responses to them may be found in the Archivo General de Simancas, Estado, Legajo 1171, a volume of 232 folios dealing largely

with Sherley in the years 1606–12. These materials are extensively summed up and cited in Luis Gil Fernández, *El Impero Luso-Español y la Persia Safávida: Tomo I (1582–1605)* (Madrid, 2006).

70. Sherley to Father Creswell, Ferrara, 8 March 1608, Archivo General de Simancas, Estado, Legajo 1491, cited in Gil Fernández, *El Impero Luso-Español y la Persia Safávida*, p. 211. Sherley quotes from Don Hieronimo de Urrea's Spanish translation, where it appears at the opening to canto 14; I cite the version of William Stewart Rose, *The Orlando Furioso, translated into English verse, from the Italian of Ludovico Ariosto*, 2 vols. (London, 1892), vol. I, p. 257, where it appears in canto 15.
71. For Pagliarini's denunciation, see Archivo General de Simancas, Estado, Legajo K. 1678, G. 7. These materials are extensively summed up in Gil Fernández, *El Impero Luso-Español y la Persia Safávida*, pp. 213–15.
72. This appears in a letter of Thomas Ferrers, formerly an important merchant in Stade, to his brother Humphrey, dated July 1598, in Edward Scott et al., *Catalogue of the Stowe manuscripts in the British Museum*, vol. I (London, 1895), p. 126. Ferrers at this time was in the service of Essex, which renders the charge all the more interesting.
73. Gil Fernández, *El Impero Luso-Español y la Persia Safávida*, pp. 224–25.
74. Davies, *Elizabethans Errant*, p. 216.
75. Archivo General de Simancas, Estado, Legajo 1164, fl. 34, cited in Davies, *Elizabethans Errant*, p. 220.
76. Anthony Sherley to Philip III, Palermo, 20 May 1610, Archivo General de Simancas, Estado, Legajo 494, cited at length Gil Fernández, *El Impero Luso-Español y la Persia Safávida*, pp. 235–38.
77. Penrose, *The Sherleian Odyssey*, pp. 162–66.
78. Ross, *Sir Anthony Sherley and His Persian Adventure*, p. 81.
79. Archivo General de Simancas, Estado, Legajo 2853, cited in Davies, *Elizabethans Errant*, p. 284. This was seemingly a transformed version of an earlier proposal he had made, in about 1607, to settle in and transform the island of Capri as a center of trade. For other proposals from the late period by Sherley, largely focusing on the Mediterranean in general (and North Africa in particular), see his "Discurso en razón de lo que pueden en general y particular los reyes y potentandos contra esta monarquía, y sobre el aumento de ella" (dated Granada, 25 March 1625), in Anthony Sherley, *Peso de todo el mundo (1622); discurso sobre el aumento de esta monarquía (1625)*, ed. Ángel Alloza Aparicio, Miguel Ángel de Bunes Ibarra, and José Antonio Martínez Torres (Madrid, 2010), pp. 219–65.
80. Francisco Henriquez de Jorquera, *Anales de Granada: Descripción del Reino y Ciudad de Granada, Crónica de la Reconquista (1482–1492), sucesos de los años 1588 a 1646*, ed. Antonio Marín Ocete, 2 vols. (Granada, 1987), vol. II, p. 740. For

some reason, Ángel Alloza Aparicio, in his introduction to Sherley, *Peso de todo el mundo*, ed. Alloza et al., p. 33, does not accept this date, and continues to prefer 1636.

81. Ross, *Sir Anthony Sherley and His Persian Adventure*, p. 81. Ross also adds that he was "quick-tempered and quarrelsome" and "gives no evidence of possessing a sense of humour."
82. Penrose, *The Sherleian Odyssey*, pp. 244–45.
83. Davies, *Elizabethans Errant*, p. 284.
84. Resende, "'Un homme d'inventions et inconstant,'" p. 235.
85. Steensgaard, *The Asian Trade Revolution*, pp. 264, 413. For Sherley's presentation of the opposition between the Aleppo route and the Hormuz route to Shah 'Abbas and the latter's response, see the correspondence between the two from 1017 H/1608 CE, in Biblioteca Nazionale, Naples, Ms. III.F.30, "Makātibāt-i Rīm-Pāpā wa dīgar pādshāhān," fls. 40r–40v, 42r–43v, reproduced in 'Abd al-Husain Nawa'i, *Shāh 'Abbās: Majmū'ah-i asnād wa makātibāt-i tārīkhī hamrāh bā yāddāsht-hā-yi tafsīlī*, 3 vols. (Tehran, 1366 H/1987–88 CE), vol. III, pp. 240–43. For the Spanish version of the shah's letter, see Gil Fernández, *El Impero Luso-Español y la Persia Safávida*, pp. 229–30.
86. The full title is *Sir Antony Sherley his relation of his trauels into Persia: The dangers, and distresses, which befell him in his passage, both by sea and land, and his strange and vnexpected deliuerances. His magnificent entertainement in Persia, his honourable imployment there — hence, as embassadour to the princes of Christendome, the cause of his disapointment therein, with his aduice to his brother, Sir Robert Sherley, also, a true relation of the great magnificence, valour, prudence, iustice, temperance, and other manifold vertues of Abas, now King of Persia, with his great conquests, whereby he hath inlarged his dominions. Penned by Sr. Antony Sherley, and recommended to his brother, Sr. Robert Sherley, being now in prosecution of the like honourable imployment* (London, 1613).
87. Xavier-A. Flores, *Le "Peso político de todo el mundo" d'Anthony Sherley, ou un aventurier anglais au service de l'Espagne* (Paris, 1963). Also see the more recent edition cited above: Sherley, *Peso de todo el mundo*, ed. Alloza et al. In what follows we will usually cite Flores's text, followed by the more recent (and modernized) edition.
88. On Olivares, see the authoritative study by John H. Elliott, *The Count-Duke of Olivares: The Statesman in an Age of Decline* (London, 1986); and, from the previous generation, the work of Gregorio Marañón, *El Conde-Duque de Olivares: La pasión de mandar* (Madrid, 1952).
89. For a panorama of early modern Iberian political thought, and the place in it of the *arbitristas*, see Xavier Gil, "Spain and Portugal," in Howell A. Lloyd, Glenn Burgess, and Simon Hodson, eds., *European Political Thought, 1450–1700:*

Religion, Law and Philosophy (New Haven, 2007), pp. 416–57. For a brief attempt to place Sherley in this context, see Ángel Alloza Aparicio, "Sir Anthony Sherley," in Sherley, *Peso de todo el mundo,* ed. Alloza et al., pp. 33–44.

90. Francisco Rodrigues Silveira, *Reformação da milícia e governo do Estado da Índia Oriental,* ed. Luís Filipe Barreto, George D. Winius, and B. N. Teensma (Lisbon, 1996). More economically oriented are the celebrated writings of Duarte Gomes Solis, such as his *Discursos sobre los comercios de las dos Indias, donde se tratan materias importantes de estado y guerra* (1622), ed. Moses Bensabat Amzalak (Lisbon, 1943).
91. "Relazione di Spagna di Pietro Contarini Cav. Ambasciatore a Filippo III dall'anno 1619 al 1621," in Nicolò Barozzi and Guglielmo Berchet, eds., *Relazioni degli Stati Europei lette al Senato dagli Ambasciatori Veneti nel secolo decimosettimo: Spagna,* vol. I (Venice, 1856), p. 581.
92. Sherley, *Relation of his Travels into Persia,* p. 10.
93. For this traveler and his richly illustrated text, *Les voyages et observations du Sieur de la Boullaye-le Gouz* (first published without illustrations in 1653, and then in its full glory in 1657), see Jacques de Maussion de Favières, ed., *Le voyages et observations du Sieur de la Boullaye le-Gouz,* (Paris, 1994); also Michele Bernardini, "The Illustrations of a Manuscript of the Travel Account of François de la Boullaye le Gouz in the Library of the Accademia Nazionale dei Lincei in Rome," *Muqarnas* 21 (2004): 55–72.
94. Flores, *Le "Peso político de todo el mundo,"* p. 55; Sherley, *Peso de todo el mundo,* ed. Alloza et al., pp. 87–88.
95. Elliott, *The Count-Duke of Olivares,* p. 681.
96. Flores, *Le "Peso político de todo el mundo,"* p. 57; Sherley, *Peso de todo el mundo,* ed. Alloza et al., p. 89.
97. Flores, *Le "Peso político de todo el mundo,"* p. 58; Sherley, *Peso de todo el mundo,* ed. Alloza et al., p. 90.
98. Flores, *Le "Peso político de todo el mundo,"* p. 59; Sherley, *Peso de todo el mundo,* ed. Alloza et al., pp. 91–92.
99. Flores, *Le "Peso político de todo el mundo,"* p. 67; Sherley, *Peso de todo el mundo,* ed. Alloza et al., p. 100.
100. Flores, *Le "Peso político de todo el mundo,"* pp. 83–84; Sherley, *Peso de todo el mundo,* ed. Alloza et al., p. 118.
101. Flores, *Le "Peso político de todo el mundo,"* p. 128; Sherley, *Peso de todo el mundo,* ed. Alloza et al., p. 166.
102. Flores, *Le "Peso político de todo el mundo,"* pp. 149–50; Sherley, *Peso de todo el mundo,* ed. Alloza et al., p. 190.
103. "The Epistle Dedicatorie," in António Galvão (Galvano), *The Discoveries of the World, from their first original unto the Year of Our Lord 1555 [. . .], corrected,*

quoted and published in England, by Richard Hakluyt, 1601, ed. Charles Ramsay Drinkwater-Bethune (London, 1862), pp. iii–vi.

104. This is the sense in which it is used by Buoncompagno da Signa (1165–1240), as also by Giordano Bruno, and by the younger Spanish contemporary of Sherley, Baltasar Gracián, in his *El Criticón* (1650s).

105. M. J. Wilks, *The Problem of Sovereignty in the Later Middle Ages* (Cambridge, 1963), pp. 63–64; Eric L. Saak, *High Way to Heaven: The Augustinian Platform between Reform and Reformation, 1292–1524* (Leiden, 2002), pp. 76–79.

106. Flores, *Le "Peso político de todo el mundo,"* pp. 67–8; Sherley, *Peso de todo el mundo,* ed. Alloza et al., p. 102.

107. Bruce Buchan, "Asia and the Moral Geography of European Enlightenment Political Thought, c.1600–1800," in Takashi Shogimen and Cary J. Nederman, eds., *Western Political Thought in Dialogue with Asia* (Lanham, Md., 2009), pp. 65–86. For two recent and rather unconvincing attempts to rescue these writers, see John M. Headley, *The Europeanization of the World: On the Origins of Human Rights and Democracy* (Princeton, N.J., 2007), and Michael Curtis, *Orientalism and Islam: European Thinkers on Oriental Despotism in the Middle East and India* (Cambridge, 2009). More nuanced, but still problematic in its curiously apologistic tone, is Joan-Pau Rubiés, "Oriental Despotism and European Orientalism: Botero to Montesquieu," *Journal of Early Modern History* 9, nos. 1–2 (2005): 109–80.

108. Earlier, in 1609, Sherley had met with strenuous objections when he proposed an audacious project to settle a group of Levantine Jews in Trapani (in Sicily), using them to produce imitations of Polish *leonico* coins for the Ottoman trade; cf. Gil Fernández, *El Impero Luso-Español y la Persia Safávida,* pp. 218–20. His proposal bears an interesting resemblance to the successful Genoese project of the 1650s and 1660s with regard to the so-called *luigini* coins, on which see Carlo M. Cipolla, "La truffa del secolo (XVII)," in Cipolla, *Tre storie extra vaganti* (Bologna, 1994), pp. 51–62.

109. Flores, *Le "Peso político de todo el mundo,"* pp. 116–17; Sherley, *Peso de todo el mundo,* ed. Alloza et al., pp. 153–54.

110. Francis Bacon, "Of Empire," in Bacon, *Works,* ed. J. Spedding et al., 7 vols. (London, 1857–59), vol. VI, pp. 419–23. On Bacon's debt to Guicciardini, see Vincent Luciani, "Bacon and Guicciardini," *PMLA* 62, no. 1 (1947): 96–113. For a general view of the literature, also see Herbert Butterfield, "Balance of Power," in Philip P. Wiener, ed., *The Dictionary of the History of Ideas,* 5 vols. (New York, 1973–74), vol. I, pp. 179–88.

111. Flores, *Le "Peso político de todo el mundo,"* p. 166, for the reference to "el zurrón de Machavele [or Maquiavelo]"; Sherley, *Peso de todo el mundo,* ed. Alloza et al., pp. 208–9.

112. Compare the view of European relations with the Muslim world presented in Iver B. Neumann and Jennifer M. Welsh, "The Other in European Self-definition: An Addendum to the Literature on International Society," *Review of International Studies* 17, no. 4 (1991): 327–48.
113. Letter from Juan Nicolás, agent of Count Anthony Sherley, to the Count-Duke of Olivares, Madrid, 11 January 1623, in Flores, *Le "Peso político de todo el mundo,"* p. 177.
114. R. A. Stradling, *Philip IV and the Government of Spain, 1621–1665* (Cambridge, 1988), pp. 61–62. Also see Stradling's further remark (p. 83) that Olivares's "vision was stimulated by the various *arbitrios* of Mariana, Álamos, and (in this context) above all the breathtaking geopolitics of Sherley."
115. Flores, *Le "Peso político de todo el mundo,"* p. 166; Sherley, *Peso de todo el mundo*, ed. Alloza et al., p. 209. On Álamos de Barrientos, also see Xavier Gil, "Spain and Portugal," pp. 444–45.
116. Cited in Rubiés, "Oriental Despotism and European Orientalism," p. 127. Botero here falls into a larger category of such observers, though his place and influence are crucial. See Aslı Çırakman, "From Tyranny to Despotism: The Enlightenment's Unenlightened Image of the Turks," *International Journal of Middle Eastern Studies* 33, no. 1 (2001): 49–68.
117. Giovanni Botero, *The Reason of State*, trans. P. J. and D. P. Waley (London, 1956), p. 85.
118. In Sherley's relative indifference to the opposition between Catholics and Protestants, he seems to have been true to his erstwhile master Essex. Petruccio Ubaldini noted (in a letter from London) for example that "even the English Catholics have a very good opinion of the Count of Essex, because though he was born and brought up a heretic . . . he has not tormented or persecuted the Catholics": cf. Crinò, "Lettere autografe inedite di Sir Henry Wotton," p. 10.

4. UNMASKING THE MUGHALS

1. In *A Treatise of Human Nature*, book 1, part 4, section 6, cited in Franco Fido, "At the Origins of Autobiography in the 18th and 19th Centuries: The *Topoi* of the Self," *Annali d'Italianistica* 4 (1986): 168–180 (on 177).
2. Margaret Meserve, *Empires of Islam in Renaissance Historical Thought* (Cambridge, Mass., 2008), pp. 1–3, 100–104.
3. For what remains the best single account of this period, see Jean Aubin, "L'avènement des Safavides reconsidéré," *Moyen Orient et Océan Indien* 5 (1988): 1–130. For an analysis of the sources, also see Aubin, "Chroniques persanes et relations italiennes: Notes sur les sources narratives du règne de Šâh Esmâ'il Ier," *Studia Iranica* 24, no. 2 (1995): 247–59.
4. Peruschi, *Informatione del regno, e stato del Gran Rè di Mogor, della sua persona,*

qualità, e costumi, e delli buoni segni, e congietture della sua conversione alla nostra santa fede (Rome, 1597). For a brief discussion of the text, see Edward Maclagan, *The Jesuits and the Great Mogul* (London, 1932), pp. 12–13.

5. Xavier-A. Flores, *Le "Peso político de todo el mundo" d'Anthony Sherley, ou un aventurier anglais au service de l'Espagne* (Paris, 1963), pp. 128–29.
6. Flores, *Le "Peso político de todo el mundo,"* pp. 130–31.
7. Sanjay Subrahmanyam, "The Company and the Mughals between Sir Thomas Roe and Sir William Norris," in Subrahmanyam, *Explorations in Connected History: Mughals and Franks* (Delhi, 2005), p. 145.
8. For a discussion, also see Joan-Pau Rubiés, "Oriental Despotism and European Orientalism: Botero to Montesquieu," *Journal of Early Modern History* 9, nos. 1–2 (2005): 109–80, especially 143–47. Rubiés argues that, contrary to recent scholarship, "there is little sense of a fundamental gap between the 'realistic' merchant [Pelsaert] and the 'orientalizing' scholar [De Laet]. If anything, De Laet stood out for his sensible and critical use of sources." While one may agree with him on the fundamental lack of difference between De Laet and Pelsaert, this somewhat heroic view of De Laet remains rather puzzling.
9. This is based on a reading of the tombstone on a visit to the site in December 2006. The graveyard is also the resting place of other Italians such as Girolamo Veroneo (d. 1640) and Hortensio Bronzoni (d. 1677). For a rare reference to Mafei, see Giuseppe Tucci, "Pionieri italiani in India," *Asiatica* 2 (1936): 3–11. Also of interest in this context are the materials relating to the Papal envoys, the Vecchietti, who visited Agra, Thatta, and Lahore in 1603–5; see R. Almagià, "Giovan Battista e Gerolamo Vecchietti, viaggiatori in Oriente," *Rendiconti dell'Accademia Nazionale dei Lincei,* 8th ser., 11 (1956): 313–50; and Francis Richard, "Les manuscrits persans rapportés par les frères Vecchietti et conservés aujourd'hui à la Bibliothèque nationale," *Studia Iranica* 9, no. 2 (1980): 291–300.
10. The classic work is that of Angelo de Gubernatis, *Storia dei viaggiatori italiani nelle Indie orientali* (Livorno, 1875); more recently, one should consult Alessandro Grossato, *Navigatori e viaggiatori veneti sulla rotta per l'India: Da Marco Polo ad Angelo Legrenzi* (Florence, 1994). For the sixteenth century, also see Luca Campigotto, "Veneziani in India nel XVI secolo," *Studi veneziani* 22 (1991): 75–116. Useful additional materials may be found in Julieta Teixeira Marques de Oliveira, *Fontes documentais de Veneza referentes a Portugal* (Lisbon, 1997). I have attempted to evaluate the place of the early sixteenth-century Italian (and especially Venetian) accounts in Sanjay Subrahmanyam, "The Birth-Pangs of Portuguese Asia: Revisiting the Fateful "Long Decade" 1498–1509," *Journal of Global History* 2, no. 3 (2007): 261–80.
11. See Joan-Pau Rubiés, *Travel and Ethnology in the Renaissance: South India through European Eyes, 1250–1625* (Cambridge, 2000).

12. Louise Bénat-Tachot and Serge Gruzinski, eds., *Passeurs culturels: Mécanismes de métissage* (Paris, 2001).
13. For the most significant recent examples, Oumelbanine Zhiri, *L'Afrique au miroir de l'Europe: Fortunes de Jean Léon l'Africain à la Renaissance* (Geneva, 1991); Dietrich Rauchenberger, *Johannes Leo der Afrikaner: Seine Beschreibung des Raumes zwischen Nil und Niger nach dem Urtext* (Wiesbaden, 1999).
14. Natalie Zemon Davis, *Trickster Travels: A Sixteenth-Century Muslim between Worlds* (New York, 2006); also see David Turnbull, *Masons, Tricksters and Cartographers: Comparative Studies in the Sociology of Scientific and Indigenous Knowledge* (Amsterdam, 2000).
15. Davis, *Trickster Travels*, p. 260. Further, communication and violence were by no means mutually exclusive options.
16. Subrahmanyam, "The Company and the Mughals between Sir Thomas Roe and Sir William Norris."
17. William Dalrymple, "Assimilation and Transculturation in Eighteenth Century India: A Response to Pankaj Mishra," *Common Knowledge* 11, no. 3 (2005): 445–85.
18. Here I refer to Blaise Cendrars, *Bourlinguer* (Paris, 1948), which opens with an extended evocation of Manuzzi and his life, based once more on William Irvine's translation. Cendrars, or Frédéric-Louis Sauser (1887–1961), was a French writer, adventurer, and traveler of Swiss origin who clearly identified with the Venetian.
19. The name appears in contemporary writings in a variety of spellings: "Manucci," "Manuchy," "Manouchy," and so on. I have finally chosen here — on the advice of Italian historians Carlo Ginzburg and Adriano Prosperi — to use Manuzzi, also the preferred spelling of the Venetian archivist and historian Piero Falchetta, who has written extensively on the subject.
20. For Manuzzi's role as an English agent, see K. V. Rangaswami Aiyangar, "Manucci in Madras," in *Madras Tercentenary Commemoration Volume* (Madras, 1939), pp. 147–52.
21. Centre des Archives d'Outre-Mer, Aix-en-Provence (henceforth CAOM), Notariat de Pondichéry, P7 (1712–13), pp. 1–19, text titled "Le testament de Nicolao Manuchy" by the archivist A. Singaravelou. Singaravelou adds: "J'ai découvert un second testament avec son codicille faits à Madras le 8 janvier 1719. C'est en portugais. Le papier a également jauni; c'est très difficile de le lire et le déchiffrer. Car le papier est en très mauvais état, dès qu'on le touche, il tombe en miettes." This is a text of four pages signed by Nicolao Manuchy and Mie de Famirante, and the codicil is signed by Manuchy and M. Quiel de Lima. It has two red seals with the arms of the Company. The text of 1712 has been published with a facsimile in Françoise de Valence, "Un testament de Niccoló Manucci (ou Manuzzi)," *Ateneo veneto*, n.s., 36 (1998): 149–61.

22. Jadunath Sarkar, *Studies in Aurangzib's Reign* (Calcutta, 1933); J. F. Richards, *Mughal Administration in Golconda* (Oxford, 1975), pp. 138, 223–24; Richards, *The Mughal Empire* (Cambridge, 1993), p. 153. The dependence on Manuzzi as a source of popular perceptions is marked at several places in Harbans Mukhia, *The Mughals of India* (Oxford, 2004); also see the remarks in Iqtidar Alam Khan, "Seventeenth-Century Assessments of Akbar," in Iqtidar Alam Khan, ed., *Akbar and His Age* (New Delhi, 1999), pp. 231–38 (especially pp. 236–37). He also appears as a crucial source of Mughal military history in Geoffrey Parker, *The Military Revolution: Military Innovation and the Rise of the West, 1500–1800* (Cambridge, 1988), pp. 129–30. For more detailed discussions of the source from the point of view of reliability, see D. Bredi, "L'immagine di un grande impero musulmano secondo un testimone italiano: La 'Storia do Mogor' di Nicolò Manucci," in Ugo Marazzi, ed., *La conoscenza dell'Asia e dell'Africa in Italia nei secoli XVIII e XIX*, vol. I, part 1 (Naples, 1984), pp. 373–95, and G.S.L. Devra, "Manucci's Comments on Indian Social Customs and Traditions: A Critical Study," in Marazzi, ed., *La conoscenza dell'Asia e dell'Africa in Italia*, vol. I, part 1, pp. 351–71.
23. See the works by Pompa Banerjee, *Burning Women: Widows, Witches, and Early Modern European Travelers in India* (New York, 2003); Andrea Major, *Pious Flames: European Encounters with Sati, 1500–1830* (Delhi, 2006); and Major, ed., *Sati: A Historical Anthology* (Delhi, 2007), on the question of satī; on Manuzzi and music at the Mughal court, see Katherine B. Brown, "Reading Indian Music: The Interpretation of Seventeenth-Century European Travel-Writing in the (Re)construction of Indian Music History," *British Journal of Ethnomusicology* 9, no. 2 (2000): 1–34, and Brown, "Did Aurangzeb Ban Music? Questions for the Historiography of His Reign," *Modern Asian Studies* 41, no. 1 (2007): 77–120.
24. Pompa Banerjee, "Postcards from the Harem: The Cultural Translation of Niccolao Manucci's Book of Travels," in Palmira Brummett, ed., *The 'Book' of Travels: Genre, Ethnology and Pilgrimage, 1250–1700* (Leiden, 2009), pp. 241–81. Reading this essay, one is reminded at times of Nabokov's celebrated remark, regarding Mary McCarthy's having "added quite a bit of her own angelica to the pale fire of Kinbote's [here, Manuzzi's] plum pudding."
25. Niccolao Manucci, *Mogul India, or Storia do Mogor*, trans. William Irvine, 4 vols. (London, 1907–8). This extensive translation then formed the basis for the abridged work, *A Pepys of Mogul India, 1653–1708; Being an Abridged ed. of the 'Storia do Mogor' of Niccolao Manucci*, trans. William Irvine, abridged by Margaret L. Irvine (London, 1913); as well as the French version by Françoise de Valence, *Niccolo Manucci, un Vénitien chez les Moghols* (Paris, 1995). Excerpts from Irvine's translation may also be found most recently in Michael H. Fisher, ed., *Beyond the Three Seas: Travellers' Tales of Mughal India* (New Delhi, 2007), pp. 116–33.
26. Piero Falchetta, "Per la biografia di Nicolò Manuzzi (con postilla casanoviana)," *Quaderni veneti* 3 (1986): 85–111.

27. Apostolo Zeno, *Memorie di scrittori veneziani*, manuscript text cited in Falchetta, "Per la biografia di Nicolò Manuzzi," pp. 88–89.
28. On this question, see Richard T. Rapp, *Industry and Economic Decline in Seventeenth-Century Venice* (Cambridge, Mass., 1976), and, more generally, Rapp, "The Unmaking of the Mediterranean Trade Hegemony: International Trade Rivalry and the Commercial Revolution," *The Journal of Economic History* 35, no. 3 (1975): 499–525. Visiting Europeans were in some measure responsible for this view of a Venice in drastic decline; cf. Gaetano Cozzi, "Venezia nello scenario europeo (1517–1699)," in Gaetano Cozzi, Michael Knapton, and Giovanni Scarabello, eds., *La Repubblica di Venezia nell'età moderna: Dal 1517 alla fine della Repubblica*, in *Storia d'Italia*, vol. XII, part 2, gen. ed. Giuseppe Galasso (Turin, 1992), pp. 168–83, which in turn carries useful reflections on contemporary texts such as Abraham-Nicolas Amelot de la Houssaye, *Histoire du Gouvernement de Venise* (Paris, 1676). A valuable general consideration is that of James S. Grubb, "When Myths Lose Power: Four Decades of Venetian Historiography," *The Journal of Modern History* 58, no. 1 (1986): 43–94.
29. See Laurence Lockhart, "The Diplomatic Missions of Henry Bard, Viscount Bellomont, to Persia and India," *Iran* 4 (1966): 97–104.
30. P. Falchetta, "Venezia, madre lontana: Vita e opere di Nicolò Manuzzi (1638–1717)," in *Storia del Mogol di Nicolò Manuzzi veneziano*, ed. Falchetta, 2 vols. (Milan, 1986), vol. I, pp. 25–27.
31. Thomas Clarke, who appears to have been one of the earliest Englishmen in Madras, arrived there from the earlier settlement of Armagon, just to the north. He was born in India, and may have himself been of mixed descent; his father, also Thomas Clarke, had served as agent in the English factory at Masulipatnam. See F. Penny, *Fort St. George, Madras: A Short History of Our First Possession in India* (Madras, 1900), pp. 12–14.
32. For the *contrat d'échange* of 3 July 1709, see Edmond Gaudart, *Catalogue de quelques documents des Archives de Pondichéry* (Pondicherry, 1931), doc. 55.
33. Staatsbibliothek zu Berlin, Codex Phillipps 1945, 3 vols., vol. I, "Avertissement au lecteur" (text in French). The Berlin volumes, which bear the mark of the Collegii Paris Societatis Jesu, were the ones used by Catrou. They are in a mixture of French and Portuguese.
34. To contextualize the work, see the useful essays by Marziano Guglielminetti, "Per un'antologia degli autobiografi del Settecento," *Annali d'Italianistica* 4 (1986): 140–51, and Fido, "At the Origins of Autobiography in the 18th and 19th Centuries."
35. On Bernier, the authoritative interpretation is that of Sylvia Murr, "La politique au 'Mogol' selon Bernier: Appareil conceptuel, rhétorique stratégique, philosophie morale," in Jacques Pouchepadass and Henri Stern, eds., *De la royauté à l'État dans le monde indien* (Paris, 1991), pp. 239–311. For the best edition of Bernier's

writings on India, see Frédéric Tinguely, ed., *Un libertin dans l'Inde moghole: Les voyages de François Bernier (1656–1669)* (Paris, 2008).

36. Manucci, *Storia do Mogor*, trans. Irvine, vol. I, pp. 208–9, contains a far briefer version of these remarks.
37. François Catrou, *Histoire générale de l'empire du Mogol depuis sa foundation, sur les mémoires portugais de M. Manouchi* (Paris, 1705); for an earlier discussion on these questions, see Subrahmanyam, "European Chroniclers and the Mughals," in Subrahmanyam, *Explorations in Connected History: From the Tagus to the Ganges* (Delhi, 2005), pp. 138–79, especially pp. 174–78.
38. Interesting, the list does not include the published mid-seventeenth-century account of François le Gouz de la Boullaye, for which see Jacques de Maussion de Favières, *Les Voyages et Observations du Sieur de la Boullaye le-Gouz* (Paris, 1994).
39. François Catrou, *Histoire des anabaptistes, contenant leur doctrine, les diverses opinions qui les divisent en plusieurs sectes, les troubles qu'ils ont causez et enfin tout ce qui s'est passé de plus considérable à leur égard, depuis l'an 1521* (Amsterdam, 1700); also see François Catrou et al., *Histoire romaine depuis la fondation de Rome, par les RR. PP. Catrou et Rouillé*, 20 vols. (Paris, 1731).
40. Staatsbibliothek zu Berlin, Codex Phillipps 1945, vol. III, fls. 133–34.
41. See the interesting remarks on the question in Piero Falchetta, "Autobiografia e autobiografismo indiretto nella *Storia del Mogol* di Nicolò Manuzzi," *Annali d'Italianistica* 4 (1986): 130–39, particularly 136–37.
42. Biblioteca Nazionale Marciana, Venice, Codex Zanetti, It. 44, fl. 338.
43. Biblioteca Nazionale Marciana, Codex Zanetti, It. 44, fl. 366 (i). This passage interrupts the section titled "Breve notizia di quel che credono, e discorrono gli Gentili di quest'India circa l'essenza di Dio."
44. Compare Manucci, *Storia do Mogor*, trans. Irvine, vol. IV, pp. 89–90.
45. Archivio di Stato di Venezia, Senato, Dispacci, Francia, Reg. 203, pp. 474–76.
46. These paintings have sometimes been referred to as "Company Painting," a term that I have some doubts about; cf. Mildred Archer, "Company Paintings in South India: The Early Collections of Niccolao Manucci," *Apollo*, n.s., 92, no. 102 (August 1970): 108–13, and Archer, *Company Paintings: Indian Paintings of the British Period* (London, 1992), pp. 14–16.
47. Bibliothèque Nationale de France, Paris, Estampes, Rés., Codex Od. 45: "Histoire de l'Inde depuis Tamerlank jusqu'à Orangzeb par Manucci."
48. For such early Mughal paintings in Europe, see R. W. Lightbown, "Oriental Art and the Orient in Late Renaissance and Baroque Italy," *Journal of the Warburg and Courtauld Institutes* 32 (1969): 228–79; Francis Richard, "Les manuscrits persans d'origine indienne à la Bibliothèque nationale," *Revue de la Bibliothèque nationale* 19 (1986): 30–46; and the fascinating set of semifinished portraits from about 1640 discussed in Otto Kurz, "A Volume of Mughal Drawings and Miniatures," *Journal*

of the Warburg and Courtauld Institutes 30 (1967): 251–71. It would also eventually be interesting to compare the Manuzzi album with the so-called Witsen Album, from Hyderabad in the 1680s; for some initial reflections in this direction, see Pauline Lunsingh Scheurleer, "Het Witsenalbum: Zeventiende-eeuwse Indische portretten op bestelling," *Bulletin van het Rijksmuseum* 44 (1996): 167–254. Scheurleer makes a valuable point about not underestimating the sheer number of Indian miniatures in the Netherlands by the late seventeenth century, but these would not have compared to the better products of the Mughal atelier.

49. See Ebba Koch, "The Hierarchical Principles of Shah-Jahani Painting," in Milo Cleveland Beach, Ebba Koch, and Wheeler Thackston, *King of the World: The Padshahnama, an Imperial Manuscript from the Royal Library, Windsor Castle* (London, 1997), pp. 130–43.
50. On this figure, and his portrait, see Jorge Flores and Sanjay Subrahmanyam, "Rei ou bode expiatório: A lenda do Sultão Bulaqi e a política mogol do Estado da Índia, 1629–1635," *Anais de História de Além-Mar* 3 (2002): 199–229.
51. There is a clear relationship between the Manuzzi collective portrait of the 'Adil Shahi dynasty and the painting usually called *The House of Bijapur* by Kamal Muhammad and Chand Muhammad (c. 1680), The Metropolitan Museum of Art, New York, Islamic Art, Accession no. 1982.213.
52. Antonio Maria Zanetti, *Latina et italica D. Marci bibliotheca codicum manuscriptorum per titulos digesta* [. . .] (Venice, 1741). Later, in the nineteenth century, three further reproductions were made of the portraits of Akbar, Shahjahan, and Aurangzeb. These appear in Giovanni Flechia and Francesco C. Marmocchi, *Storia delle Indie orientali; opera ornata delle vedute delle principali città e dei più cospicui monumenti dell'India, dei ritratti degli uomini celebri, e di disegni delle più caratteristiche usanze*, 2 vols. (Turin, 1862).
53. Angelo Legrenzi, *Il Pellegrino nell'Asia, cioè Viaggi del dottor Angelo Legrenzi fisico e chirurgo, cittadino Veneto* (Venice, 1705), vol. II, pp. 223–27; citation in Grossato, *Navigatori e viaggiatori veneti*, pp. 115–16. On Legrenzi and Manuzzi, also see the discussion in Manucci, *Storia do Mogor*, trans. Irvine, vol. I, pp. lxxiii–lxxvi.
54. Archivio di Stato di Venezia, Senato, Dispacci, Francia, Reg. 203, fls. 271v–72v.
55. On the bezoar stone, see Jorge M. dos Santos Alves, "A pedra-bezoar: Realidade e mito em torno de um antidoto," in Jorge M. dos Santos Alves, Claude Guillot, and Roderich Ptak, eds., *Mirabilia Asiatica: Produits rares dans le commerce maritime* (Wiesbaden, 2003), pp. 121–34.
56. Falchetta, "Venezia, madre lontana," pp. 34–35. We do find later traces of a certain Portuguese-speaking lady called Catherine Manouchy in Madras and Pondicherry, who may have been the widow of this nephew. For her will, see CAOM, 22 Miom 227, doc. 104, dated 18 July 1747. She appears to have been married to the well-known jewel trader Pierre Ballieu, and also related by marriage to the Deita y Salazar family.

57. Biblioteca Nazionale Marciana, Codex It. VI. 135 (=5772), fl. 63; Manucci, *Storia do Mogor*, trans. Irvine, vol. IV, pp. 260–61.
58. On Martin, see Alfred Martineau, ed., *Mémoires de François Martin, fondateur de Pondichéry (1665–1696)*, 3 vols. (Paris, 1931), where Manuzzi rarely finds explicit mention. However, Manuzzi served as a witness for the marriage of Agnès Marguerite Desprez, Martin's granddaughter, and Claude Boyvin d'Hardancourt, at Pondicherry on 21 February 1705; cf. Gaudart, *Catalogue de quelques documents*, no. 44. Further, Martin does mention Manuzzi (or "Manouchy") in several letters dating around 1700, such as one in Archives Nationales, Paris, Colonies, C2 66, fl. 28.
59. Biblioteca Nazionale Marciana, Codex Zanetti It. 44 (=8299), fl. 156v/290. The section of the text is translated rather loosely in Manucci, *Storia do Mogor*, trans. Irvine, vol. II, pp. 278–79, from the Portuguese version.
60. Manucci, *Storia do Mogor*, trans. Irvine, vol. III, p. 168.
61. Manucci, *Storia do Mogor*, trans. Irvine, vol. IV, p. 75.
62. For a sense of the milieu that Manuzzi frequented in Madras, see Søren Mentz, *The English Gentleman Merchant at Work: Madras and the City of London, 1660–1740* (Copenhagen, 2005). Much valuable material can also be found in Henry Davison Love, *Vestiges of Old Madras, 1640–1800; Traced from the East India Company's Records Preserved at Fort St. George and the India Office, and from Other Sources*, 4 vols. (London, 1913). I return here to themes I have dealt with earlier in Subrahmanyam, "Madras, Chennai and São Tomé: An irregular urban complex in south-eastern India (1500–1800)," in Clara García Ayluardo and Manuel Ramos Medina, eds., *Ciudades mestizas: Intercambios y continuidades en la expansión occidental, siglos XVI a XIX* (Mexico City, 2001), pp. 221–39.
63. Staatsbibliothek zu Berlin, Codex Phillipps 1945, vol. II, fl. 153v; my translation differs somewhat from Manucci, *Storia do Mogor*, trans. Irvine, vol. II, p. 304. Compare the comments of Charles de Bussy somewhat later in the eighteenth century on what he terms the *fourberie* of the Indians; Subrahmanyam, "Profiles in Transition: Of Adventurers and Administrators in South India, 1750–1810," *Indian Economic and Social History Review* 39, nos. 2–3 (2002): 197–231.
64. Biblioteca Nazionale Marciana, Codex It. 135 (=5772), fl. 24–27; also see Manucci, *Storia do Mogor*, trans. Irvine, vol. IV, pp. 187–93.
65. "I advise the reader that the Gentiles of whom I speak, and whose customs and politics I describe, are the inhabitants of a province which is called Madurey, and they are the most cowardly and weak people that there are in the Indies, as one can see in their manner of making war"; Biblioteca Nazionale Marciana, Codex Zanetti, It. 44 (=8299), fl. 219v/394.
66. Biblioteca Nazionale Marciana, Codex Zanetti, It. 44 (=8299), p. 390.
67. Many of these paintings, and extensive sections of Manuzzi's comments (unfortunately often modernized beyond recognition), were published in Tullia

Gasparrini Leporace, *Usi e costumi dell'India dalla 'Storia del Mogol' di Nicolò Manucci Veneziano* (Milan, 1963).

68. British Library, Oriental and India Office Collections, Original Correspondence, vol. LXVI, part 1, no. 6790, letter from Nicolas Manuch to John Pitt, 1/11 December 1699 (this concerns a request that Manuzzi should accompany the embassy of Sir William Norris to Aurangzeb). The letter is quoted fully in Manucci, *Storia do Mogor*, trans. Irvine, vol. I, p. lxi. Also see Lavinia Mary Anstey, "More about Nicolao Manuchy," *The Indian Antiquary* 49 (March 1920): 52–53.
69. Biblioteca Nazionale Marciana, Codex It. VI. 136 (=8300), fl. 145.
70. Biblioteca Nazionale Marciana, Codex It. VI. 136 (=8300), fl. 67. The description, but not the painting, is commented on (and traced to earlier texts) in Banerjee, *Burning Women*, pp. 101–3.
71. Biblioteca Nazionale Marciana, Codex It. VI. 136 (=8300), fl. 85.
72. Biblioteca Nazionale Marciana, Codex Zanetti, It. 44 (=8299), fl. 219v/p. 394.
73. Manucci, *Storia do Mogor*, trans. Irvine, vol. II, p. 452 (editor's notes).
74. A. Gorla, *Viaggio di un frate converso carmelitano scalzo,* cited in Falchetta, "Venezia, madre lontana," p. 33. This view interestingly contradicts the claim in the Fort St. George Records of March 1703 that it was "the generall opinion of all that the aforesaid Nicolo Manuch is very poor," perhaps again a strategic claim made by Manuzzi to have his dues on the renewal of his lease reduced (Manucci, *Storia do Mogor*, trans. Irvine, vol. I, p. lxiii).
75. H. H. Dodwell, *Records of Fort St George: Minutes of the Proceedings in the Mayor's Court of Madrasapatam (June–December 1689 and July 1716 to March 1719)* (Madras, 1917). "Preface": "A still more interesting person who appears here is 'Dr Manuch' with his characteristic suit against a 'Moorman' to recover winnings at backgammon. The date of the suit shows moreover that the time of Manucci's death must be assigned to a later period than Mr. Irvine supposed."
76. Falchetta, "Per la biografia di Nicolò Manuzzi," p. 99.
77. C. Biron, *Curiositez de la nature et de l'art* (1703), cited in Françoise de Valence, *Médecins de fortune et d'infortune: Des aventuriers français en Inde au XVIIe siècle: Témoins et témoinages* (Paris, 2000), pp. 64–65; also see D. V. Subba Reddy, "Medical Adventures and Memoirs of Manucci, an Italian quack doctor in India in the second half of the 17th century," *The Indian Journal of History of Medicine* 7, no. 1 (1962): 42–50. Most recently, see the brief essay by Philip J. Sykes, Paolo Santoni-Rugiu, and Ricardo F. Mazzola, "Nicolò Manuzzi (1639–1717) and the First Report of Indian Rhinoplasty," *Journal of Plastic, Reconstructive and Aesthetic Surgery* 63 (2010): 247–50.
78. For a discussion of these claims, see Subrahmanyam, "European Chroniclers and the Mughals," pp. 176–78.
79. This issue has been discussed earlier in respect of the Portuguese chronicler

Gaspar Correia in Maurice Kriegel and Sanjay Subrahmanyam, "The Unity of Opposites: Abraham Zacut, Vasco da Gama and the Chronicler Gaspar Correia," in Anthony Disney and Emily Booth, eds., *Vasco da Gama and the Linking of Europe and Asia* (Delhi, 2000), pp. 48–71.

80. For the significance of this work, see Lynn Hunt, Margaret Jacob, and Wijnand Mijnhardt, eds., *Bernard Picart and the First Global Vision of Religion* (Los Angeles, 2010).
81. Picart, *The Ceremonies and Religious Customs of the Various Nations of the Known World; together with Historical Annotations and several curious discourses equally instructive and entertaining*, vol. III (containing the ceremonies of the idolatrous nations) (London, 1734), pp. 408–42.
82. See *Voyages de Mr Dellon, avec sa relation de l'Inquisition de Goa, augmentée de diverses pièces curieuses*, 3 vols. (Cologne, 1709/1711).
83. Anonymous review of the *Voyages de Mr Dellon* in the *Journal des Sçavans* 38 (1709): 598–605. On Dellon more generally, see Charles Amiel and Anne Lima, eds., *L'Inquisition de Goa: La relation de Charles Dellon (1687)* (Paris, 1997).
84. "An Historical Dissertation on the Gods of the East-Indians," in Picart, *The Ceremonies and Religious Customs*, vol. III, p. 409.
85. Biblioteca Nazionale Marciana, Venice, Codex Zanetti, It. 44, fls. 366 (b)–(i) in Italian, followed by a more extended version in French, fls. 367–406; excerpts may be found in *Storia del Mogol di Nicolò Manuzzi*, ed. Falchetta, vol. II, pp. 170–210; and the English translation by Irvine in Manucci, *Storia do Mogor*, vol. III, pp. 1–71.
86. Staatsbibliothek zu Berlin, Codex Phillipps 1945, vol. III, fls. 48r–69v.
87. See the text published in Willem Caland, ed., *Twee oude fransche verhandelingen over het Hindoeïsme* (Amsterdam, 1923), pp. 3–92. Caland suggests that this text was itself a revised and reworked version of an account first prepared by Roberto de Nobili in about 1644.

5. BY WAY OF CONCLUSION

1. Letter from Anthony Sherley to Margaret Clifford, Countess of Cumberland, Venice, 20 July 1602, in Evelyn Philip Shirley, *The Sherley Brothers: An historical memoir of the Lives of Sir Thomas Sherley, Sir Anthony Sherley, and Sir Robert Sherley, Knights* (London, 1848), pp. 38–39.
2. See the useful remarks in Carlo Ginzburg, "Latitude, Slaves, and the Bible: An Experiment in Microhistory," *Critical Inquiry* 31, no. 3 (2005): 665–83.
3. Cf. Sanjay Subrahmanyam, "Holding the World in Balance: The Connected Histories of the Iberian Overseas Empires, 1500–1640," *The American Historical Review* 112, no. 5 (2007): 1359–85.

4. Tzvetan Todorov, *La conquête de l'Amérique: La question de l'autre* (Paris, 1982); Todorov, *The Conquest of America: The Question of the Other*, trans. Richard Howard (New York, 1984).
5. Bernard S. Cohn, *Colonialism and Its Forms of Knowledge: The British in India* (Princeton, N.J., 1996), pp. 18–19.
6. Clifford Geertz, *The Interpretation of Cultures* (New York, 1973), p. 89.
7. For a more extended discussion, see Sanjay Subrahmanyam, "Par-delà l'incommensurabilité: Pour une histoire connectée des empires aux temps modernes," *Revue d'histoire moderne et contemporaine* 54, no. 5 (2007): 34–53; also, the earlier comments in Daniel Carey, "Questioning Incommensurability in Early Modern Cultural Exchange," *Common Knowledge* 6, no. 3 (1997): 32–50.
8. See Sumit Guha, "Speaking Historically: The Changing Voices of Historical Narration in Western India, 1400–1900," *The American Historical Review* 109, no. 4 (2004): 1084–1103 (quotation on 1090).
9. See Simon Schaffer, Lissa Roberts, Kapil Raj, and James Delbourgo, eds., *The Brokered World: Go-betweens and Global Intelligence, 1770–1820* (Uppsala, 2009).
10. Georg Simmel, "The Stranger," in Kurt Wolff, ed. and trans., *The Sociology of Georg Simmel* (New York, 1950), pp. 402–8; Simmel, "Exkurs über den Fremden," in Simmel, *Soziologie: Untersuchungen über die Formen der Vergesellschaftung* (Berlin, 1908), pp. 509–12. There is of course an extended literature on the subject, and on the uses and misuses of Simmel; cf. S. Dale McLemore, "Simmel's 'Stranger': A Critique of the Concept," *The Pacific Sociological Review* 13, no. 2 (1970): 86–94.
11. Steven Shapin, *A Social History of Truth: Civility and Science in Seventeenth-Century England* (Chicago, 1994), pp. 127–28.
12. See the helpful discussion in John Martin, "Inventing Sincerity, Refashioning Prudence: The Discovery of the Individual in Renaissance Europe," *The American Historical Review* 102, no. 5 (1997): 1309–42.
13. Compare the case of an almost exact contemporary, discussed in Mercedes García-Arenal and Gerard Wiegers, *A Man of Three Worlds: Samuel Pallache, a Moroccan Jew in Catholic and Protestant Europe*, trans. Martin Beagles (Baltimore, 2003).
14. See Perez Zagorin, *Ways of Lying: Dissimulation, Persecution, and Conformity in Early Modern Europe* (Cambridge, Mass., 1990); also Jon R. Snyder, *Dissimulation and the Culture of Secrecy in Early Modern Europe* (Berkeley, 2009).

Index

Library of Congress Cataloging-in-Publication Data
Subrahmanyam, Sanjay.
Three ways to be alien : travails and encounters in the early modern world / Sanjay Subrahmanyam.
p. cm.—(The Menahem Stern Jerusalem lectures)
Includes bibliographical references and index.
ISBN 978-1-58465-991-4 (cloth: alk. paper)
ISBN 978-1-58465-992-1 (pbk.: alk. paper)
ISBN 978-1-61168-019-5 (e-book)
1. India—Colonization—History—16th century. 2. Middle East—Colonization—History—16th century. 3. Identity (Psychology)—Social aspects—History—16th century. 4. 'Ali bin Yusuf 'Adil Khan, d. ca. 1567. 5. Sherley, Anthony, Sir, 1565–1635? 6. Manucci, Niccolao, 1639–1717. 7. Iranians—India—Goa (State)—History—16th century. 8. Italians—Mogul Empire. 9. British—Middle East—History—16th century.
I. Title. II.Series.
DS498.S84 2011
954.02'54–dc22 2011000130